The Selected Poetry and Prose of Andrea Zanzotto

The Selected Poetry and Prose of Andrea Zanzotto

A Bilingual Edition

Edited and translated by Patrick Barron

With additional translations by
Ruth Feldman   Thomas J. Harrison   Brian Swann
John P. Welle   Elizabeth A. Wilkins

The University of Chicago Press | Chicago and London

ANDREA ZANZOTTO (b. 1921), widely regarded as Italy's most important living poet, is the author of more than twenty books of poems and collections of prose. His most recent English-language book is *Peasants Wake for Fellini's* Casanova *and Other Poems* (1997).

PATRICK BARRON is assistant professor of English at the University of Massachusetts, Boston. He is the coeditor and cotranslator of *Italian Environmental Literature: An Anthology* (2003) and the recipient of the Rome Prize, a Fulbright grant, and a translation award from the National Endowment for the Arts.

The University of Chicago Press, Chicago 60637
The University of Chicago Press, Ltd., London
© 2007 by The University of Chicago
All rights reserved. Published 2006
Printed in the United States of America

15 14 13 12 11 10 09 08 07 06   1 2 3 4 5

ISBN-13: 978-0-226-97884-0 (cloth)
ISBN-10: 0-226-97884-2 (cloth)

Italian poems © Copyright Andrea Zanzotto. All rights reserved.
Published in Italy by Arnoldo Mondadori Editore, Milano.

This pulication was made possible thanks to the support of the Italian Ministry of Foreign Affairs, the Istituto Italiano di Cultura of Chicago, Director Tina Cervone, and the Istituto Italiano di Cultura of Los Angeles, Director Francesca Valente.

Library of Congress Cataloging-in-Publication Data

Zanzotto, Andrea, 1921–
        [Selections English and Italian 2006]
        The selected poetry and prose of Andrea Zanzotto / edited and translated
    by Patrick Barron ; with additional translations by Ruth Feldman ... [et al.].
    — Bilingual ed.
        p. cm.
        English and Italian.
        Includes bibliographical references and index.
        ISBN-13: 978-0-226-97884-0 (cloth : alk. paper)
        ISBN-10: 0-226-97884-2 (cloth : alk. paper)
        I. Barron, Patrick, 1968– II. Feldman, Ruth. III. Title.
    PQ4851.A74A2 2006
    851'.914—dc22

                                                                    2006028853

Contents

Selected Poetry

Illustrations

Translator's Note and Acknowledgments

Without missing a beat despite faltering in his step, Zanzotto called out "One, two, three" in his inimitably kind and sprightly voice as he reached the short, steep slope. My hands instinctively went up and were suddenly upon the poet's back: as bid, I ever so gently pushed, helping him to the summit of the grassy knoll. We were soon next to the "unstable house," an abandoned building along the Soligo River in the hamlet of Solighetto not far from Zanzotto's home, and the subject of the last poem in this book. Zanzotto vividly described the site, its former occupants, and an old woman who lived in another mysterious house tucked into the trees closer to the river—barely perceptible from where we stood. He was interested in everything, from the rustling leaves to the graffiti of teenagers scrawled on the house and a nearby bench. I strained to understand and remember as many details as possible, to link them with his poetry. Many remained, many more did not; but most important, I felt a connective energy emanating from the poet, his poetry, and his place that has not diminished, but rather increased as I have slowly attempted to transform "indizi" into "indications" and "parole" into "words."

I hope here to have earned a measure of the trust that Zanzotto placed in me—to have achieved in translation a glimmer here and there of the brilliance of his original poetry and prose. The way has indeed been steep and challenging, but rewarding, leading to "new heights" as well as "certain circular chasms."[1] I have attempted to follow as faithfully as possible Zanzotto's own voice, searching for stirring cross-lingual musicality, suggestive and multifaceted meanings, and most of all, the nearly intangible, kinetic unleashing of the poetic energy stored in the original texts. I am particularly grateful that my efforts are here joined by those of

1. See Andrea Zanzotto, "Da un'altezza nuova" and "(Certe forre circolari . . .)," *Le poesie e prose scelte* (Milan: Mondadori, 1999), 169, 562.

Ruth Feldman, Thomas J. Harrison, Brian Swann, John P. Welle, and Elizabeth A. Wilkins.

A number of these translations originally appeared in earlier publications:

Translations by Ruth Feldman and Brian Swann appeared in *Selected Poetry of Andrea Zanzotto* (Princeton University Press, 1975); of these, "Eclogue III" and "Elegy in Petèl" first appeared in *boundary 2* 2, no. 3 (spring 1974): 490–506, and "From the Sky" in *Nimrod* 18, no. 2 (1974): 45–46; reprinted by permission of Princeton University Press, *boundary 2,* and *Nimrod.*

Translations by Thomas J. Harrison appeared in *The Favorite Malice* (Out of London Press, 1983); courtesy of Thomas J. Harrison.

Elizabeth A. Wilkin's translation of "Glances, Facts and Senhals" appeared in *Forum Italicum* 17, no. 2 (1984): 290–97; courtesy of *Forum Italicum.*

Translations by Ruth Feldman and John P. Welle appeared in *Peasants Wake for Fellini's* Casanova *and Other Poems* (University of Illinois Press, 1997); used with permission of the University of Illinois Press.

Translations by Patrick Barron of "A Book of Eclogues," "By Now," and "Through the New Window" appeared in *ISLE: Interdisciplinary Studies in Literature and Environment* 7, no. 2 (2000): 269–72, and were reprinted in *Italian Environmental Literature: An Anthology* (Italica, 2003), in which the following translations also appeared: "Eclogue I" and "Eclogue II"; "Subnarcosis," "High, Other Language, Beyond Idiom?" "Noplace," and "Towards the Palù" appeared in *Ecopoetics* 2 (2002): 160–69; "Evenings of the Festival Day" appeared in *Two Lines: A Journal of Translation* 10 (2003): 5–15; and "The Euganean Hills" appeared in *ISLE: Interdisciplinary Studies in Literature and Environment* 12, no. 1 (2005): 139–45.

Acknowledgment is due to the two principal collections of Zanzotto's work: *Poesie (1938–1986),* edited by Stefano Agosti, and *Le poesie e prose scelte,* edited by Stefano Dal Bianco and Gian Mario Villalta (both published by Mondadori, in 1993 and 1999, respectively). These volumes, carefully prepared and annotated, provided valuable editorial guidance; both contain extensive Zanzotto bibliographies. The following prose pieces are from *Le poesie e prose:* "A Poetry Determined to Hope," "Some Perspectives on the Poetry of Today," "Self-portrait," "From 'Intervento': A Conversation with Middle School Students in Parma," "Between the Recent Past and Distant Present," "Poetic and Bodily Experience," "Between Minimal and Maximal Languages," and "The Euganean Hills." The following pieces are from *Sull'Altopiano e prose varie* (Vicenza: Neri Pozza, 1995): "Sundials," "January," "Rebirth of the Hills," and "June."

Figure 3, "Andrea Zanzotto" (1996), by Tullio Pericoli, is published courtesy of the artist. For figure 12, photograph of Nino by Vincenzo Cottinelli, see http://www.vincenzocottinelli.it. Figure 21, portrait of Andrea Zanzotto (drawing, 2005), is by Manuela Mariani.

I am very grateful to the National Endowment for the Arts; the Istituto Italiano di Cultura, Chicago; and the Istituto Italiano di Cultura, Los Angeles, for their generous support of this book. I must also thank the American Academy in Rome for fostering my work in such a warmly collegial and inspiring environment. My deepest thanks go to all those who gave me assistance and inspiration during the long process of bringing this book to fruition: to Giorgio Spano, Erika Valsecchi, Franco Manca, Michael P. Branch, Cheryll Glotfelty, Nida Caselli, Annie Barron, Timothy Padayachee, Kalmia Smith, Byron Smith, Whitney Smith, Christoph Greger, and Dina Viggiano for their helpful editorial suggestions; to Randy Petilos, my editor at the University of Chicago Press, for his enduring support of this project; to Giovanni Zanzotto for helping speed lines of communication and for generously showing me the countryside around Pieve di Soligo; to Marisa Zanzotto for her kind assistance in locating many of the illustrations that appear in this book; to Andrea Zanzotto for welcoming me to his home and for providing invaluable advice and guidance during the stages of both selection and translation; and to my wife, Manuela Mariani, for her loving support and many hours spent poring over half-born translations.

Patrick Barron

Introduction

> . . . *what delight*
> *what joy of seeing and not seeing,*
> *of diving into the mind and leaving it behind,*
> *the signifier has guided and piloted*
> *the user in dazzling tongue-twisters*
> *nothing-twisters.*[1]

Thus ends one of Andrea Zanzotto's recent poems, composed in the early months of the new millennium and expressive of a lifetime of expansive, daring, and profoundly moving writing that from its remote past to continuous present teems with vibrant meditations on "the infinities / that here converge / that from here wander off."[2] Born on October 10, 1921, in Pieve di Soligo, a small village in the hilly farm country of the Veneto in northern Italy, Zanzotto studied literature in Padua, took part in the resistance during the Second World War, lived for two years in Switzerland and France after hostilities had ended, and then returned to Pieve di Soligo where he has remained ever since—working as a teacher and administrator for many years.

Zanzotto's prolific writing career engages many themes, from linguistics and landscape to political historiography and the natural sciences. He has long been regarded as one of Europe's leading contemporary poets. In a 1954 review of Zanzotto's first published book, *Dietro il paesaggio* (Behind the landscape), Giuseppe Ungaretti sung his praises, calling him a "free poet" and comparing

---

1. Translated from Andrea Zanzotto, "lievissime rotelle del 2000"; this poem appears in print for the first time in this volume in the section of "New Poems," pp. 352–353.

2. Translated from Andrea Zanzotto, "Non si sa quanto verde," *Meteo* (Rome: Donzelli, 1996), 19.

him to the foremost writers in the history of Italian letters.[3] With
the appearance of *La Beltà* (Beauty) in 1968, Eugenio Montale
dubbed him the most important Italian poet born in the twentieth
century.[4] To date, Zanzotto has written fifteen books of poetry,
two collections of literary criticism, and two volumes of prose,
and has also translated the work of a number of French writers,
including Alain Borne, Michel Leiris, George Bataille, Honoré de
Balzac, and Henri Michaux. His own work has been translated into
many languages, including German, Romanian, French, Spanish,
and English. His awards include the Saint Vincent Prize (1950),
the Cino Del Duca Prize (1959), the Viareggio Prize (1979), the
Librex-Montale Prize (1983), the Accademia dei Lincei Prize (1987),
the Stadt Münster Prize for European Poetry (1993), the Pandolfo
Poetry Prize (1998), the Bagutta Prize (1999), and the Friedrich
Hölderlin Prize (2005).

Zanzotto is one of a few, rare figures in contemporary Italian
literature who straddles generations and historical-geographical
realities—specifically the shift from a prewar, largely agrarian, and
dialectal Italy to the current highly industrialized and urbanized
one. His poetry carries tones of both earlier and recent voices,
from Dante and Petrarch, to Giacomo Leopardi and Ugo Foscolo,
to Pier Paolo Pasolini and Vittorio Sereni, and is informed by both

3. Giuseppe Ungaretti, "Piccolo discorso sopra *Dietro il Paesaggio* di Andrea
Zanzotto," *Vita d'un uomo. Saggi e interventi* (Milan: Mondadori, 1974), 699.
    4. John P. Welle, introduction, *Peasants Wake for Fellini's* Casanova *and Other
Poems* (University of Illinois Press, 1997), vii.

modern and postmodern currents of philosophical and psychological thought, including the work of Jacques Lacan, Roland Barthes, Martin Heidegger, and Sigmund Freud. Other important influences include Friedrich Hölderlin, Rainer Maria Rilke, Federico García Lorca, Paul Éluard, Paul Celan, and Mario Luzi. With a lifelong familiarity with a single place by now uncommon in many writers, his poetry delves beneath the surfaces of language and landscape to explore the complex mesh of culture and nature evident in his native village and the surrounding countryside— concentrations of energy within clustered locales that he terms "archipelagoes of places."[5]

Such attention is especially evident in what he calls his "pseudo-trilogy," considered by many to be his masterpiece: *Il Galateo in bosco* (The Woodland book of manners), *Fosfeni* (Phosphenes), and *Idioma* (Idiom; 1978–1986). In turn, each of these books focuses on differing, yet overlapping aspects of Zanzotto's home region: *Il Galateo in bosco,* on the Montello Woods to the south and their impossibly tangled human and nonhuman remains; *Fosfeni,* on the Dolomites to the north and their elemental purity; and *Idioma,* on the dialectal and vernacular landscape surrounding Pieve di Soligo and the nearby Piave River. Taken together, these books create something of an impossible yet highly focused map, lacking fixed itineraries but providing an intense understanding of the vibrating, interwoven, and concentrated vitalities that stretch, tension-filled, from lauded/abused woodland, to rarified alpine heights, to thoroughly humanized countryside. As Zanzotto eloquently states,

> There is a true geographical correspondence that is implicit in my writings. *Il Galateo in bosco* coincides with the Montello Woods, whose rich verdure I see to the south, and which represent and symbolize to me the snarls of the human and nonhuman, history and nature; to the north, on the other hand, I see the initial, abstract outlines of the Dolomites, which carry me to a rarified, suspended world. They can be perceived as slides pointed skyward, inviting "uphill slaloms" towards a timeless, mathematical light. Then there exists, like the bellybutton of the world and daily

5. Translated from Andrea Zanzotto, "Colli Euganei," *Le poesie e prose scelte* (Milan: Mondadori, 1999), 1079.

centrality, the reality of the little village where I live. This, it seems to me, is composed of fragments of various types, each with a remarkable uniqueness, and yet also joined together in a story formed of a choral quality that is all the same unsettled, veering towards the falsetto. My village is like a garden, here and there devastated, map and palimpsest, gestures fixed in an eternal instant, a blinking of eyes, a sudden opening of narrow streets that are always here and yet curving elsewhere.[6]

The most chthonic book in the trilogy, *Il Galateo in bosco,* plumbs the wonderful horrible depths of the Montello Woods, laden with geologic, human, and nonhuman remains, all jumbled together. The Montello Woods's human history is varied, ranging from traces of the Neolithic to roots of modern civilization to signs of the direst moments of the recent past. In the sixteenth century the area was home to many humanists and artists—including Giovanni Della Casa, whose *Galateo overo de' costumi* (Galateo, or on Manners, 1558), which Zanzotto "cites" in his own title, was a popular codification of the modes of speech and manners proper for civilized society. In contrast, today the woods are traversed by the "linea degli Ossari" (line of the Ossuaries), filled with the remains of many thousands of soldiers who died there during the First World War. The title *Il Galateo in bosco* places together two intractable and irreconcilable entities: culture and nature, or codified language and the inarticulate scratchings on (and under) the forest's surface. For Zanzotto, the Montello is many things: sacred, wild, war-scarred, tomb-marked, sylvan, primeval, dangerous, degraded, and welcoming—a place of contrasts, a home for plants and animals, a resting place for the scattered dead, and a refuge for the marginalized. To travel the Montello, as Zanzotto explains to Marco Paolini, "is to perpetually follow a history that has turned into a geographic map, in the landscapes, in the tragedies that have affected the earth and its people."[7]

And yet, such close attention to localized human society, language, and culture has been a hallmark of Zanzotto's entire

6. Translated from Andrea Zanzotto, "Percorso di Zanzotto: Dalla *Beltà* al *Galateo in Bosco* e dintorni," *Ateneo Veneto* 18, nos. 1–2 (1980): 175–76.

7. Translated from Marco Paolini, *Bestiario Veneto: Parole mate* (Pordenone: Edizione Biblioteca dell'Imagine, 1999), 102.

production, from his first verse written in the late 1930s, to early books *Dietro il paesaggio* and *Vocativo* (Vocative, 1957), to the most recent, *Sovrimpressioni* (Superimpressions, 2001). This long period of activity, stretching over more than six decades, contains various shifts in poetic form and the use of language. His early work is focused on an idyllic and protecting, if tragically war-torn, landscape—a temporary refuge from political and social problems—within which he eloquently, if oftentimes painfully, examines the human psyche. With clear hermetic and symbolist influences, this verse digs beneath the surfaces of his surroundings in part to seek out and sooth the self, and in part to celebrate natural beauty, with the widespread use of traditional poetic forms such as the elegy and eclogue.

The title of Zanzotto's first collection, *Dietro il paesaggio*, indicates what has become an enduring desire to indeed go behind the landscape, into it, and out upon it, to literally wrap it around the self—as is expressed in the closing lines of the poem "Ormai" (By Now), in which the landscape is conceived of as a type of protecting cloak: "Here all that's left is to wrap the landscape around the self / and turn your back."[8] Zanzotto's recognition of the total encirclement of the self by one's surroundings reveals a deep rootedness, at once warmly familiar and yet also uneasily enclosing. The self is seen as a space within space, frequented by all

8. Translated from Andrea Zanzotto, "Ormai," *Le poesie e prose scelte*, 46.

5

manner of other beings, including the microbiological; ideas and energy emanating from both the immediate environs as well as from other thinkers and poets; and matter, from the fragrance of sweet honey to the booming electric currents of distant lightning. The body becomes the base unit for measuring space and time on the most intimate of levels: the organismic. All modes of perception, including poetic imagination, are revealed as integral tools to understanding the flux of internal-external reality.

With *Vocativo* (Vocative, 1959), uncertainty emerges over the relevance of pastoral poetry to the present-day landscape, as well as over the ability of language to accurately represent either the external world or the individual psyche. Marking a period of crisis, this collection exhibits an uneasy split between reality and language, with increasing doubts as to the authenticity of poetry. As Zanzotto explains to Beverly Allen, the vocative, previously understood as an active and reciprocated

> invocation of the gods . . . becomes a pure and simple grammatical given, the vocative case. Therefore, the language that, in its adventure, went forth from the human mind in order to become text in the belief that it was weaving a colloquy fell backwards with radar effect, we might say, but one that was tragically traumatic because it found no response, an effect in which the word became a pure sign without a signified, in which the signified oscillated extremely, or in which the signified had to be sought in territories quite different from those indicated on the surface by the sign.[9]

No longer a safe refuge, the landscape in *Vocativo* becomes troubling. Intense questioning of traditional language use and the fixed meanings of words lead to an intense dilemma, the unknotting of which is slowly worked at in successive books in the attempt to re-communicate with the muses, the self, and the land. From this point onward, Zanzotto's struggle with self, matter, language, and identity intensifies, through *IX Ecloghe* (*IX Eclogues*, 1962), and culminates in *La Beltà* (Beauty, 1968) and *Pasque* (Easters, 1973).

In these later works, Zanzotto shifts his attention from nature as a protecting shield to increasingly confront a vast range of con-

---

9. Beverly Allen, "Interview with Andrea Zanzotto: Pieve di Soliogo: July 25, 1978," *Stanford Italian Review* 4, no. 2 (fall 1984): 259.

tradictory indications in both language and landscape. At the heart of this exploration stands his hometown Pieve di Soligo, perched on the edge of, if not crashing headlong into, the postmodern world. Scattered throughout are variously decaying or still vibrant elements of a fast diminishing agricultural society, including the local Solighese dialect—important to Zanzotto both as a means of daily communication and one of artistic expression. His first published dialectal poetry appeared in *Filò* (*Peasants Wake*, 1976), a project that grew from a collaboration with filmmaker Federico Fellini to write a chant-like accompaniment for two scenes of the film *Casanova* in a pseudo-Venetian dialect. Fellini describes the proposed "recitation" in a letter to Zanzotto, as a "sad and scoffing prayer, frightened and mischievous, as old as the world and eternally childish" for a scene in which "a rite is enacted at night on the Grand Canal [in Venice] from whose depths a gigantic and black head of a woman must emerge: a kind of lagoon deity, the Great Mediterranean Mother, the mysterious female who lives in each of us."[10] This work formed the basis for further collaborations with Fellini on the films *La città delle donne* (The City of Women, 1980) and *E la nave va* (And the Ship Sails On, 1983). Later work, including many dialectal poems in *Idioma*, exhibit Zanzotto's desire to expand the semantic field while remaining in close contact with his local linguistic roots.

Early signs of Zanzotto's incipient "glossolalia," his voracious appetite for myriad forms of linguistic expression, appear in *IX Ecloghe*, in which scientific and technological terms and Latinate phrasings are scattered throughout poems eclectically modeled after Virgilian and Petrarchan antecedents. The focus of this book is as much upon the surrounding landscape as upon the pastoral literary tradition that it takes as a model. In essence, *IX Ecloghe* is a close examination of the nature of poetry (and its converse), as well as an investigation of history and science, whose increasing importance at mid-twentieth century for the poet demanded comment. The nine eclogues of the book, each accompanied by a short lyric poem, take the traditional shape of a series of dialogues. However, instead of shepherds, Zanzotto presents two somewhat mysterious voices: *"a"* (presumably the poet himself) and *"b"*

10. Andrea Zanzotto, *Peasants Wake for Fellini's* Casanova *and Other Poems* (Chicago: University of Illinois Press, 1997), 5.

(Polyphemus, representing lyric poetry). In these tension-filled colloquies, Zanzotto frequently examines the validity of traditional poetics. The discussion generated is largely contradictory and unsettled, more often than not producing disturbing and open-ended discoveries rather than comforting resolutions.

In the first poem of the volume, "A Book of Eclogues," Zanzotto challenges and yet simultaneously pays homage to the elevated, formal tones of earlier writers (such as Virgil and Dante), while admitting to feeling trapped in their familiar, even seductive, models. He seems to apologize for the "parenthesis within innumerable parentheses," of which this prefatory poem is the first example of many to come. There is a danger of going nowhere, of continual, pointless self-searching and deluding digression. And yet, this struggle to find a song that does not lie, even if it is "out of tune," is necessary if Zanzotto hopes to uncover an impossible "diagram of the 'soul'" or to fruitfully come to terms with "a land that is always / sprouting feathers and raving of green and of springtimes."[11]

This difficult task is made all the more challenging by histori-

11. Translated from Andrea Zanzotto, "Un libro di Ecloghe," *Le poesie e prose scelte,* 201.

cal powers, against which Zanzotto struggles here and in poems to come. As he states, "when I wrote a book entitled *IX Ecloghe*, it was in fact an homage (a presumptuous one, perhaps) to the great shadow of Virgil that reflects in itself all the contradictions of the meek man, the man far removed from any form of prevarication and violence who himself still gets pulled by circumstances to the center of power."[12] This conflict with power, conducted from the margins of accepted consciousness and meaning, must direct its attention toward the localized indications of past human activity, often of war and degradation.

For Zanzotto the true subject of an eclogue, rather than an idealized landscape in an Arcadian reverie divorced from historiographical reality, is not only "things sublime," but also the "death rattle and filth" as they become "human studies."[13] The nonhuman and the human are thus drawn inextricably together in a web of time and space as Zanzotto increasingly confronts sociopolitical and historical realities, whose "artifacts" lie semihidden within the landscape all around him—including the thousands of corpses of First World War soldiers interred in and around the Montello Woods. Rather than seek an elevated subject matter and pure diction, Zanzotto here signals what will become in later work a radical shift in attention to all aspects (including the most fragmented and disturbing historical depths and details) of the landscape, as well as every conceivable form of speech. Soon he will embrace the idea that literally everything speaks and, as such, is fit for verse.

Zanzotto's bent for experimentalism indeed emerged with full force soon thereafter in 1968 with the publication of *La Beltà*, the beginning of what Glauco Cambron referred to as his "verbal fireworks."[14] In it scientific terminology is joined with slogans from advertising, the personalized blabblings of *"petèl"* (dialectal-styled baby talk), and fragmented quotations from such varied personages as Kafka, Hölderlin, Molière, Rorschach ink-blot test experts, and the local farmer-philosopher Nino. Montale wrote that the book acted "like a drug on the discerning intellect of the reader," and Pasolini found that in confronting it one is put in an unprec-

12. Allen, "Interview with Andrea Zanzotto," 255.
13. Translated from Andrea Zanzotto, "Un libro di Ecloghe," *Le poesie e prose scelte*, 201.
14. Glauco Cambon, foreword, *Selected Poetry of Andrea Zanzotto* (Princeton: Princeton University Press, 1975), xiii.

andrea Zanzotto

edented condition of estrangement from known semantic fields and reading habits.[15]

In *Beltà* Zanzotto indeed plunges into the cracks of linguistic and epistemological margins, exploding his poetic diction and syntax outward into the unknown. In doing so, he embraces the odd, scattered fragments of speech and meaning collected from his immediate environs, an array of old and recent literary and philosophic sources, and various forms of graphic, journalistic, and sound media. This metalinguistic investigation examines existence while working to undermine language conceived as a fixed or immutable source of meaning. Reflecting the disorienting social and cultural upheaval of the 1960s, the book grapples with the decline in agricultural folk society and local dialects, the swelling ranks of a new urban proletariat, the seemingly uncontrollable growth of consumer society, and the steadily worsening degradation of the landscape. Zanzotto can no longer rely on traditional means of communication but must invent, including the excluded and bending the apparent; he must break apart as much as build.

15. Translated from Eugenio Montale, "La poesia di Andrea Zanzotto," *Corriere della Serra*, June 1 1968, 3. Pier Paolo Pasolini, *"La Beltà* (appunti)," *Nuovi Argomenti* 21 (1971): 23–26.

In his next book, *Pasque,* Zanzotto begins to employ various graphic elements in his poetry, from little zigzagging arrows to circled words, which in later works expand to include tiny sketches of rain, pathways, playing cards, mathematical symbols, and road signs—all of which complicate the text, pointing to what exists outside it, "beyond all prepositions known and unknown."[16] In his attempt to utilize every conceivable form of language, from invented to dialectal terms, Zanzotto undertakes, as he puts it, a "search, through the movement of language, for the various points of flight, the instincts" that will enable him to "understand the world of the gods to be that whole world of instincts that certainly go back to the soma, to the body, to physicality, and that unite us to the general ecosystem."[17] In his poem "Subnarcosis," even the endless, early morning chirping of birds, full of scintillating if disturbing supralinguistic and supralogical meaning, are fair game for Zanzotto's omnivorous poetics. Like birds, his "scattered species" of sleep are forever departing, into and out upon the earth.[18] The world calls, and he calls back: a renewed colloquy ensues with matter through intertwined time and space.

While *Beltà* and subsequent books exhibit signs of influence from the radical experimentalism of the *Novissimi* and *Gruppo 63* poets, especially their calling into question of the efficacy of language, Zanzotto's verse has largely struck off on its own, remaining less politicized and more tied to place and local tradition than much of the work of the neo-avant-garde. Likewise, his axial themes concerning the self, language, and landscape have evolved alongside an increasingly challenging poetics that has consistently engaged with the past. While he has become one of the most experimental of writers, he has nonetheless remained dexterously playful with traditional verse forms. His respect and affection for centuries-old, provincial ways of life in and around Pieve di Soligo are constants, expressed without embarrassment alongside the most ingenious of recent poetic and philosophical exploits. The fact that Zanzotto and his poetry are so rooted in a specific locale, dialect, and culture provides him with various measures of both "safety" and the temptation to test limits. As such, he constantly

16. Translated from Andrea Zanzotto, "Al mondo," *Le poesie e prose scelte,* 301.
17. Allen, "Interview with Andrea Zanzotto," 259.
18. Translated from Andrea Zanzotto, "Subnarcosi," *Le poesie e prose scelte,* 391.

ventures into the mysterious connections between place, language, and identity, insistently and creatively pushing the edges of accepted meaning and linguistic coherency—a role, he believes, that is central to poetry: "That which is not involved with marginalization is not poetry . . . [yet] precisely when it is fully engaged, the force from which poetry is born touches 'the edge,' the boundary, and perhaps even crosses over all that which one was able to suspect at the beginning."[19]

In his two most recently published books, *Meteo* (1996) and *Sovrimpressioni,* Zanzotto increases his focus upon often overlooked elements of common beauty surviving within a landscape devastated by rampant traffic and insensitive development: small weeds and flowers that flourish in degraded areas such as vacant lots and roadsides, abandoned buildings that were once bustling houses, taverns, and inns, and disappearing field patterns and canal systems indicative of an older way of life more closely attuned to the earth and its seasons. As in *Idioma,* there also appear in these volumes elegiac remembrances of deceased dear friends and relatives, including Pasolini, Zanzotto's younger brother Ettore, and Nino. *Meteo* (a term that in the language of the Italian media means "weather forecast") is a collection of what Zanzotto calls in his introductory note to the book "uncertain fragments . . . provisionally organized according to themes that blend one into the other—not according to a precise temporal sequence, but perhaps a 'meteorological' one."[20] Indeed, the volume pays close attention to the subtlest changes in the atmosphere and on the ground, with pointed mediations on the humblest elements of everyday life, such as the clustered tendrils of invasive clematises in the poem "Settlements and Sites" that represent "the superfluous / and relentless gathering-in-place / and intensity of place."[21] New to this collection are a number of poems, including "Lanugos," "Legends," and "Topinambùr," consisting of series of concentrated three-line stanzas that loosely resemble haiku.

The themes of *Meteo* and of *Sovrimpressioni* are often very topical, ranging from the debate over genetically modified crops

19. Translated from Andrea Zanzotto, "Poesia?" *Le poesie e prose scelte* (Milan: Mondadori, 1999), 1201.

20. Translated from Andrea Zanzotto, *Meteo* (Rome: Donzelli, 1996), 81.

21. Translated from Andrea Zanzotto, "Sedi e siti," *Meteo,* 65.

and the war in Bosnia, to the internet and the onset of the new millennium. Zanzotto calls *Sovrimpressioni* a gathering of "'works adrift' that tend here and there to cluster in relatively uniform groups—which at once shake off, and yet are also implicated in the current atmosphere, whipped up with frenzy and all manner of excess that cause everything to bend towards an omnivorous and annihilating plethora."[22] The description, seemingly of wind-blown flowers or clouds, aptly describes the wonderfully mindful, evanescent poems, at times joyous, at others grieving, yet always connected to the capricious shifts of temperature, light, and moisture within and just "beyond" Pieve di Soligo and its encircling Piave Valley. As indeed is Zanzotto himself, simultaneously sensitive to the nearest and tiniest, continually metamorphosing elements of his everyday existence, and yet driven to attempt the exceptional, to reveal myriad connections between the psyche, language, landscape, and culture through the most innovative and unpredictable poetic means.

As Carlo Mazzacurati warmly notes, "Andrea Zanzotto is the most radical and at the same time the gentlest person I've ever met. Everything about his person seems to be ruled by extreme

22. Translated from Andrea Zanzotto, *Sovrimpressioni* (Milan: Mondadori, 2001), 133.

and unexpected contrasts. Suffering and lightness, fragility and depth."[23] In this sense person and poetry seem to merge, with the lasting impression that stands out from meeting Zanzotto and reading his work being one of an endearing humbleness coupled with a courageous daring, of an enduring desire to go beyond while remaining rooted to home. He challenges us to slow our frenetic pace and quicken our thoughts, to embrace the most familiar realities, however variously and eternally disturbing, comforting, prickly, and exhilarating they may be. And above all, while remaining painfully aware of life's dangers and disappointments, he constantly dives into uncertainty and beauty, giving us both space and reason to hope.

23. Carlo Mazzacurati, *Ritratti: Andrea Zanzotto* (Padua: Vesna Film, 2000).

Selected Poetry

da A che valse? Versi, 1938–1942

---

from What was the point?:
Verse, 1938–1942
[1970]

Nell'era della silenziosa pace
vitrei villaggi nelle aperte valli
del cielo nascono.

I sonni in figura di monti
aspettano con le celate correnti
i viandanti dai passi gravi
sospinti dallo stimolo del vento.

Nei giorni delle insonni primavere
mi verrà contro il vento che abbaglia,
mi spingerà ai febbrili amori
dimenticati alle mura
delle umane città.
Le porte aperte mostreranno
oscuri vestiboli
interminabili cortili.
Nubi azzurrognole come ghiaccio
saranno lontano, dove le sentinelle
come monumenti
al nulla fanno la guardia.

A questo ponte
finisce il freddo del prato
finisce il freddo del cielo
e della cieca luce,
finisce il freddo del tuo volto
e del tuo cuore simile a una croce,
finisce il sole con spine.

*

In the age of silent peace
translucent villages are born
in the open valleys of the sky.

Slumbers in the shape of summits
await with secret currents
the heavy steps of wayfarers
nudged along by the wind's urging.

*

In the days of sleepless springs
the dazzling wind will hit,
spurring me to feverish loves
forgotten at the walls
of human cities.
The open doors will reveal
dim vestibules
endless courtyards.
Clouds blue as ice
will distantly linger, where the sentinels
like monuments
keep watch over nothing.

*

At this bridge
the chill of the field ends
the chill of the sky
and the blind light ends,
the chill of your face
and your cross-like heart ends,
the thorny sun ends.

Le danze segrete delle acque
e degli alberi
intorno al sole domato
io sento nel freddo del prato
che affonda sotto il ponte.

I sense the secret dances of the waters
and the trees
around the tamed sun
in the cold of the field
that sinks under the bridge.

1/VII   Carl White 1949

da Dietro il paesaggio

---

from Behind the Landscape
[1951]

Indizi e luna

La stella della primavera
il dolce succo
trae negli alberi giovani.
La verde sera al suo specchio s'adorna,
ha grandi insegne ormai la città.
Cieli di giardino
sorgete ancora dai vostri spazi:
quella ch'era bambina e sorella
dalla sua casa
comprende e vede
l'antico gelo dei monti,
si stringe al petto il cuore
esile come rosa.
Dai portici, mercati
effondono troppo colmi
non colta e non venduta
la messe del loro bene,
indizi angosciosi di festa
giacciono agli angoli delle piazze.
Negli orti e nelle serre più lontane
si sfogliano e si smarriscono
le acque e la madre luna.
Gli abitanti camminano
abbagliati dal sonno.

Quanto a lungo

Quanto a lungo tra il grano e tra il vento
di quelle soffitte
più alte, più estese che il cielo,
quanto a lungo vi ho lasciate
mie scritture, miei rischi appassiti.
Con l'angelo e con la chimera
con l'antico strumento
col diario e col dramma
che giocano le notti

Indications and Moon

The star of the spring
draws the sweet sap
into the young trees.
The green evening dresses up in its mirror,
by now the signs of the city loom large.
Garden skies
you still rise up from your spaces:
she who was child and sister
from her house
understands and sees
the ancient frost of the mountains,
grasps to her breast her heart
faint as a rose.
From the porticos, markets
pour forth excesses
the harvest of their goods,
fallow and unsold,
distraught signs of celebration
wallow about in the corners of piazzas.
In the farthest gardens and greenhouses
the waters and mother moon
lose leaves and wander off.
The residents walk about
dazzled with drowsiness.

How Long

How long amid the wheat and the wind
of those garrets
higher and wider than the sky,
how long I have left you
my writings, my withered risks.
With the angel and chimera
with the ancient tool
with the diary and drama
that the nights play

a vicenda col sole
vi ho lasciate lassù perché salvaste
dalle ustioni della luce
il mio tetto incerto
i comignoli disorientati
le terrazze ove cammina impazzita la grandine:
voi, ombra unica nell'inverno,
ombra tra i dèmoni del ghiaccio.
Tarme e farfalle dannose
topi e talpe scendendo al letargo
vi appresero e vi affinarono,
su voi sagittario e capricorno
inclinarono le fredde lance
e l'acquario temperò nei suoi silenzi
nelle sue trasparenze
un anno stillante di sangue, una mia
perdita inesplicabile.

Già per voi con tinte sublimi
di fresche antenne e tetti
s'alzano intorno i giorni nuovi,
già alcuno s'alza e scuote
le muffe e le nevi dai mari;
e se a voi salgo per cornici e corde
verso il prisma che vi discerne
verso l'aurora che v'ospita,
il mio cuore trafitto dal futuro
non cura i lampi e le catene
che ancora premono ai confini.

Ormai

Ormai la primula e il calore
ai piedi e il verde acume del mondo

I tappeti scoperti
le logge vibrate dal vento ed il sole
tranquillo baco di spinosi boschi;

one after the other with the sun
I left you up there to save
from the burning light
my uncertain roof
the bewildered chimney-tops
the terraces where the crazed hail walks:
you, solitary shadow in the winter,
shadow among the demons of ice.
Noxious moths and butterflies
mice and moles dropping into hibernation
grasped and whetted you,
Sagittarius and Capricorn
trained cold lances at you
and Aquarius tempered in its silences
in its transparencies
a year dripping with blood, one of my
inexplicable losses.

Already for you with sublime tints
of fresh antennae and roofs
the new days crop up all around,
already someone rises up and shakes
the mold and the snows from the seas;
and if I climb to you along ledges and cables
towards the prism that gives form to you
towards the dawn that shelters you,
my heart transfixed by the future
ignores the lightning flashes and chains
that still press in at the edges.

By Now

By now the primrose and the warmth
at your feet and the green insight of the world

The uncovered carpets
the loggias shaken by wind and sun
tranquil worm of the thorny woods;

il mio male lontano, la sete distinta
come un'altra vita nel petto

Qui non resta che cingersi intorno il paesaggio
qui volgere le spalle.

Là sovente nell'alba

La sovente nell'alba
dall'inferno mi destava
il rombo lieve e il tremito
degli azzurri vulcani.
Tra i monti specchi eccelsi del primordio
impigliava le gracili corna
il cervo nato dalla neve;
pullulavi alle finestre
lava di primavera,
vivente a me scendevi tra le spire
degli evi deformi.

O golfo della terra
a me noto per sempre,
dalle cui pieghe antiche
spogli d'ombre balzano eventi;
freddo rifugio cui gl'insoliti
fiumi cingono il grembo,
i tuoi sparsi elementi sono
la mia solitaria gloria,
i raggi del tuo sole
non maturano che neve.
Ma ancora negli abissi
tuoi cercarti m'è caro,
in ogni tua forma giaccio sepolto,
del mio sangue ogni tua fonte esulta.

Tu clemente ricorderai le immagini
della mia vita.

my distant pain, distinct thirst
like another life in the breast

Here all that's left is to wrap the landscape around the self
and turn your back.

There Often in the Dawn

There often in the dawn
the light rumble and tremor
of azure volcanoes
awoke me from hell.
Amidst the towering mountains primeval mirrors
the deer born of the snow
entangled his slender antlers;
spring's lava
you swarmed at the windows,
living, you descended to me amidst the whorls
of disfigured ages.

O gulf of earth
forever familiar to me,
from whose ancient folds
events spring naked of shadows;
cold refuge whose womb
the extraordinary rivers encircle,
your scattered elements are
my solitary glory,
your sun's rays
ripen nothing by snow.
But in your abysses
I still love to search for you,
in your every form I lie buried,
in my blood your every springhead exults.

Temperate, you will remember the images
of my life.

Serica

Schiava d'altre stagioni
e della notte caverna di fango
cadde la luna;
dalle dighe che guidano le tenebre
dal musco che occlude le valli
dai rotti cancelli dell'alba
si manifesta e sgorga
acqua cruda di primavera.

Ma il vostro sonno sazio
di cibo, così mi sostenta,
larve beate,
che la terra ieri diroccata
pesa di rose, esce il sole
dal bocciolo di neve,
vigore acquista ovunque
buona calma dell'azzurro.

Nella ricchezza del mattino
vento e seta
trama silenzi d'alberi, dagli alti
parapetti delle selve
dei monti e della neve.

Nelle stanze moltiplicate
da parvenze e solitudini
sui piani eccelsi delle grate
tra le mani lucide del cibo

lunghi resti da voi l'insidia
innumerevole delle formiche.

Distanza

Or che mi cinge tutta la tua distanza
sto inerme dentro un'unica sera

Silky

Slave of other seasons
and of the cavernous muddy night,
the moon fell;
from the embankments that guide the shadows
from the moss that clogs the valleys
from the broken gates of dawn
spring's raw waters
rise up and gush out.

But your sleep sated
with food, thus sustains me,
beatific larvae,
the earth yesterday ragged,
weighed down with roses, the sun emerges
from the germinating snow,
vigor gains everywhere
the benevolent calm of the azure.

In the richness of the morning
wind and silk
weave silences of trees, from the high
parapets of the forests
of the mountains and the snow.

In the rooms multiplied
by flickerings and seclusions
over the hallowed surfaces of the latticework
amidst the hands glimmering with food

far from you remain the incalculable
hazards of the ants.

Distance

Now that all your distance surrounds me
I stand defenseless inside a lone evening

Odora il miele sulla mensa
e il tuono è nella valle,
molto affanno tra l'uno e l'altro

Io sono spazio frequentato
dal tuo sole deserto,
vieni a chiedermi dove
gridami solitudine

E questo azzurro guasto di sgomenti
e di luci di monti
per sempre m'ha appreso a memoria.

Adunata

Indugia ancora la parvenza
dei soldati selvaggi
sulle porte, ed ostili
insegne sui fortilizi
alza la sera, chiama piazze a raccolta.

Un arso astro distrusse questa terra
profonda in pozzi e tane
s'avventa l'ombra dell'estate
da vicoli e da altane
e dai rotti teatri.

Nel disegno dei pavimenti
nelle crepe delle caserme
nelle clausure delle palestre
un morbo splende,
il vetro seme del gelo traligna,
il vino e l'oro sui deschi appassisce.

Ma, gloria avara del mondo,
d'altre stagioni memoria deforme,
resta la selva.

The honey is redolent on the table
and thunder sounds in the valley,
much unease between one and the other

I am frequented space
deserted by your sun,
come, ask me where
shout solitude at me

And this azure sky marred with dismay
and mountain lights
forever knows me by heart.

Gathering

The apparition of the wild
soldiers still lingers
on the doors, and evening
hoists hostile banners over fortresses
summoning piazzas to the assembly.

A burnt star destroyed this earth
deep in wells and lairs
the shadow of summer hurls itself
from alleyways and terraces
and broken theaters.

In the design of pavements
in the cracks of barracks
in the seclusion of gymnasiums
a sickness shines,
the glass seed of the frost degenerates,
wine and gold decay on the tables.

But, mean glory of the world,
misshapen memory of other seasons,
the forest remains.

Nel mio paese

Leggeri ormai sono i sogni,
da tutti amato
con essi io sto nel mio paese,
mi sento goloso di zucchero;
al di là della piazza della salvia rossa
si ripara la pioggia
si sciolgono i rumori
ed il ridevole cordoglio
per cui temesti con tanta fantasia
questo errore del giorno
e il suo nero d'innocuo serpente

Del mio ritorno scintillano i vetri
ed i pomi di casa mia,
le colline sono per prime
al traguardo madido dei cieli,
tutta l'acqua d'oro è nel secchio
tutta la sabbia nel cortile
e fanno rime con le colline

Di porta in porta si grida all'amore
nella dolce devastazione
e il sole limpido sta chino
su un'altra pagina del vento.

L'acqua di Dolle

Ora viene a consolarmi
con una lunga visita
l'acqua di Dolle
che portò dieci colline al paese
sfuggì tra le api e i lor castelli di acume
toccò le forme sensitive
di un'isola di pura sabbia,
ora viene quest'acqua ch'io sospiro
perché traspare dalle tue

In My Land

With dreams by now buoyant,
loved by all
I remain in my land,
craving sugar;
beyond the piazza of the red sage
the rain steals off
and noises melt away with
the laughable sorrow
for which you so fancifully feared
this error of the day
black as a harmless serpent

The windows and apple trees
of home gleam on my return,
the hills are first
over the sky-soaked finish line,
the golden water is all in the pail
the sand all in the courtyard
together rhyming with the hills

Shouts of love fly from door to door
amid the sweet devastation
lit by the limpid sun bent over
another page of the wind.

The Water of Dolle

Now to console me
with a long visit
comes the water of Dolle
that carried ten hills to town
escaped amidst the bees and their acute castles
touched the sensitive shapes
of an island of pure sand,
now comes this water I yearn for
because it glimmers up through your

membra gemelle;
perché a lungo
indugiò nello scrigno d'ombra
dove il fico s'affaccia guardiano
e il sole non fa più musco né felce,
dove sono già aperte
le scene da festa del cielo.
Acqua ignara della creta
che già fuoresce dai suoi viluppi,
fiera del rosso momentaneo
dei fiori celebrati da quest'ora,
tu vai dovunque lambendo e tentando
le più ritrose solitudini:
lasciatemela mia,
per la mia lampadina di chiocciola
per l'orto di che il nano è mezzadro,
lei dal fittissimo alfabeto
lei che ha i messaggi
di nobili invasioni
degli astri che ritornano dalle alpi
ormai pingui d'argento,
lei che va promettendo
una notte fresca come un domani.

L'amore infermo del giorno

L'amore infermo del giorno
i monti fa deserti
e inaccessibili ormai.
I cimiteri oscuri diluvi
hanno accolto l'odore delle macerie,
le innumerevoli gale
della pioggia si assottigliano
e vanno ai cieli di carta
delle girandole e delle tende.
A lungo esita il verde
nelle soste dei prati
e tra i suoi fregi fiordalisi,

twin limbs;
because for so long
it lingered in the shadowy coffer
where the fig tree stands sentinel
and the sun no longer spawns moss or fern,
where the festive scenes of the sky
are already open.
Water oblivious of the clay
that already seeps from its snarls,
proud of the ephemeral red
of the flowers celebrated by this hour,
you go everywhere lapping and touching
the most reluctant solitudes:
let it stay mine,
for my snail's lamp
for the dwarf sharecropper's garden,
water from the densest alphabet
water with messages
of noble invasions
of stars returning from the Alps
by now laden with silver,
water that promises
a night cool as a tomorrow.

The Infirm Love of Day

The infirm love of day
makes mountains deserts
and inaccessible now.
The cemeteries dark deluges
have gathered the smell of rubble,
the rain's countless galas
thin out
and go to paper skies
of Catherine wheels and tents.
Green hesitates a long time
in the fields' pauses
and among its fleur-de-lys friezes,

l'ombra è caduta nelle piazze
si è fatta freddi umidi cervi.
In città deboli di muffa
nate sotto i venti
nelle vetrine e nei gioielli
fanciulle non vedute
schiudono il loro sopore
di semplice crisantemo.
Stanca allenta le dita
cerule e svela i puri
lineamenti la neve
dietro balconi e corti.
Dal suo vaso odoroso
il vespero ricciuto di germogli
indugia sopra il lento
discendere del mondo.

Là sul ponte

Là sul ponte di San Fedele
dove la sera abbonda
di freddo fieno
e dove la pioggia raccoglie
tutte le sue vele madide
c'è da ieri una fanciulla bionda
che ha un nome come una corona
e che ha perduto per sempre
una mano per salutare una rosa.

Sulle rive oscure del fieno
c'è una nave di pioggia
abbandonata dalla notte

Dalle stretture delle sorgenti
là si libera talvolta
la dalia abbigliata di rosso

the shadow has fallen in piazzas
has become cold damp deer.
In cities weak with mustiness
born under the winds
in windows and in jewels
unseen girls
unfold their simple
chrysanthemum stupor.
Tired snow slackens its blue
fingers and unveils
pure features
behind courtyards and balconies.
From its fragrant vase
twilight curling with shoots
lingers above the world's
slow descent.

Translated by Ruth Feldman and Brian Swann

There on the Bridge

There on the bridge of San Fedele
where the evening teems
with cold hay
and where the rain collects
all of its damp sails
since yesterday a fair-haired girl has rested
who has a name like a garland
and who has forever lost
a hand to greet a rose.

On the dim banks of hay
there sits a ship of rain
abandoned by the night

From the narrow windings of springs
the dahlia decked out in red
at times breaks free

e illumina la crisalide
intricata del sole.

Là un animale azzurro
deperisce nella sua tana
e l'estate legata dalla neve
non conosce altro frutto che se stessa.

Perché siamo

Perché siamo al di qua delle alpi
su questa piccola balza
perché siamo cresciuti tra l'erba di novembre
ci scalda il sole sulla porta
mamma e figlio sulla porta
noi con gli occhi che il gelo ha consacrati
a vedere tanta luce ed erba

Nelle mattine, se è vero,
di tre montagne trasparenti
mi risveglia la neve;
nelle mattine c'è l'orto
che sta in una mano
e non produce che conchiglie,
c'è la cantina delle formiche
c'è il radicchio, diletta risorsa
profusa alle mie dita,
a un vento che non osa disturbarci

Ha sapore di brina
la mela che mi diverte,
nel granaio s'adagia un raggio amico
ed il vecchio giornale di polvere pura;
e tutto il silenzio di musco
che noi perdiamo nelle valli
rende lento lo stesso cammino
lo stesso attutirsi del sole

and illuminates the sun's
intricate chrysalis.

There an azure animal
wastes away in its den
and summer bound by snow
knows no other fruit than itself.

Because We Are

Because we are on this side of the Alps
on this small rise
because we grew up among November grass
the sun warms us at the door
mother and son at the door
we with eyes the frost has consecrated
to see so much light and grass

Mornings, if it's true,
the snow of three transparent
mountains awakens me;
mornings there's the kitchen-garden
that fits into a hand
and yields only shells,
there's the ants' cellar
there's the red chicory, prized resource
prodigal under my fingers,
under a wind that doesn't dare disturb us

The apple I enjoy
tastes of hoar-frost,
in the granary a friendly ray lies down
and the old newspaper of pure dust;
and all the silence of moss
which we lose in the valleys
slows the same walk
the same muffling of the sun

che si coglie a guardarci
che ci coglie su tutte le porte

O mamma, piccolo è il tuo tempo,
tu mi vi porti perch'io mi consoli
a là v'è l'erba di novembre,
là v'è la franca salute dell'acqua,
sani come acqua vi siamo noi;
sana azzurra sostanza
vi degradano tutte le sieste
cui mi confondo e che sempre più vanno
comunicando con la notte

Né attingere al pozzo né alle alpi
né ricordare come tu non ricordi:
ma il sol che splende come cosa nostra,
ma sete e fame all'ora giusta
e tu mamma che tutto
sai di me, che tutto hai tra le mani.

Con la scorta di te e dell'erba
e di quella lampada precaria
di cui distinguo la fine,
sogno talvolta del mondo e guardo
dall'alto l'inverno del nord.

Dietro il paesaggio

Nei luoghi chiusi dei monti
mi hanno raggiunto
mi hanno chiamato
toccandomi ai piedi

Sulle orme incerte delle fontane
ho seguito da vicino
e senza distrarmi

that catches itself looking at us
that catches us at all the doors

Oh mother, your time is small,
you take me there to console myself
and there is the November grass,
there the frank health of water,
there we are healthy as water;
all the siestas in which I lose myself
and which are always communicating
more with night step down
to that healthy blue substance

To haul neither from well nor Alps
nor to remember as you don't remember:
but the sun shining like something that belongs to us,
but thirst and hunger at the right time
and you mother who know everything
about me, who hold it all between your hands.

With you and the grass as guide
and that precarious lamp
of which I perceive the end,
I dream sometimes of the world and look
from on high at the northern winter.

Translated by Ruth Feldman and Brian Swann

Behind the Landscape

In the closed mountain places
they reached me
called to me
touching my feet.

On the uncertain traces of fountains
I followed the Pole's
soft shadows from nearby

le tenebre tenere del polo
ho veduto da vicino
le spoglie luminose
gli ornamenti perfettissimi
dei paesi dell'Austria.

Hanno fatto l'aria tutta fresca
di ciliegi e di meli nudi
hanno lasciato soltanto
che un piccolo albero crescesse
sulla soglia della sua tristezza
hanno lasciato fuggire in un riverbero
un tiepido coniglio di pelo.

Per le estreme vie della terra caduta
assistito da giorni tardi e scarsi
discendo nel sole di brividi
che spira da tramontana.

Nella Valle

Oltre la mia porta le ultime colline
dell'anno e della guerra
s'alzano al vento di san Silvestro,
un uomo che non subisce
le leggi della notte
e che ha il mignolo d'oro
s'annuncia sulle strade
presagendo i suoi doni,
io vado ai ponti del presepe.
E l'ambra sottilmente
è cresciuta dovunque
è cresciuta la gioia
di chi non sa parlare
che per conoscere
il proprio oscuro matrimonio
con il cielo e le selve;
le mense ed i giardini

undistracted
and saw from nearby
the shining remains
the most perfect ornaments
of Austrian villages.

They cooled the air
with bare cherry and apple trees
left only
a small tree to grow
on the threshold of its sadness
and let a warm furry rabbit
escape in a gleam.

Through the farthest ways of the fallen earth
assisted by late and scarce days
I descend in the sun of shivers
that blows in with the north wind.

In the Valley

Beyond my door the last hills
of the year and of the war,
Saint Silvester's wind rises up,
a golden-fingered man
refusing to put up with
the laws of the night
heralds himself on the streets
divining his gifts,
I go to the bridges of the manger.
Amber has subtly
grown everywhere,
grown too is the joy
of those unable to speak
except to know
their own dark marriage
with the sky and the woods;
the tables and the gardens

traboccano di riccioli d'indivia
di lumache dolcissime
di zuccheri preziosi,
una stella dai suoi paesi
di solitario cristallo
ha osato sporgersi più acuta,
l'insetto sale al puro volto affranto
e diviene farfalla
e delude la fredda polvere
fuochi sicuri scarabei
si accampano con le alpi nuove
e col cielo formato dal domani

Nella valle scricchiolano porte
e botole, nella valle
mi hanno preparato il caro pasto
hanno rifatto il mio letto
di cruda indivia e di vischio.

overflow with curly endives
the sweetest snails
and precious sugars,
from its lands
a star of reclusive crystal
has dared to lean out more keenly,
the insect rises up to the pure disconsolate face
and becomes butterfly
deluding the cold dust,
assured fires scarabs
encamp with the new alps
and the sky formed from tomorrow

In the valley doors and trapdoors
are creaking, in the valley
they've cooked me the dear meal
remade my bed
of raw endives and mistletoe.

da Elegia e altri versi

from Elegy and Other Poems
[1954]

Partenza per il Vaud

Nuovi i tuoni, nuovo l'emigrante:
e non mi so decidere a partire
per voi alberi zolle e declivi,
per voi mie piccole nozioni.

Là germina la selva di molti uccelli,
la pioggia, paese ignaro, mi sta di fronte,
la resurrezione dirada le nevi di marzo,
è la stanza alitata dalla calce.

Ah, più volte l'aurora in sé confuse e spense
col sopore del domani le partenze tentate,
ha una campanella ogni sera il cimitero,
con lei le mie sorelle m'accarezzano.

Riposo potrò chiamarti, cielo? E vento
te, piangere concorde di pendici e di liane
verso il freddo Montello, parallele
ombre e certezze della mia giornata?

Giace il fardello, tu sei già, remota
nel marzo che t'invola, oltre le siepi,
ed il sole non è più che la viola
lacrimosa che tace nel bicchiere.

da Ore calanti

I

Quale lento riflesso, quale vitrea memoria
di sé ai prati affranti va tentando
questo scorcio di maggio calante?

E a me tu sempre nell'angolo oscuro
della mia sorte distruggi quel lume

Departure for Vaud

New the thunderclaps, new the emigrant:
and because of you trees clods and hollows,
because of you my little notions,
I can't make up my mind to leave.

There sprouts the forest of myriad birds,
the rain, unknowing expanse, stretches ahead of me,
the resurrection dissipates the snows of March:
a room permeated with lime.

Ah, many times with the drowsiness of tomorrow
the aurora confused and stifled attempted departures,
every evening my sisters caress me
with the cemetery bell.

Sky, will I be able to call you repose? And you
wind, concerted weeping of slopes and vines
towards the cold Montello, parallel
shadows and certainties of my day?

The satchel awaits, you are already beyond the hedges
far off in the March that spirited you away,
and the sun is nothing but the teary
violet that falls silent in the glass.

from Waning Hours

I

What slow reflex, what vitreous memory
of itself upon the smitten meadows
is this remnant of waning May seeking?

And you, always in the dark corner
of my destiny, strip that light from me

Tace il fianco beato del colle,
guarda incerto il papavero
le dissolte forze delle erbe

Prati affranti, affranti di tante acque,
grilli residui dello spazio vinto,
e non raggiungeranno il crudo azzurro
né il felice giro dei monti

Tu, mia morte, fredda riporti
e cara quest'ombra di maggio
ed una sera divenuta un raggio
che triste si sfibra a illimpidirsi.

III

Ormai m'apparve il senso dell'estate,
serena è forse l'ombra tua
tra quelle del paese dei ciliegi piovosi,
alla sorgente s'accordano i boschi,
foglia con foglia ombra con ombra
la mia stagione è tutta qui

E tutto il mondo è l'orto mio
dove raccolgo a sera
dolci bacche accecate e caute acque,
dal fedele azzurro del Nord
un soffio incrina l'estate leggera
e le immagini pigre dei monti,
la nube è tanto più del suo profumo

Tardivo canta l'uccello ai ciliegi
domestica mi segue l'ortica.

V

Arrischiata luce
prati che v'induceste
lungi nel grembo di una sera

Rinviene l'acqua e indovina Pedeguarda
indovina la nube nera

The blissful hillside is silent
as the poppy watches in uncertainty
the unraveled forces of the grasses

Smitten meadows, smitten with myriad rivulets,
vestigial crickets of vanquished space,
who will attain neither the raw azure
nor the happy circling of the peaks

You, my death, carry back this shadow
of May cold and dear
as an evening-turned-ray
wears itself in sadness thin and clear.

III

By now the feeling of summer has come to me,
your shadow is serene perhaps
amidst the dark flickerings of sodden cherry trees,
the woods harmonize with the wellspring,
leaf with leaf shadow with shadow
my season is all here

And all the world is my garden
where I gather in the evening
sweet darkened berries and cautious waters,
from the stalwart azure of the North,
a gust ruptures the mild summer
and the lazy shapes of the mountains,
the cloud is much more than its perfume

The evening bird sings to the cherry trees
as the common nettle pursues me.

V

Reckless light
meadows where you grew resolved
distant in the lap of an evening

The water revives and divines Pedeguarda
divines the black cloud

che su Dolle scavalca con l'estate
infausta, e al verde umano al verde vano
delle chine la mia poca vita
si fa grande di tante
profonde fantasie di colline.

that straddles Dolle with the ominous
summer, and towards the human green the vain green
of the slopes my little life
grows large with myriad
resounding fantasies of hills.

da Vocativo

---

from Vocative
[1957]

Fiume all'alba

Fiume all'alba
acqua infeconda tenebrosa e lieve
non rapirmi la vista
non le cose che temo
e per cui vivo

Acqua inconsistente acqua incompiuta
che odori di larva e trapassi
che odori di menta e già t'ignoro
acqua lucciola inquieta ai miei piedi

da digitate logge
da fiori troppo amati ti disancori
t'inclini e voli
oltre il Montello e il caro acerbo volto
perch'io dispero della primavera.

Caso vocativo

I

O miei mozzi trastulli
pensieri in cui mi credo e vedo,
ingordo vocativo
decerebrato anelito.
Come lordo e infecondo
avvolge un cielo
armonie di recise ariste, vene
dubitanti di rivi,
e qui deruba
già le lampade ai deschi
sostituisce il bene.
Come i cavi s'ingranano a crinali
i crinali a tranelli a gru ad antenne
e ottuso mostro
in un prima eterno capovolto
il futuro diviene.

River at Dawn

River at dawn
infertile shadowy tenuous water
don't steal my sight away
not the things that I fear
and live by

Vague water incomplete water
you smell of worms and passings
you smell of mint and already I look away
water restless firefly at my feet

from many-fingered loggias
from flowers overly loved you break away
you cant upwards and fly
beyond the Montello and its dear coarse face
because I despair of the springtime.

Vocative Case

I

O my mutilated toys
thoughts in which I believe and see myself,
greedy vocative
decerebrated longing.
How filthy and infertile
a sky enfolds
harmonies of cut ears of corn, uncertain
veins of streams,
and here it already
steals lamps from tables
and substitutes the good.
As wires mesh with ridges
ridges with snares with cranes with antennas
and the future becomes
a dull monster in a past
continually capsizing.

Il suono il movimento
l'amore s'ammollisce in bava
in fisima, gettata
torcia il sole mi sfugge.
Io parlo in questa
lingua che passerà.

II

Anni perduti sotto la rotta vampa
pomeridiana dei cicloni,
anni dove l'attesa mi dissolse,
dove straziato il ritorno invocai;
là dietro la mia vita,
presso l'addentante
torrenziale condanna
che mezzogiorno ormai vieta e la vana
perennità del sole.
Tremo e piango tra i boschi?
O grumi verdi, ostile
spessore d'erompenti pieghe,
terra—passato di tomba—
donde la mia
lingua disperando si districa
e vacilla; vacilla se dal dorso
attonito del monte
smuove le sue lebbrose fronti il cielo.
Ah passaggio mio fervido, accorato
amoroso passaggio. Vedo felci
avanzare e sciuparsi nelle nere
correnti, e tra vaganti
inferni, gorghi atomici, il pudore d'ortica
e il vino e il dolce lavoro di Dolle
deprimere il suo lume,
la vite inclinarsi disossata
sventurata sulle case, l'uva
chiudere il vento e il giorno.

Sound movement
love softening in slaver
in whim, thrown
torch the sun escapes me.
I speak in this
tongue that will pass.

II

Years lost under the broken
afternoon blaze of cyclones,
years where waiting dissolved me
where tormented I invoked return;
there behind my life,
near the biting
torrential condemning
that noon now forbids and the empty
endlessness of the sun.
Do I shake and cry in the woods?
Oh green clots, hostile
thickness of bursting folds,
earth—grave's past—
whence my
despairing tongue disentangles itself
and sways; sways if from the astonished
spine of the mountain
the sky stirs its leprous brows.
Ah my fervid passing, brokenhearted
amorous passing. I see ferns
approach and wilt in the black
currents, and amidst wandering
hells, atomic vortexes, I see the nettle's modesty
the wine and the easy work of Dolle
lower its lamp,
and the limp vine tilt
luckless over the houses, and the grape
close the wind and the day.

Colloquio

*«Ora il sereno è ritornato le campane suonano per il vespero ed il le
ascolto con grande dolcezza. Gli ucelli cantano festosi nel cielo
perché? Tra poco e primavera i prati meteranno il suo manto verde,
ed io come un fiore appasito guardo tutte queste meraviglie.»*
SCRITTO SU UN MURO IN CAMPAGNA

Per il deluso autunno,
per gli scolorenti
boschi vado apparendo, per la calma
profusa, lungi dal lavoro
e del sudato male.
Teneramente
sento la dalia e il crisantemo
fruttificanti ovunque sulle spalle
del muschio, sul palpito sommerso
d'acque deboli e dolci.
Improbabile esistere di ora
in ora allinea me e le siepi
all'ultimo tremore
della diletta luna,
vocali foglie emana
l'intimo lume della valle. E tu
in un marzo perpetuo le campane
dei Vesperi, la meraviglia
delle gemme e dei selvosi uccelli
e del languore, nel ripido muro
nella strofe scalfita ansimando m'accenni;
nel muro aperto da piogge e da vermi
il fortunato marzo
mi spieghi tu con umili
lontanissimi errori, a me nel vivo
d'ottobre altrimenti annientato
ad altri affanni attento.

Sola sarai, calce sfinita e segno,
sola sarai fin che duri il letargo
o s'ecciti la vita.

Colloquy

"Now it has cleared the bells ring for vespers and I listen to them with great peace. Why do the birds Sing festive in the sky? Spring soon and the meadows will put on their green mantle, and I like a withered flower stand looking at all these wonders."
WRITTEN ON A COUNTRY WALL

Through deluded autumn,
through woods losing their
color I appear, through the prodigal
calm, far from work
and from sweaty evil.
Tenderly
I smell the dahlia and the chrysanthemum
fructifying everywhere on the moss's
back, on the submerged pulse
of frail gentle waters.
Improbable existing from hour
to hour aligns me and the hedges
to the last quiver
of the dear moon;
the intimate valley light
puts forth vocal leaves. And
in a perpetual March the Vesper
bells, the wonder
of buds wood-birds
and languor, in the steep wall
in the scratched strophe you beckon me gasping;
in the wall breached by rains and worms
fortunate March
you explain to me with humble
distant errors, to me in the quick
of October otherwise destroyed
attentive to other sufferings.

You'll be alone, worn lime and mark,
you'll be alone as long as lethargy lasts
or life rouses.

Io come un fiore appassito
guardo tutte queste meraviglie

E marzo quasi verde quasi
meriggio acceso di domenica
marzo senza misteri

inebetì nel muro.

I paesaggi primi

Dal mio corpo la coltre di neve
rimuovi, padre, e il sole
sei che brusco mi anima:
e alle mie dita
componi frutti e fiori intensi
in un soffice inverno che pur duole
pur duole ovunque su in collina?
Dal tuo pennello fervido,
ma talvolta più algido che specchi
che cieli perduti nei cieli,
lavorano di luci
e muschi i paradisi ed i presepi
che tutt'intorno hai già, che sulla
bianca parete a me seduci,
tu modesto signore
di Lorna che creasti e che ti crea,
tu artefice
di me, di un mai sopito amore.

Da un'altezza nuova

I

Ancora, madre, a te mi volgo,
non chiedermi del vero,

I like a withered flower
stand looking at all these wonders.

And March, almost green almost
noon lit with Sunday
March that holds no mysteries

stunned in the wall.

The First Landscapes

From my body, father, you lift
the mantle of snow, you are
the brusque sun that animates me:
and at my fingertips
do you arrange vivid fruits and flowers
in a mild winter that languishes still
languishes everywhere high in the hills?
With your fervid brush
but at times colder than mirrors
than skies lost in skies,
the elysiums and crèches
teeming with lights and mosses
that you already have around you, that you lure
to me on the white wall,
you modest lord
of Lorna which created you and which creates you,
you crafter
of me, of a never-tiring love.

From a New Height

I

Again, mother, I turn to you,
don't ask the truth of me,

non di questo precluso
estremo verde ch'io ignorai
per tanti anni e che maggio mi tende
ora sfuggendo; alla mia inquinata
mente, alla mia disfatta pace.
Madre, donde il mio dirti,
perché mi taci come il verde altissimo
il ricchissimo nihil,
che incombe e esalta, dove
beatificanti fiori e venti gelidi
s'aprono dopo il terrore—e tu, azzurro,
a me stesso, allo specchio che evolve
nel domani, ancora mi conformi?
Ma donde, da quali tue viscere
il gorgoglio fosco dei fiumi,
da quale ossessione quelle erbe
che da secoli
a me impone?
Amore a te, voce a te, o disciolto
come nevi silenzio, come raggi
rasi dal nulla: sorgo, e questo gemito
che stringe, questo fiore che irrora
di rosso i prati e le labbra, questa porta
che senza moto si disintegra
in canicole ed acque . . .

.   .   .   .

E, come da un'altezza nuova,
l'anima mai non ti ricorda—
in scalinosi
sogni, in impervie astenie,
tra dolce fumo e orti approfonditi
là sotto il lago, là nelle rugiade
traboccanti, dall'occhio
ereditati ancora,
ancora al tocco triste
dell'alba lievitanti . . .

II

Un senso che non muove ad un'immagine,
un colore disgiunto da un'idea,

nor this closed
last green I did not know
for so many years and which May now fleeing
offers to me; to my polluted
mind, my shattered peace.
Mother, whence my speaking to you,
why do you keep silent like the high green
the rich nihil,
that impends, exalts, where
beatifying flowers and icy winds
open after the terror—and you, sky,
do you still adapt me to myself,
to the mirror that evolves into tomorrow?
But whence, from what viscera of yours
the dark gurgle of rivers,
from what obsession those grasses
that for centuries
you impose on me, wretched?
Love to you, voice to you, or silence
melted like snows like rays
scraped from nothing: I rise and this groan
that binds, this flower that sprinkles
fields and lips with red, this door
that motionless crumbles
into dog days and waters . . .

. . . .

And, as from a new height,
my soul does not remember you—
in dreams of
steps, in impervious asthenias,
between mild smoke and deep-dug gardens
there under the lake, there in the overflowing
dew, still
inherited by the eye
still rising at the sad
touch of dawn . . .

    II

A sense that does not move to an image,
a color detached from an idea,

un'ansia senza testimoni
o una pace perfetta ma precaria:
questo è l'io che mi désti, madre e che ora
appena riconosco, né parola
né forma né ombra?
Al vero—al negro bollore dei monti—
con insaziate lacrime
ancora, ancora sottratto
per un giorno all'aculeo del drago,
ritorno e non so
non so tacere.

. . . .

Nulla dunque compresi
del brancicare avido di bestie
d'insetti e fiori e soli,
nulla m'apparve del lavoro
là sussurrato e sparso
nei campi, aggrinzito nel nido,
né il sudore m'apparve, l'altrui vigile
combustione, ed io solo
io trasceso
in un feroce colloquente vuoto
fronte a fronte mi attinsi?

Calda la mano accarezza ancora il frutto.
Nel vicolo il bambino e l'artigiano.
Vivo il lume degli occhi nel profondo.
Questo fu mio, né mai seppi, mai vidi?
Per voi non m'allietai né piansi ancora?
Madre ignora il tuo volto ma non l'ansia
proliferante sempre
in ogni piega in ogni bene in ogni
tuo rivelarmi,
ma non l'amore senza riparo
che da te, mostro o spirito, m'avvolge
e aridamente m'accalora.

an unwitnessed anxiety
or a peace perfect but precarious:
is this the I you gave me, mother, that now
I scarcely recognize, not word
not shape not shadow?
To truth—to the black seethe of mountains—
with tears still unsated,
still saved for a day from the dragon's sting,
I return and I don't know
I don't know how to keep silent.

. . . .

I understood nothing, then,
of the greedy groping of beasts
insects flowers and suns,
nothing appeared to me of the work
whispered and strewn there
in the fields; shriveled in the nest
neither did sweat appear to me, others' watchful
combustion, and I alone
I, transcended in a fierce speaking void,
brow to brow did I attain myself?

The warm hand still strokes the fruit.
In the side-street child and workman.
Lively the eyes' light in the depths.
Was this mine and did I never know, never see?
Did I still not rejoice not weep for you?
Mother your face was unknown to me but not the anxiety
always multiplying
, in each crease in every good in all
your revelings to me,
but not the irreparable love
which from you, monster or spirit, enfolds
and warms me aridly.

Translated by Ruth Feldman and Brian Swann

Esistere psichicamente

Da questa artificiosa terra-carna
esili acuminati sensi
e sussulti e silenzi,
da questa bava di vicende
—soli che urtarono fili di ciglia
ariste appena sfrangiate pei colli—
da questo lungo attimo
inghiottito da nevi, inghiottito dal vento,
da tutto questo che non fu
primavera non luglio non autunno
ma solo egro spiraglio
ma solo psiche,
da tutto questo che non è nulla
ed è tutto ciò ch'io sono:
tale la verità geme a se stessa,
si vuole pomo che gonfia ed infradicia.
Chiarore acido che tessi
i bruciori d'inferno
degli atomi e il conato
torbido d'alghe e vermi,
chiarore-uovo
che nel morente muco fai parole
e amori.

Impossibilità della parola

Se con te, sorella, se in tua vece
giacendo corpo di vetro, dal vetro
della bara dal basso
dolce e pauroso, il mondo
veduto avessi, ieri, tra bisbigli
di campane e il compianto di novembre
—come in un vecchio film venne narrato—
se il tuo silenzio col mio mutato avessi,

Existing Psychically

From this artful earth-flesh
thin sharp senses
and starts and silences,
from this slaver of events
—suns that collided with threads of eyelashes
sparsely fringed wheat-spikes across the hills—
from this long instant
swallowed by snows, swallowed by wind,
from all this which was not
spring not July not autumn
but just sickly glimmer
just psyche,
from all this which is nothing
and is everything that I am:
in this way truth groans to itself,
wants to be an apple that swells and soaks.
Sour brightness that weaves
the stings of hell
of atoms and the murky
struggle of seaweed and worms,
egg-gleam
that in the dying slime makes loves
and words.

Translated by Ruth Feldman and Brian Swann

Impossibility of the Word

If with you, sister, if in your place
prostrate body of glass, from the glass
of the coffin from the gentle
and fearful deep, if only I had seen
the world, yesterday, amidst whisperings
of bells and November's lament
—as if recounted in an old film—
if only I had altered your silence with mine,

non maggiore l'affanno, non la morte
maggiore: e consumato
lo stanco equivoco ora mi dorrei?
E se per te compagno, se in tua vece
i folgoranti prati
la terra tagliente la neve
saziata avessi,
nel tuo grido quale grido mio
per te, dal cuore lacerato, quale
fatale e fosco giorno a lieto volto
a aperto petto salutato avrei.
Che mi trattenne lungi
da voi, dal vostro sonno
sterile o dalla vostra
umile apoteosi? Forse quella
che dicono sporca speranza—
e al gioco spinto ancora
da viscere agitate
di presente, di fisici conati,
non disertai da questo
esistere ove terra
tocca e beve la mente, dove il sole
è un lontano martirio.
Non disertai, né seguirvi mi fu dato
oltre l'accadimento
lo schema atono afoso delle lacrime.

Speranza e fede, virtù che dai cieli
discendono, assai più che il fuoco offeso
di carità. Voci ed occhi traditi
assai, ma più tu offesa
carità senza potenza, sgomenta
anima; né te volli salvare
per alla fine perderti, pietoso
non fui troppo di me se prime e verdi
sempre, nelle ombre mie,
speranza carità fede non foste voi
quella che pietà di noi si dice.
E se un giorno dal fango,
da una veglia impossibile,

the worry no greater, no greater
the death: and the weary
equivocation consumed, would I regret it now?
And if for you friend, if in your place I had
the glimmering meadows
the keen earth
the sated snow,
in your cry like my cry
for you, from the rent heart, what
dark and fatal day would I have greeted
with a cheerful face an open breast.
Who kept me far
from you, from your sterile
sleep or humble
apotheosis? Perhaps that
which they call grimy hope—
and still driven to the game
by restless viscera
of present, of physical strainings,
I did not abandon this
existence where the mind
and earth touch and drink, where the sun
is a distant martyrdom.
I did not abandon, nor was I allowed to follow you
beyond the happening
the stifling toneless scheme of tears.

Hope and faith, virtues that from the skies
descend, far beyond charity's aggrieved
fire. Oft-deceived eyes
and voices, but more so you, vexed
and powerless charity, dismayed
soul; nor did I want to save you
only in the end to lose you; I was not
too merciful with myself if first and always
green, in my shadows,
hope charity faith you were not
that which we call mercy upon us.
And if one day from the mud,
from an impossible vigil,

o da una sede non umana,
o da un'innominabile certezza
io-non-io ripensassi a questo spazio
gocciola, astuta pietra, a questa
sacra e feroce brevità di cose
e sensi e segni, se il fuoco di Marte
cogliessi avvolto alle sue sere e mari
di salutari effimere salsedini
e fanciulle protese ad abbracciare
il luccichio degl'inferi
e l'opera che edifica e ricade
in sé come in un sogno, forse anch'io
—reo di speranza e d'amore—
se tu fossi, sarei, tu ch'è da folli
il nominare, da folli il tacere?
Stipato avello, attesa, eco, di testa
mozza: al più blasfemo
dei silenzi equivale.
Ma donde in suoni che nulla
non di te colmi insegnano, non cieli
né opere né volti né lo stesso
adusto loro contraddirsi,
io mi trascino e tento?
Dai mattini orribili tu liberami
dalla luce infinita che non leva
a sé le mie scomposte
passioni, i gesti invano ripetuti,
ai mattini toglimi, ai risvegli
nel raggiante terrore,
tu risveglio perpetuo su te stesso.

Prima del sole

Ancora lo stupore, io me stesso
parlo a me stesso e la valle rilevo
e i profondi suoi veri.
Io stupore che cresce che torna
dopo le offese,

or from a nonhuman place
or an unnamable certainty
I-not-I were to rethink this space
drop of water, wise stone, this
sacred and fierce brevity of things
senses and signs, if I were to gather
the fires of Mars enveloped in its evenings and seas
of salutary ephemeral saltiness
and girls leaning to embrace
the shimmer of hells
and the work that builds and falls back
into itself as in a dream, perhaps I too
—guilty of hope and of love—
if you were, would I be, you for whom it is madness
to name, madness to remain silent?
Crowded grave, waiting, echo, of severed
head: equivalent to the most blasphemous
of silences.
But where in sounds which teach
nothing if not filled with you, not skies
nor works nor faces nor the same
dry contradicting of theirs,
do I drag myself and strive?
Free me from the horrible mornings
from the infinite light that does not lift
to itself my jumbled
passions, the futilely repeated gestures,
free me from the mornings, the reawakenings
in radiant terror,
you, perpetual reawakening upon yourself.

Before the Sun

Again the stupor, I myself
speak to myself and observe the valley
and its actual depths.
I—stupor—who grows, returns
after the wrongs,

quando ogni oppressione
già è velata passione che s'attende,
quando ogni dorso d'erbe
o vivificatrice
acqua m'appaghi o fiotto
lucido eccelso di nubi,
od ombra
non attingibile mi leghi,
quando occhi guardano guardati
ma ancora eccederebbe il sole

Stupore che in sé e nelle cose
dolorando, godendo s'instaura . . .

Dal cielo

Se in te mi esprime il risveglio
se io tutto
avvampo e sono mente,
io tuo seno, realtà:
brevi figure tra cui svolse
il suo debole senso la mia vita,
lieto e aspro rifugio
che l'alba senza affanni e il sole
già sommuove di pura meraviglia,
ecco il dono e l'azzurro
usciti in forza dalla morte,
ecco supero il corpo
mio impoverito e il respiro
e tutto da te riconosco,
cielo, felicità di fibre miti
di felci e brine,
conclusiva diafana ebrietà,
intransigente e fulgida
causa che stai nel vero.

Dal cielo è questa penombra
dove senza termine è la fede

when every oppression
is already knowing veiled passion,
when every blade of grass
or vivifying
wellspring contents me or sublime
lustrous spouting of clouds,
or intangible
shadow binds me,
when watched eyes watch
but still the sun seems to surpass

Stupor—which in itself and things
suffering, enjoying—sets in . . .

From the Sky

If the awakening expresses me in you
if all of me
blazes and is mind,
I your breast, reality:
brief shapes among which my life
unfolded its frail meaning,
happy and rough refuge
that effortless dawn and sun
already stir with pure wonder,
here are the gift and the blue
sprung in force from death,
here I overcome this impoverished
body and breath of mine
and I acknowledge everything from you,
sky, happiness of soft
fern-fibers and hoar-frost,
final diaphanous rapture,
uncompromising brilliant source
that stands in the truth.

From the sky is this half-shadow
where even the faith of the insect—

anche dell'insetto che procede
dalla foglia invernale alla stella
che ardendo gocciò nella valle,
dal cielo è questo scrigno di paesi
dormenti tra le presenze oscure
e feconde dei monti,
dal cielo è l'ordine tenace e leggero
delle viti sui colli
dov'io tacqui e sorrisi,
e dal cielo è la strada
che già mi balza dalle mani
verso il lavoro e la ventura
mentre turge la fiamma dentro il vetro
e di tintinni brulicano i boschi.

Da te azzurra remota corona,
assedio e sostegno,
è la mia noncuranza
ed il grido onde volgo
le ormai facili spalle,
da te s'irradia la mia pace
al di là delle ortiche
insonni, dei bronchi in agguato,
e se m'adagio e ascolto
il sussurro di sagra che fa nostro l'inverno
se porgo orecchio alla lusinga
bisbigliata dai gerani
già oltre il ghiaccio di gennaio,
dal cielo io dico ogni mio moto
ogni verde d'atti scintillanti
ogni luce d'atti incerti e immaturi
per pienezza d'amore,
e in amore già accolte le colline
io sempre rinascendo
insieme riconduco al cielo.

Mani, lingua, respiro,
dal cielo è questo mio conoscervi,
dal cielo vita immemore
ti componi al tuo sguardo e il tuo sguardo

proceeding from winter leaf to the star
that dripped burning into the valley—is endless,
from the sky is this coffer of villages
sleeping among the dark and fruitful
presences of mountains,
from the sky is the tenacious and light order
of vines on the hills
where I fell silent and smiled,
and from the sky is the path
that already leaps from my hands
toward work and chance
while the flame swells inside the glass
and the woods swarm with ringing.

From you remote blue crown,
siege and support,
is my indifference
and the cry from which I turn
my back, easy now;
from you my peace radiates
beyond sleepless
nettles, brushwood lying in wait,
and if I stretch out and listen
to the murmur of the feast that makes winter ours
if I turn my ear to the seductions
whispered by geraniums
already beyond January ice,
from the sky I tell each of my motions
each green of sparkling ants
each light of acts uncertain and unripe
through fullness of love,
and the hills already embraced in love
I eternally in rebirth
bring them back together to the sky.

Hands, tongue, breath,
from the sky comes my knowledge of you,
you—oblivious life—create yourself
from the sky at your glance

dal cielo si compone.
E in volto di mattino si riannuncia
a sé quanto da sé fu oppresso:
vedere, udire, ancora
a me nuovi ritornano?
E questo io posso donde
la faglia senza fondo mi divelse
e, fatto sangue, nelle congiunture
nuove che il mondo affermano,
viventi sensi, muovere a me stesso?
Riproposte realtà
qui dal vuoto che smuore
vi attendo perché io sia. Dal cielo
è la pietà che il mondo fa consistere.

and your glance is created from the sky.
What oppressed itself in the morning face
is announced again:
seeing, hearing, do they
still return fresh to me?
And this me, from where
the bottomless rock-fault uprooted me,
and, made into blood, in the new
conjunctions that affirm the world,
living senses—can I move to myself?
Reproposed realities
from the paling void
I wait here for you
so that I may exist. From the sky
comes the mercy that makes the world persist.

Translated by Ruth Feldman and Brian Swann

4/25   C. W. Lewis

da IX Ecloghe

---

from IX Eclogues
[1962]

Un libro di Ecloghe

Non di dèi non di prìncipi e non di cose somme,
non di te né d'alcuno, ipotesi leggente,
né certo di me stesso (chi crederebbe?) parlo.
Né indovino che voglia tanta menzogna, forte
come il vero ed il santo, questo canto che stona
ma commemora norme s'avvince a ritmi a stimoli:
questo che ad altro modo non sa ancora fidarsi.
Un diagramma dell'«anima»? Un paese che sempre
piumifica e vaneggia di verde e primavere?
Giocolieri ed astrologi all'evasione intenti,
a liberar farfalle tra le rote superne?
Trecentomila parti congiunte a fil di lama,
l'acre tricosa macchina il futuro disquama?

Faticosa parentesi che questo isoli e reggi
come rovente ganglio che induri nell'uranico
vacuo soma, parentesi tra parentesi innumeri,
pronome che da sempre a farsi nome attende,
mozza scala di Jacob, «io»: l'ultimo reso unico:
e dunque dèi e prìncipi e cose somme in te,
in te potenze, cose d'ecloga degne chiudi;
in te rantolo e fimo si fanno umani studi.

Ecloga I
I lamenti dei poeti lirici

Persone: *a, b*

a: Alberi, cespi, erbe, quasi
   veri, quasi all'orlo del vero,
   dal dominio del monte che la gran luce simula
   sempre tornando, scendendo
   a incristallirvi
   in oniriche antologie:
   mite selva un lamento
   mite bisbigliate un accorato

A Book of Eclogues

Not of gods not of princes and not of things sublime,
not of you nor of anyone, readable hypothesis,
nor of myself (who would believe it?) do I speak.
Nor can I guess why so much lying is needed, strong
as the true and the sacred, this song which is out of tune
but commemorates rules, draws itself towards rhythms and stimuli:
this which still cannot entrust itself to another mode.
A diagram of the "soul"? A land that is always
sprouting feathers and raving of green and of springtimes?
Jugglers and astrologers intent on escape,
on freeing butterflies among ethereal wheels?
Three hundred thousand parts joined along a knife blade,
the bitter jumbled machine which disrupts the future?

Exhausting parenthesis that isolates and supports this
like a burning ganglion that endures in the Uranic
vacuous burden, parenthesis within innumerable parentheses,
pronoun forever waiting to become noun,
Jacob's severed ladder, "I": the last made singular:
and thus gods and princes and things sublime in you,
in you powers, things worthy of an eclogue you enclose;
in you death rattle and filth become human studies.

Eclogue I
Lament of the lyrical poets

Personae: *a, b*

a: Trees, bushes, grasses, almost
    real, almost on the edge of the real,
    from the dominion of the mountain which the vast light simulates,
    always returning, descending
    to crystallize
    in oneiric anthologies:
    gentle forest you whisper
    a gentle lament, an aggrieved

ostinato non utile dire.
Significati allungano le dita,
sensi le antenne filiformi.
Sillabe labbra clausole
unisono con l'ima terra.
Perfettissimo pianto, perfittissimo.

. . . .

E tenta di valere, accenna, avvampa
l'altra mano dell'uomo.
Da lei protesa
rugge, accelera il razzo a dipanare
il metallo totale dei cieli.
Per lei fibrilla il silenzio, incellulisce.
Oh aquiloni orientati
più su dell'infanzia, più del punto che brilla,
mano da un fuoco a un altro, mano bisturi.
Mano dove gli strati serpeggiano nel coma,
dove il ventre della terra accampa
profili irriferibili,
funzioni insospettate, osceni segni,
foglie e corpi di sofismi, il libro
che non scrisse, la penna, non illustrò, il colore.
Autopsie, autopsie.
Mano da un fuoco a un altro, mano bisturi.

. . . .

Ma pure, ecco, «le mie labbra non freno»
insinui, selva,
tu molto umiliata,
tu quasi viva, più che viva, quasi viva
—le tue foglie movendo
bagliori come d'insetto nel lago
albuminoso che fu notte fu giorno
occhio in gioia occhio in lutto . . .

. . . .

Chiedono, implorano, i poeti,
li nutre Lazzaro alla sua mensa,
come cigni biancheggiano.

obstinate useless speaking.
Meanings elongate fingers,
senses stretch out their wiry antennae.
Syllables lips clauses
unite with the deep earth.
Most perfect lament, most perfect.

. . . .

Attempting to be of value,
man's other hand beckons, burns.
From it propelled
the rocket roaring, accelerating to unravel
the total metal of the skies.
Through it silence seeps, forms cells.
Oh kites steered
higher than infancy, higher than the shining point,
hand from one fire to another, scalpel hand.
Hand where the layers creep in the coma,
where the earth's belly advances
inexplicable profiles,
unsuspected functions, obscene signs,
leaves and bodies of sophisms, the book
the pen didn't write, color didn't illustrate.
Autopsies, autopsies.
Hand from one fire to another, scalpel hand.

. . . .

And yet, look, "I do not curb my lips"
you insinuate, forest,
you much humiliated,
you almost alive, more than alive, almost alive
—your leaves moving
gleams as if of insects in the albuminous
lake that was night was day
eye in joy eye in grief . . .

. . . .

They ask, implore, the poets,
Lazzaro feeds them at his table,
like white swans they shine.

Invocano l'amata
l'iddio la pia vittima le orme
che s'addentrano al simbolo
(morì quel simbolo, morì).
Nomi hanno, date con interrogativo,
schede, schemi,
cadaveri com'elitre
in oniriche antologie.
Perfettissimo pianto, perfettissimo.
I poeti tra cui
se tu volessi pormi
«cortese donna mia»
sidera feriam vertice.

b: Come per essi, basterà la tua
confessione, immodesta, amorosa,
e quasi vera e più che vera
come il canone detta:

a: «Ma io non sono nulla
nulla più che il tuo fragile annuire.
Chiuso in te vivrò come la goccia
che brilla nella rosa e si disperde
prima che l'ombra dei giardini sfiori,
troppo lungo, la terra.»

Ecloga II
La vita silenziosa

a M.

I

Sediamo insieme ancora
tra colli, nella domestica selva.
Tenere fronde dalle tempie scostiamo,
soli e cardi e vivaci prati scosto
da te, amica. O erbe che salite
verso il buio duraturo, verso

They invoke the loved one
the god the pious victim the tracks
which penetrate the symbol
(it died that symbol, it died).
They have names, dates with a question mark,
filing cards, diagrams
cadavers like the wing-casings of insects
in oneiric anthologies.
Most perfect lament, most perfect.
The poets among whom
if you wished to place me
"cortese donna mia"
sidera feriam vertice.

b: As for them, your confession,
    immodest, loving, is enough,
    and almost true and more than true
    as the canon dictates:

a: "But I am nothing
    nothing more than your fragile assent.
    Closed in you I will live like a drop
    that gleams in a rose and is scattered
    before the gardens' shadow withers,
    stretched too long upon the earth."

Eclogue II
The silent life

to M.

I

Again we sit together
amidst hills, in the domestic wood.
We brush branches from our foreheads,
suns and thistles and vivacious meadows I brush away
from you, friend. Oh grasses that climb
towards enduring dark, towards

qui omnia vincit.
E venti estinguono e rinnovando
a ogni volgere d'ore e d'acque
le anime nostre.
Ma noi sediamo intenti
sempre a una muta fedele difesa.
Tenera sarà la mia voce e dimessa
ma non vile,
raggiante nella gola
—che mai l'ombra dovrebbe toccare—
raggiante sarà la tua voce
di sposalizio, di domenica.
Non saremo potenti, non lodati,
accosteremo i capelli e le fronti
a vivere
foglie, nuvole, nevi.
Altri vedrà e conoscerà: la forza
d'altri cieli, di pingui
reintegratrici
atmosfere, d'ebbri paradossi,
altri moverà storia
e sorte. A noi
le madri nella cucina fuochi
poveri vegliano, dolce
legna in cortili cui già cinge il nulla
colgono. Poco latte
ci nutrirà finché
stolti amorosi inutili
la vecchiezza ci toglierà, che nel prossimo
campo le mal fiorite aiole
prepara e del cuore
i battiti incerti, la pena
e l'irreversibile stasi.

· II

Ma tu conoscerai del mio sorriso
l'implorazione ferma
nei millenni come una ferita,
io del tuo l'alba ad ogni alba.

qui omnia vincit.
And winds extinguish and renew
at every turn of hours and waters
our souls.
But we sit intent
always in a silent, loyal defense.
Kind will my voice be and restrained
but not cruel,
shining in the throat
—which never should the shadow touch—
shining will your voice be
of the wedding, of Sunday.
We will not be powerful, nor praised,
we will draw near hair and brows
to live
leaves, clouds, snows.
Others will see and know: the strength
of other skies, of rich
restorative
atmospheres, of intoxicated paradoxes,
others will shift history
and fate. For us
mothers in kitchens watch over
poor fires, gather mild
firewood in courtyards walled by
nothingness. A little milk
will nourish us until,
foolish useless loving,
old age carries us off,
that in the next field
prepares the poorly blooming flowerbeds
and in the heart
uncertain beats, the pain
and the irreversible stasis.

II

But you will know from my smile
the pleading, fixed
like a wound through the millennia,
I, from yours, the dawn at every dawn.

Germoglio lieve ti conoscerò:
quanto aprirai, quanto ci appagherai
di lievi avvenimenti.
Droghe innocue, bufere di marzo;
orti d'iridi e cera, sinecure
per menti e mani molli d'allergie;
letture su pulviscolo d'estati,
letture su piogge, tra spine infinite di piogge.
Talvolta Urania il vero
come armato frutto ci spezzerà davanti:
massimi cieli,
voli che la notte
solstiziale riattizza,
gemme di remotissimi
odî e amori, d'idrogeno
sfolgorante fatica:
deposti qui nell'acqua di un pianeta
per profili di colchici e libellule.

Forse alzerò fino a te le mie ciglia
fino a te la mia bocca cui l'attesa
alterò dire, esistere.
E anche nella terra,
domani, l'ultimo mio indizio
inazzurrirà di stellari entusiasmi,
di veloci convulse speranze.

Avremo lontananze capovolte
specchi che resero immagini rubate
fiori usciti da mura ad adorarti.
Saremo un solo affanno un solo oblio.

Ecloga III
La vendemmia

I

Autunno, presto. E il colchico
sui prati e la luna che si fa avanti regina

I will know you as a light bud:
how much you will unfold, how much you will gratify us
with light events.
Innocuous drugs, March storms;
gardens of rainbows and wax, sinecures
for minds and allergy-softened hands;
readings on the fine dust of summer,
readings on rains, amidst innumerable thorns of rain.
Sometimes Urania will split truth
before us as if it were armored fruit:
maximum skies,
flights that the solstitial
night sets blazing again,
gems of the remotest
hates and loves, of hydrogen
raging travail:
laid down here in the water of a planet
through profiles of saffron and dragonflies.

Perhaps I will raise my eyes up until I see you,
until to you my mouth reaches, that in waiting,
changed speech, existence.
And even in the earth,
tomorrow, my last sign
will turn blue with starred enthusiasms,
with swift convulsive hopes.

We will have distances reversed
mirrors that returned stolen images
flowers sprouting from walls to adore you.
We will be a single care, a single oblivion.

Eclogue III
Grape-Harvest

I

Autumn, soon. Meadow-saffron
in the fields and moon proceeding, queenly.

e il molto frutto nei notturni adyti
e i ruscelli lucenti millepiedi.
Cose vive, ahi, vite che ora
mi pare di avere perdute. Chi, tardo,
si tratterrà a cantarvi?
Ma in qualche luogo m'attendete, con qualche
segno dell'umano, il più limpido, al limite.
Morbido fianco dell'erba,
fianco di luna nel giorno,
pace in ripresa, lenti alberi,
autorità e sostanza.
Si, è un'ubriachezza stolta
questa, non durerà. Col dolce
colchico e il sonno che oltre me traspare
come una lata ricchissima rosa
riavrò anche il supremo il superfluo l'azzurro.
In esso
mi ripristino: basta
così poco alla precaria anima
(rifrazione che ora
cade falsa, e non so la ragione)
così poco per tornare,
per essere: raggio
che s'acqueta d'un cielo ove cadere.

     II

In autunno era il tempo
del grande guadagno,
molto anelata vendemmia, quando
esistevi, poesia: pura.
Un moto, un modo, ultimo, dell'azzurro
che di sé si contenta e fa contenti
anche i vinti, i divisi.
Eri, non eri: mutila
in ciò, più che colpevole;
tu come luna sempre oltre la selva,
sempre col vano raggio
pur tra la selva a spanderti. Ma ora
in altre sere vai, fonte imbarbarita,
in altri alvei, difetto e perdizione.

Much fruit in nocturnal sanctums
and the brooks, shining millipedes.
Living things, alas, lives that now
seem lost to me. Who, late,
will stay to sing of you?
But somewhere you wait for me at the limit
with some mark of the human, the clearest.
Soft flank of grass,
moon's flank in day,
peace renewing, slow trees,
authority and substance.
Yes, it is a foolish rapture this,
it will not last. With the sweet
meadow-saffron and sleep which shines beyond me
like a wide rich rose
I will recover too the supreme the superfluous the blue.
In this
I renew myself: so little
suffices for the precarious soul,
(refraction that now
falls false—I don't know why)
so little needed to return,
to be: ray
that is content with a sky in which to fall.

II

Autumn was the time
of the large yield,
much longed-for grape-harvest, when
you existed, poetry: pure.
A movement, a mode, the last, of the blue
that content with itself
makes even the vanquished, the divided content.
You were, you were not: maimed
in this, more than guilty
you moonlike forever beyond the forest,
forever with your vain ray
shedding light even within the forest. But now
you move in other evenings, barbarized spring,
in other channels, defect and perdition.

Interferenze s'aprono s'appuntano
ove decadde l'inarticolato
cuore tuo, il tuo ritmo
che la tempia fedele—lei sola—auscultava.
Qui. M io sono immune
e incolpevole: tanto oso dire.
E io posso all'azzurro serbarti
—solo talvolta
(come all'autunno, padre, giaciglio, cibo)—
all'azzurro di ierofania
che ogni passione avalla, ogni informità soffoca.
Madore, fumo, lume
d'immagini, d'incontri, di conati

.   .   .   .

.   .   .   .

Parola d'ordine
d'altri milioni d'anni, d'altri defunti eoni,
triviale slogan. Noi

.   .   .   .

Per la finestra nuova

Brilla la finestra del verde lungamente
lungamente composto, sogno a sogno,
orti o prati non so; ma quanta brina
prima ch'io mi convinca, quanta neve.

Verde del grano che alzi il capo e irridi
tra l'incerto oro e il vuoto:
tu, mia finestra, e tu, cielo, che porti
a me tra placidi astri gli squillanti satelliti

che il gioco umano ha lanciati, con lampi
di fantascienza, a vagheggiare in orbite

Interferences open point themselves
where that inarticulate heart of yours
declined, your rhythm sounded by
the faithful forehead—it alone.
Here. But I'm immune
and blameless: that much I dare say.
And I can preserve you for the sky
—only at times
(as in autumn, father, pallet, food)—
in the blue of hierophany
that confirms every passion, stifles every lack of form.
Moisture, smoke, light
of images, meetings, efforts.

. . . .
. . . .

Password
of other millions of years, of other dead aeons,
trivial slogan. We

. . . .

Translated by Ruth Feldman and Brian Swann

Through the New Window

The window shines with lengthening green
long shaped, dream by dream,
orchards or meadows I don't know: but how much frost
before it convinces me, how much snow.

Green of the wheat that raises its head and laughs
between uncertain gold and emptiness:
you, my window, and you, sky, that carry
to me amidst quiet stars the blaring satellites

that the human game launched, with lights
of science fiction, to wander above the hills

leggiere i colli, e li vede a piè fermo
il bue sul campo arato e la vite e la luna.

O mia finestra, purezza inestinguibile.
Per farti spesi tutto ciò che avevo.
Ora, non lieto, in povertà completa,
ancora tutti i tuoi doni non gusto.

Ma tra poco
tutto mi darai quel che anelavo.

Ecloga IV
Polifemo, Bolla fenomica, Primavera

Animula vagula blandula

IMPERATORE ADRIANO

Persone : *a, Polifemo*

a: «Dolce» fiato che muovi
    le nascite dal guscio, il coma, il muto;
    «dolce» bruma che covi
    il ritorno del patto convenuto;
    uomo, termine vago,
    impropria luce, uomo a cui non rispondo,
    salto che il piede spezza sopra il mondo.

Godono i prati acqua silenzio e viole;
da fiale laghi, nevi si versano.
Occhio, pullus nel guscio: ho veduto
nell'errare del mondo errante il sole.

Mondo, termine vago, primavera
che mi chiami nel tuo psicoide fioco.
Ancora un poco è giusto
ch'io stia al gioco, stia al fiato,
all'afflato,
di lutea passibile cera,
di, e mondo primavera.

in light orbits, seen in turn by the unmoving
ox in the ploughed field, vines and the moon.

Oh my window, inextinguishable purity.
To make you I spent all that I had.
Now, not content, in complete poverty,
I still do not enjoy all of your gifts.

But before long
you will give me all that I longed for.

Eclogue IV
Polyphemus, Phenomenological Bubble, Spring

Animula vagula blandua
EMPEROR HADRIAN

Personae: *a, Polyphemus*

a: "Sweet" breath that moves
    births from the shell, the coma, the mute;
    "sweet" mist that hatches
    the return of the established pact;
    man, vague term,
    unfit light, man I don't respond to,

    leap which shatters the foot above the world.
    The meadows savor water silence and violets
    lakes spill from phials, snows.
    Eye, pullus in the shell: I have seen
    the sun wandering in the world's wandering.

    World, vague term, Spring,
    you call to me in your thin psychoid.
    It's right for me to stay with the game
    a little longer, stay with the breath,
    with the afflatus,
    of soft saffron wax,
    I, and Spring world.

E vengo dritto, obliquo,
vengo gibboso, liscio;
come germe che abbonda
di dente ammicco e striscio
e premo alle lane onde ammanta
il dì le sue fetali clorofille.
M'adergo, prillo, come a musicale
sferza la trottola. Poi che qui tutto è «musica».
Non uomo, dico, ma bolla fenomenica.
Ah, domenica è sempre domenica.

Le bolle fenomeniche alle mille
stimolazioni variano s'incupano
scintillano. Sferica
è anche la speranza, anche la sete.
Abiuro dalle lettere consuete.
O primavera di cocchi e di lendini,
primavera di lìquor, dèi, suspense,
«vorrei trovare
parole nuove»:
ma il petalo e la frangia, ma l'erba e il lembo muove,
muovono al gioco i giocatore. Monadi
radianti, folle, bolle a corimbi e tu
tondo comunque, a tutta volta, estremo
occhio di Polifemo.

Po.: No, qui non si dissoda, qui non si cambia testo,
qui si ricade, qui
frigge nel cavo fondo della vista
il renitente trapano, la trista
macchina, il giro viziosissimo.
E qui su questo,
assestandomi, giuro:
io Polifemo sferico monocolo
ebbro del vino d'Ismaro primavera,
io donde cola, crapula, la vita
(oh: vino d'Ismaro; oh: vita; oh: primavera!).

And I come straight, oblique,
I come humped, smooth;
like well-toothed seed
I nod and crawl
and press on wools with which day
cloaks its fetal chlorophylls.
I rise, spin like a top
to a musical whip. Since here everything is "music."
Not man, I say, but phenomenological bubble.
Ah, Sunday is always Sunday.

The phenomenological bubbles vary at a thousand
stimulations darken
sparkle. Hope too
is spherical, and so is thirst.
I renounce the usual literature.
Oh Spring of cocci and nits,
Spring of liquors, gods, suspense,
"I'd like to find
new words":
but petal and fringe, but grass and grass-edge move,
the players move to the game. Radiant
monads, throngs, corymb-like bubbles and you
still round, a full circle, infinite
eye of Polyphemus.

Po.: No, here one doesn't break new ground, here one doesn't tinker
     with the text,
    here one relapses, here
    the reluctant drill, the perverse
    machine, the most vicious circle
    sizzles in the deep socket of my sight.
    And here taking my stance
    on this, I swear:
    I, Polyphemus, spherical one-eyed being
    drunk with the Spring wine of Ismarus,
    I from whom dribbles—debauchery—life
    (oh: wine of Ismarus; oh: life; oh: Spring!).

Translated by Ruth Feldman and Brian Swann

La quercia sradicata dal vento
nella notte del 15 ottobre MCMLVIII

Nel campo d'una non placabile
idea,
d'una sera che il vento era tutto,
sì, tutto, e mi premeva
col suo gelo verso il più profondo
di quell'idea di quel sogno,
tricosa Gordio
da atterrire il filo della spada.
Nel seno d'energia
di quella inibizione nera
che faceva le cose sempre più
sempre più terra nella terra.
Vedi: troppo vicine le mie stanze
sono a te, quercia: resisti
ora, sull'orlo, sta
anche per tutto il mio
mancare.

. . . .

Ti rinvenimmo
attraverso la squallida bocca del giorno,
rovesciata. Nel basso,
empito umbrifero, plurimo,
di calme e aromi chi ti spiegavi fin là,
sino alla fonte mai vista del fiume
sino all'infanzia fantastica balbettante degli avi.
Ai nostri abietti piedi
tu ch'eri la vetta cui corre
l'occhio e il tempo al riposo.

E ora il sole allarga aride ali
sul paese svuotato di te.

. . . .

. . . .

Quercia, come la messe
d'embrici e vetri, la dispersione

The Oak Uprooted by the Wind

in the night of October 15 MCMLVIII

In the field of an implacable
idea,
of an evening whose wind was everything,
yes, everything, and with its chill
it spurred me towards the lowest depths
of that idea of that dream,
Gordian snarl
to terrify the sword's edge.
In the breast of energy
of that black inhibition
that always made things ever more
ever more earth within the earth.
See: my rooms are too close
to you, oak: resist
now, on the edge, stay
despite all my
failings.

.   .   .   .

We found you
aslant the day's squalid mouth,
knocked down. Laid-low,
dark multifarious impetus,
of scents and serenities which you unfurled as far as there,
as far as the unseen source of the river
as far as the fantastic childhood stammering about ancestors.
At our abject feet
you who were the summit to which
the eye and time run to rest.

And now the sun spreads dry wings
over the countryside emptied of you.

.   .   .   .
.   .   .   .

Oak, like the harvest
of roof tiles and windows, the scattering

per selciati ed asfalti
—nostre irrite grida, irriti aneliti—,
quercia umiliata ai piedi
miei, di me inginocchiato
invano a alzarti come si alza il padre
colpito, invano
prostrato ad ascoltare
in te nostri in te antichissimi
irriti aneliti, irriti gridi.

Così siamo

Dicevano, a Padova, «anch'io»
gli amici «l'ho conosciuto».
E c'era il romorio d'un'acqua sporca
prossima, e d'una sporca fabbrica:
stupende nel silenzio.
Perché era notte. «Anch'io
l'ho conosciuto.»
Vitalmente ho pensato
a te che ora
non sei né soggetto né oggetto
né lingua usuale né gergo
né quiete né movimento
neppure il né che negava
e che per quanto s'affondino
gli occhi miei dentro la sua cruna
mai ti nega abbastanza

E così sia: ma io
credo con altrettanta
forza in tutto il mio nulla,
perciò non ti ho perduto
o, più ti perdo e più ti perdi,
più mi sei simile, più m'avvicini.

along cemented and asphalted surfaces
—our hopeless cries, futile gasps—,
oak humbled at my
feet, as I kneel
in vain to lift you as one lifts a stricken
father, prostrate
in vain to listen
in you to our in you ancient
futile gasps, futile cries.

That's How We Are

Friends were saying, in Padua, "me too"
"I knew him."
And there was the nearby muttering of dirty water
and of a dirty factory:
stupendous in the silence.
Because it was night. "Me too
I knew him."
Acutely I thought
of you who now
are neither subject nor object
nor usual speech nor slang
nor stillness nor movement
not even the nor that negated
—and for all that my eyes
penetrate its needle eye—
never negates you enough

So be it: but I
believe with as much
force in all my nothingness,
thus I haven't lost you
or, the more I lose you and you lose yourself,
the more you are like me, the nearer you come.

Notificazione di presenza sui colli Euganei

Se la fede, la calma d'uno sguardo
come un nimbo, se spazi di serene
ore domando, mentre qui m'attardo
sul crinale che i passi miei sostiene,

se deprecando vado le catene
e il sortilegio annoso e il filtro e il dardo
onde per entro le più occulte vene
in opposti tormenti agghiaccio et ardo,

i vostri intimi fuochi e l'acque folli
di fervori e di geli avviso, o colli
in sì gran parte specchi a me conformi.

Ah, domata qual voi l'agra natura,
pari alla vostra il ciel mi dia ventura
e in armonia pur io possa compormi.

Epilogo
Appunti per un'Ecloga

Persone: *a, b, c, d, e*

b: (*materia, macchie, pseudo-braille*)

a: L'anancasma che si chiama vita:
macchie, macchine, muscoli, ceneri,
spasmi, fu il corso di quella partita
in cui perdesti te stesso e il tuo stesso perderti

c: (*codici vari per tutti i suoni*)

a: Non tesi, terra, energia, spirito
nemmeno, non carme civile o intimo.
In chiave di fuoco o di tenebre.
Ma retina o reticolo,

Notifying One's Presence in the Euganean Hills

If faith, the nimbus-like calmness
of a glance, if spaces of serene
hours I demand, while here I linger
my steps sustained upon this ridge,

if I condemn the chains
and the ancient sorcery, philter and dart
where within the most occult veins
in clashing torments I freeze and burn,

your secret fires and demented waters
of fervors and chills I foretell, O hills
so much do you mirror and shape me.

Ah hills of such tamed harsh nature,
with an equal fate might the sky confront me
so that I too in harmony might remake myself.

Epilogue
Notes for an Eclogue

Personae: *a, b, c, d, e*

b: (*matter, marks, pseudo-braille*)

a: The anancasm that we call life:
marks, machines, muscles, ashes,
spasms, was the way that game went
in which you lost yourself and your losing of yourself

c: (*various sounds for all the sounds*)

a: Not thesis, earth, energy, not even
spirit, not civil or intimate ode.
In key of fire or of darkness.
But retina or reticulum,

ma poi trama ed omento: convenzione
prima in cui tutto si rifà ragione.

d: (*catena di dattili, spondei etc.*)

a: O quale e quanto in quella viva stella
pur vinse, quale e quanto si sospinse
oltre le soglie della sua stessa luce;
al di là del silenzio quale e quanto t'induce!

e: (*simboli matematici etc.*)

a: Integrando, sul limite, sospinti
solo minimamente sopra il suolo
dell'impossibile, impossibilmente
qui, e pure qui a dire l'impossibile
e il possibile. E reversibilmente

. . . .

Avverbio in «mente», lattea sicurezza

but then weaving and omentum: first
convention in which everything is remade into reason.

d: (*chain of dactyls, spondees, etc.*)

a: O what and how much in that living star
also beaten, what and how much thrust
beyond the thresholds of its own light;
what and how much propelled beyond silence!

e: (*mathematical symbols etc.*)

a: Integrating, at the edge, spurred on
only minimally above the ground
of the impossible, impossibly
here, and also here to say the impossible
and the possible. And reversibly

. . . .

Adverb ending in "-ly," milky security

da La Beltà

from Beauty
[1968]

La perfezione della neve

Quante perfezioni, quante
quante totalità. Pungendo aggiunge.
E poi astrazioni astrificazioni formulazione d'astri
assideramento, attraverso sidera e coelos
assideramenti assimilazioni—
nel perfezionato procederei
più in là del grande abbaglio, del pieno e del vuoto,
ricercherei procedimenti
risaltando, evitando
dubbiose tenebrose; saprei direi.
Ma come ci soffolce, quanta è l'ubertà nivale
come vale: a valle del mattino a valle
a monte della luce plurifonte.
Mi sono messo di mezzo a questo movimento-mancamento radiale
ahi il primo brivido del salire, del capire,
partono in ordine, sfidano: ecco tutto.
E al tua consolazione insolazione e le mia, frutto
di quest'inverno, allenate, alleate,
sui vertici vitrei del sempre, sui margini nevati
del mai-mai-non-lasciai-andare,
e la stella che brucia nel suo riccio
e la castagna tratta dal ghiaccio
e—tutto—e tutto-eros, tutto-lib. libertà nel laccio
nell'abbraccio mi sta: ci sta,
ci sta all'invito, sta nel programma, nella faccenda.
Un sorriso, vero? E la vi(ta) (id-vid)
quella di cui non si può nulla, non ipotizzare,
sulla soglia si fa (accarezzare?).
Evoè lungo i ghiacci e le colture dei colori
e i rassicurati lavori degli ori.
Pronto. A chi parlo? Riallacciare.
E sono pronto, in fase d'immortale,
per uno sketch-idea della neve, per un suo guizzo.
Pronto.
Alla, della perfetta.

«È tutto, potete andare.»

The Perfection of the Snow

How many perfections, how many
how many totalities. Stinging it adds.
And then abstractions astrifications astral formulations
star-frost, across sidera and coelos
star-frosts and assimilations—
I would proceed in the perfected
beyond the glaring dazzle, the full and the empty,
I would search out proceedings
standing out, avoiding   .
the doubtful and dark; I would know I would say.
But how it suffuses us, how great is the snowy fertility
how much is it worth: in the valley of morning in the valley
on the mountain of many-springed light.
I put myself into the middle of this radial movement-missing
ah the first shiver of ascending, of understanding,
they depart in order, they challenge: that's all.
And your consolation insulation and my own, fruit
of this winter, trained, allied,
on the vitreous vertices of forever, on the snowy edges
of never-never-did-I-let-go,
and the star burning in its husk
and the chestnut pulled from the ice
and—all—and all-eros, all-lib. liberty in the snare
it's there in my embrace: it goes along,
it goes along with the invitation, the program, the whole affair.
A smile, right? And the li(fe) (id-vid)
about which you can do nothing, cannot hypothesize,
it gets (caressed?) on the threshold.
Evoè there along the ices and cultures of colors
and the reassured workings of golds.
Hello? Who's speaking? Hang up.
And I'm ready, in an immortal phase,
for a "sketch-idea" of snow, for one of its glimmerings.
Hello.
To the, of the perfect.

"That's all, you may go."

Sì, ancora la neve

«Ti piace essere venuto a questo mondo?»
Bamb.: «Sì, perché c'è la STANDA»

Che sarà della neve
che sarà di noi?
Una curva sul ghiaccio
e poi e poi . . . ma i pini, i pini
tutti uscenti alla neve, e fin l'ultima età
circondata da pini. Sic et simpliciter?
E perché si è—il mondo pinoso il mondo nevoso—
perché si è fatto bambucci-ucci, odore di cristianucci,
perché si è fatto noi, roba per noi?
E questo valere in persona ed ex-persona
un solo possibile ed ex-possibile?
Hölderlin: «siamo un segno senza significato»:
ma dove le due serie entrano in contatto?
Ma è vero? E che sarà di noi?
E tu perché, perché tu?
E perché e che fanno i grandi oggetti
e tutte le cose-cause
e il radiante e il radioso?
Il nucleo stellare
là in fondo alla curva di ghiaccio,
versi inventive calligrammi ricchezze, sì,
ma che sarà della neve dei pini
di quello che non sta e sta là, in fondo?
Non c'è noi eppure la neve si affisa a noi
e quello che scotta
e l'immancabilmente evaso o morto
evaso o morto.
Buona neve, buone ombre, glissate glissate.
Ma c'è chi non si stanca di riavviticchiarsi
graffignare sgranocchiare solleticare,
di scoiattolizzare le scene che abbiamo pronte,
non si stanca di riassestarsi
—l'ho, sempre, molto, saputo—
al luogo al bello al bel modulo
a cieli arcaici aciduli come slambròt cimbrici

Yes, the Snow Again

"Are you glad you came into this world?"
Child: *"Yes, because there's the 5 and 10."*

What will happen to the snow
what will happen to us?
A curve on the ice
and then and then . . . but the pines, the pines
all emerging to meet the snow, and until the last age
surrounded by pines. Sic et simpliciter?
And why is it—the piney world the snowy world—
and why has the world become tiny totty-wotties, odor of human tots
why has it become us, stuff for us?
And this having value as a person and ex-person
a single possible and ex-possible?
Hölderlin: "we are a sign without interpretation":
but where do the two series come into contact?
But is it true? And what will happen to us?
And you why, why you?
And why and what do the big objects do
and all the things-causes
the radiant and the shining?
The stellar nucleus
there at the end of the ice-curve,
verses inventions calligrams riches, yes,
but what will happen to the snow to the pines
to that which isn't and is there, way down?
There is no us and yet the snow stares at us
and the thing that scalds
and the unavoidably fugitive or dead
fugitive or dead.
Good snow, good shadows—slide slide. Please.
But there are those who don't tire of clinging again
of snitching munching tickling
squirreling the scenes we have ready,
who never tire of readjusting
—I've always been well aware of it—
to the place to the lovely to the lovely pattern
to archaic skies acidulous as Cimbric gibberish

al seminato d'immagini
all'ingorgo di tenebrelle e stelle edelweiss
al tutto ch'è tutto bianco tutto nobile:
e la volpazza di gran coda e l'autobus
quello rosso sul campo nevato.
Biancaneve biancosole biancume del mio vecchio io.
Ma presto i bambucci-ucci
vanno al grande magazzino
—ai piedi della grande selva—
dove c'è pappa bonissima e a maraviglia
per voi bimbi bambi con diritto
e programma di pappa, per tutti
ferocemente tutti, voi (sniff, sniff
gnam gnam yum yum slurp slurp:
perché sempre si continui l'«umbra fuimus fumo e fumetto»):
ma qui
ahi colorini più o meno truffaldini
plasmon nipiol auxol lustrine e figurine
più o meno truffaldine:
meglio là, sottomano nevata sottofelce nevata . . .
O luna, ormai,
e perfino magnolia e perfino
cometa di neve in afflusso, la neve.
Ma che sarà di noi?
Che sarà della neve, del giardino,
che sarà del libero arbitrio e del destino
e di chi ha perso nella neve il cammino
(e la neve saliva saliva—e lei moriva)?
E che si dice là nella vita?
E che messaggi ha la fonte di messaggi?
Ed esiste la fonte, o non sono
che io-tu-questi-quaggiù
questi cloffete clocchete ch ch
più che incomunicante scomunicato tutti scomunicati?
Eppure negli alti livelli
sopra il coma e il semicoma e il limine
si brusisce e si ronza e si cicala-ciàcola
—ancora—per una minima o semiminima
biscroma semibiscroma nanobiscroma
cose e cosine

to the seed-bed of images
to the blocking of small darknesses and edelweiss stars
to everything that's all white all noble:
and the nasty fox with the big tail and the bus
the red one on a snowy field.
Snow-white sun-white white mass of my old me.
But soon the tiny totty-wotties
go to the big 5 and 10
—at the foot of the big woods—
where you find absolutely delicious pap
for you children babies with pap
rightly on your program, for everyone
fiercely everyone, you (sniff sniff
gnam gnam yum yum slurp slurp:
so that the "umbra fuimus fumo e fumetto" may always continue):
but here
alas pretty colors more or less tricky
plasmon nipiol auxol sequins and figurines
more or less tricky
better there, underhand fallen-snow underfern fallen-snow . . .
Oh moon, now,
and even magnolia and even
the swirling snow-comet, the snow.
But what will happen to us?
What will happen to the snow, the garden,
what will happen to free will and destiny
and to those who have lost their way in the snow
(and the snow rose rose and she was dying)?
And what are they saying there in life?
What messages does the source of messages have?
And does the source exist, or is it only
I-you-these down here
these clippety cloppety cl cl
more than non-communicating excommunicated everyone
    excommunicated ?
And yet on the high levels
above the coma and the semi-coma and the threshold
there is a rustling and buzzing and cicada-chatter
—still—for a minim or semi-minim
demisemiquaver semidemisemiquaver minisemidemiquaver

scienze lingue e profezie
cronaca bianca nera azzurra
di stimoli anime e dèi,
libido e cupìdo e la loro
prestidigitazione finissima;
è così, scoiattoli afrori e fiordineve in frescura
e «acqua che devia
si dispera si scioglie s'allontana»
oltre il grande magazzino ai piedi della selva
dove i bambucci piluccano zizzole . . .
E le falci e le mezzelune e i martelli
e le croci e i designs-disegni
e la nube filata di zucchero che alla psiche ne viene?
E la tradizione tramanda tramanda fa passamano?
E l'avanguardia ha trovato, ha trovato?
E dove il fru-fruire dei fruitori
nel truogolo nel buio bugliolo nel disincanto,
dove, invece, l'entusiasmo l'empireirsi l'incanto?

Che si dice lassù nella vita,
là da quelle parti là in parte;
che si cova si sbuccia si spampana
in quel poco in quel fioco
dentro la nocciolina dentro la mandorletta?
E i mille dentini che la minano?
E il pino. E i pini-ini-ini per profili
e profili mai scissi mai cuciti
ini-ini a fianco davanti
dietro l'eterno l'esterno l'interno (il paesaggio)
dietro davanti da tutti i lati,
i pini come stanno, stanno bene?

Detto alla neve: «Non mi abbandonerai mai, vero?»

E una pinzetta, ora, una graffetta.

things and thingies
sciences languages and prophecies
white black blue news
of stimuli souls and gods,
libido and greed and their very subtle sleight of hand;
that's how it is, squirrels smells and snowdrops in coolness
and "water that swerves
despairs dissolves wanders off"
beyond the big store at the foot of the forest
where tiny tots pick jujubes . . .
And the sickles and crescents and hammers
and crosses and designs-drawings
and the cloud of spun sugar that comes from them to the psyche?
And does tradition transmit transmit pass from hand to hand?
And has the avant-garde found, found?
And where is the con-consuming of the consumers
in the trough the dark slop-bucket the disenchantment;
where, instead, is the enthusiasm the rising to the Empyrean the
    ecstasy?

What are they saying up there in life,
there from those parts there in part;
what is being hatched peeled opened up
in that little in that dimness
inside the small nut inside the small almond?
And the thousand milk-teeth that gnaw it?
And the pine-tree. And the pines-ines-ines by profiles
and profiles never cleft never sewed
ines-ines at the side in front
behind the eternal the external the internal (the landscape)
behind before on all sides,
the pines how are they, are they all right?

Said to the snow: "You'll never abandon me, right?"

And small pincers, now, a small clamp

Translated by Ruth Feldman and Brian Swann

Alla Stagione

I

Inanellatamente e in convergenza pura
è il fatto stagionale. Questa perla perlifera,
sistema ed argomento
qui, tutto intorno al qui, ottimo.
E poi fare cenno alla matta, alla storia-storiella
e alla fa-favola, femmine balbe, sorelle.
Se ne va, te ne vai; oh stagione.
Non sei la stagione, non sapevo.

II

E ti chiudi nei tuoi grandi colori
e i colori nelle grandi ombre
e porti via te stessa
e me e non-me nell'alta involuzione
pregio di un silenzio:
cui s'appone l'ardore di un rumore
fragilissimo o il cammino di una madre-mamma
tra le dalie e i crisantemi
lacunosi leggermente imprecisi e scalpito
d'animaletti con carrettelle e sistri
appena in incidenza quasi per una svista.
E sei l'invitante e obbedisci
al goduto invito, me e non-me e non-noi.
La mami-madre là sul versante ha una forbicina d'argento.
Là sul versante opposto mi è lecito decidere
l'araldizzata minutaglia—quanta amicizia—
che s'iscrive al patito, al passibile, in un ritorno vero.
Decoro, décor, scena da cui, su via su via:
l'alito e l'invito
allo scarnito convolvolo alla zucca alla fragola,
a quanto consumarsi ad un tessuto amava,
tessuto e tensione che si ritira
e nel ritirarsi lascia grandi
sé me stesso non-me e voi
vivi al superlativo—che pingui, che quiete—
morti al superlativo mummi-mummie-muschi

To the Season

I

In endless rings and in pure convergence
is the seasonal fact. This pearl-bearing pearl,
system and subject
here, all around the here, excellent.
And then an allusion to the joker, to the story-fib
and to the fa-fable, stammering women, sisters.
It vanishes, you vanish; oh season.
You aren't the season, I didn't know.

II

And you close yourself in your large colors
and the colors in large shadows
and carry away yourself
and me and non-me in the high involution
value of a silence:
to which is fixed the fervor of a most
fragile noise or the walking of a mother-mama
between dahlias and chrysanthemums
full of lightly imprecise gaps and thudding feet
of little animals with barrows and rattles
hardly in incidence almost by mistake.
And you are the inviter and obey
the welcome invitation, me and not-me and not-us.
The momma-mother there on the slope has a small silver earwig.
There on the opposite slope I'm allowed to decide
the heraldic frippery—how much friendship—
which inscribes itself on the suffered, the sufferable, in a real return.
Decorum, décor, scene from which, up and away away:
breath and invitation
to the thin bindweed the pumpkin the strawberry,
to that which loved to be consumed to a fabric,
texture and tension that shrinks
and, in the shrinking, leaves large
selves myself not-me and you
superlatively alive—what fatness, what quiet—
superlatively dead mum-mummies-mosses

e me e non-me e voi nell'inclusione
in grandi colori e i colori in grandi ombre beatitudine

Già fu beato questo ritirarsi

III

Già fu beato, là fu beato,
grande beatitudine in circospezione
o in un'altra espansione
più accorta e difficile in vasi e valli perlifere
in silenzio esclusivo perlifero.
Interpretare questa parsimonia
questo sonno. Riferirsi alla grama
deiezione, ad un pomo ad un fico a uno spino.
Dire, molte cose, di stagione, usando l'infinito:
tante dolcezze.
Ma durano al becco felice all'ala pulita
all'occhio all'ingegno dell'augello?
Difendere quella cruna quel grimaldello quel mulinello.
Bene fosti e ben sei: ma il proposito
vano e il vano amore dove compenso e come?
Dal tessuto foglioso delle tue chiome
dalle calde simbiosi dagli aiuti dai cibi.
Esser beato—contro me—mi prescrivi
anche se è malfamato ciò che dice beato,
se la fa-favola in disparte s'imbalba,
se, fuori-stagione, mattamente la storia
clio clio pavoncella fa su e disfa
l'opus maxime oratorium.
Ma cavalchi, bel cavaliere errante:
aromi sodi, chimismi riposti
lunghi dal fallire, raggi, preminenze, nascenze.
– – – – – – – – – – – – – – – – – –

Perché siete immortali
perché sono immortale perché
francamente immortale tu sei

e l'uso dell'infinito

and me and not-me and you in the inclusion
in large colors and the colors in large shadows beatitude

Once it was blessed, this shrinking

III

Once it was blessed, blessed there,
grand beatitude in circumspection
or in another expansion
shrewder and difficult in vases and pearl-bearing valleys
in exclusive pearl-bearing silence.
To interpret this parsimony
this sleep. To refer to the wretched
excrescence, to an apple a fig a thorn.
To say, many things, of the season, using the infinite:
so much softness.
But do they survive for the bird's happy beak the clean wing
the eye the wits?
To defend that needle's eye that picklock that whirlpool.
Well you were and well you are: but the empty proposition
and the vain love where's recompense and how?
By the leafy web of your hair
by the hot symbioses by the aids the foods.
To be blessed-against me-you command me
even if what is called blessed has a bad name,
if the fa-fable stammers to one side,
if, out of season, madly history
clio clio lapwing enwraps and unwraps
the opus maxime oratorium.
But you ride, fine knight errant:
dense aromas, secret chemisms
far from failing, rays, preeminences, births.
— — — — — — — — — — — — — — — —

Because you are immortal
because I am immortal because
frankly you are immortal

and the use of the infinitive

Translated by Ruth Feldman and Brian Swann

da Possibili prefazi o riprese o conclusioni

II

Quell'io che già tra selve e tra pastori.
Perfido, perfido.
Purissimi fenomeni
selezionato insieme
che luci e pallide verità e risorse
forti o dubbie.
Là in fondo all'orto dove dicevano
non arriva non arriva.
Là sto sgambettando a perdifiato, non non
non mi cogliete. Là ero a perdifiato
là. E tutta la mia fifa nel fifàus:
tutto fronzuto trotterellante di verdi visioni
e le debolezze e la grazia di fioretti e germogli
e—oh i frutti, che frutti, fruttame
e—oh i collicelli, morbido da portare al naso da fiutare
assimilare come faceva quel vecchio: io,
quell'io che già tra selve e tra pastori   vecchio,
quell'io che faceva vino e miele,
ed il covo straricco e la calda fichina,
oh bello, tutto bello.
La vita bisogna lasciarla più avanti.
Ecco un'altra cosa, vedine l'esordio.
E questa non è, neppure un non, un neppure;
non aperte elitre su zinnie non rinfocolate
nevi non dissonanza o tono,
la gran cosa si sgrana, in sortita:
ma il valore vedrò, il valore davanti
e alle mie spalle in uguale quiete-inquietudine.
Perfidia, perfido, perfidamente.

III

In un'omogenea tesi l'elemento
mio migliore, la paura,
si confonde all'eroe. Al cielo, a lassù.
Chissà che tesori credetti portare
e lecita per essi la più fifante fifa,

from Possible Prefaces or Resumptions
or Conclusions

II

That "I" which already amidst woods and shepherds.
Treacherous, treacherous.
Purest phenomena
picked together
that pale truths and lights and forceful
resources or doubts.
There at the farthest edge of the garden where they were saying
he won't make it, he won't make it.
There I'm racing off at breakneck speed, don't don't
don't catch me. There I was at breakneck speed
there. And everything my fear in the fifàus:
everything leafy cantering about with green visions
and the weakness and the grace of flowerets and sprouts
and—oh fruits, what fruits, piles of fruit
and—oh hillocks, soft enough to bring under one's nose and sniff
to assimilate as that old "I" used to do
that "I" which already amidst woods and shepherds   old,
that "I" which made wine and honey,
and the sumptuous hideout and warm little box,
oh beautiful, all beautiful.
Life must leave it farther ahead.
Here's something else, look at the beginning.
And this is not, not even a not, a not even;
unopened wing-sheaths on unawakened zinnias
snows not dissonance or tone,
the great thing crumbles, sallying forth:
but I'll see the worth, the worth ahead
and at my shoulders in equal ease-unease.
Treacherous, treacherous, treacherously.

III

In a uniform thesis my best
element, fear,
is bewildered within the hero. In the sky, up there.
Who knows what treasures I thought to bring
for which the most fearful fear is warranted,

non so che mi sostenga a tanta riffa·
a tanta zuffa per poi sfuggire in dire;
premiatemi cose e non cose per l'animazione
sospettata nei vostri conversari,
per tanto appostamento auscultazione,
per avervi messe in agio di ritmare e rimari;
all'altezza là vi s'induceva
vi si faceva monte proteso vivanda vaticinio.
         Canagliescamente accanitamente oltreponte
                         (oltrefavole oltremiti).
Ora che chiuso alle distinzioni
sono più inerme che mai alla distinzione finale
rivolgo il sale nella ciotola: perplesso:
il granulame il lucore
che dedussi da tutto
—malgrado tutto nonostante—
—forse, benché, così—
produco questa quiete marginale.

Al mondo

Mondo, sii, e buono;
esisti buonamente,
fa' che, cerca di, tendi a, dimmi tutto,
ed ecco che io ribaltavo eludevo
e ogni inclusione era fattiva
non meno che ogni esclusione;
su bravo, esisti,
non accartocciarti in te stesso in me stesso

Io pensavo che il mondo così concepito
con questo super-cadere super-morire
il mondo così fatturato
fosse soltanto un io male sbozzolato
fossi io indigesto male fantasticante
male fantasticato mal pagato
e non tu, bello, non tu «santo» e «santificato»
un po' più in là, da lato, da lato

I don't know what sustains me with so much struggle
and so much unrest to then escape in talk;
award me with things and non-things for the suspected
animation in your conversings,
for much ambush auscultation,
for having put you at ease with rhythm-marking and rhyming;
at that height there it persuaded you
it made you outstretched mountain viand divination.
            Roguishly ruthlessly beyondbridge
                        (beyondfables beyondmyths).
Now closed to distinctions
I am more defenseless than ever against the final distinction
I turn the salt in the bowl: perplexed:
the granules the light
that I deduced from everything
—in spite of everything notwithstanding—
—perhaps, even though, thus—
I make this marginal respite.

To the World

World: Be, and be good;
exist nicely,
do that, try to, aim at, tell me all,
and there I was upending eluding
and every inclusion was no less
effective than every exclusion;
come on, old chum, exist,
don't curl up in yourself in myself

I thought that the world thus conceived
with this super-falling super-dying
the world thus adulterated
was only a me ill-hatched from a cocoon
was me ill-digested fantasizing
ill-fantasized ill-paid
and not you, dear, not you "sainted" and "sanctified"
a little more over there, to the side, to the side

Fa' di (ex-de-ob etc.)-sistere
e oltre tutte le preposizioni note e ignote,
abbi qualche chance,
fa' buonamente un po';
il congegno abbia gioco.
Su, bello, su.

Su, münchhausen.

L'elegia in petèl

Dolce andare elegiando come va in elegia l'autunno,
raccogliersi per bene accogliere in oro radure,
computare il cumulo il sedimento delle catture
anche se da tanto prèdico e predico il mio digiuno.
E qui sto dalla parte del connesso anche se non godo
di alcun sodo o sistema:
il non svischiato, i quasi, dietro:
vengo buttato a ridosso di un formicolio
di dèi, di un brulichio di sacertà.
Là origini—Mai c'è stata origine.
Ma perché allora in finezza e albore tu situi
la non scrivibile e inevitata elegia in petèl?
«Mama e nona te dà ate e cuco e pepi e memela.
Bono ti, ca, co nona. Béi bumba bona. È fet foa e upi.»
Nessuno si è qui soffermato—Anzi moltissimi.
Ma ogni presenza è così sua di sé
e questo spazio così oltrato oltrato . . . (che)
«Nel   quando │ O saldamente costrutte Alpi
    E il principe │ Le   »
appare anche lo spezzamento saltano le ossa arrotate:
ma non c'è il latte petèl, qui, non il patibolo,
mi ripeto, qui no; mai stata origine mai disiezione.
Non spezzo nulla se non spezzato ma sùbito riattato,
spezzo pochissimo e do imputazione—incollocabili—
a mimesi ironia pietà;
qui terrore: ma ridotto alla sua più modica modalità.
Per quel tic-sì riattato, così verbo-Verbo,

Be sure to (ex-des-res etc.)-ist
and beyond all prepositions known and unknown,
you should have some *chance,*
behave nicely for a bit;
give the mechanism some play.
Come on, dear, come on.

Come on, Münchhausen.

The Elegy in Petèl

It's sweet to go elegizing as autumn moves in elegy,
to collect oneself and thus securely collect clearings in gold,
to compute the mass the sediment of seizures
even though for so long I've preached and I predict my fast.
And here I stand on this side of connected things even if I don't
    benefit
from anything solid or any system:
the still sticky, the almosts, behind:
I'm thrown against a swarm
of gods, a seething of holiness.
There—beginnings. There never was a beginning.
But why then in fineness and whiteness of dawn do you place
the unwriteable and unavoided elegy in petèl?
"Mama e nova to dà ate e cuco e pepi e memela.
Bono ti, ca, no nova. Béi bumba bona. È fet foa e upi."
No one has lingered here—In fact too many have.
But every presence is so much its own
and this space gone so far far beyond . . (that)
"in the   when | Oh solidly constructed Alps
    And the prince | The   "
even the fracture shows, wheel-racked bones jump
but there is no petèl milk, here, no gallows;
I repeat, here no; there never was a beginning, never a break-up.
I break nothing not already broken but quickly mended,
I break very little and—though they're unplaceable—accuse
mimesis irony compassion;
terror here: but reduced to its most modest means.

faccio ponte e pontefice minimo su
me e altre minime faglie.

L'assenza degli dì, sta scritto, ricamato, ci aiuterà
—non ci aiuterà—
tanto l'assenza non è assenza gli dèi non dèi
l'aiuto non è l'aiuto. E il silenzio sconoscente
pronto a tutto,
questo oltrato questo oltraggio, sempre, ugualmente
(poco riferibile) (restio ai riferimenti)
(anzi il restio, nella sua prontezza):
e il silenzio-spazio, provocatorio, eccolo in diffrazione,
si incupidisce frulla di storie storielle, vignette
di cui si stipa quel malnato splendore, mai nato,
trovate pitturanti, paroline-acce a fette e bocconi, pupi,
barzellette freddissime fischi negli orecchi
(vitamina a dosi alte per trattarli
ma non se sono somatismi di base psichica),
e lei silenzio-spazio
e lei allarga le gambe e mostra tutto;
vedo il tesissimo e libertino splendore
e il fascino e il risolino e il fatto brutto
e correre la polizia e—nel vacuum nell'inane
ma raggiante—il desiderio di denaro fresco si fa più ardente
di dominio fresco di ideologia fresca;
anzi vedo a braccetto Hölderlin e Tallemant des Réaux
sovrimpressione   sovrimpressiono
ma pure
ma alla svelta
ma tutto fa brodo
(cerchiamo, bambini, di essere buoni
nel buon calore, le tue brune tettine,
il pretestuarsi per ogni movimento
in ogni momento,
calore non mai tardo nel capire
come credono «certe persone»
anzi astuto come uno di voi
quanto imbroglia grilli erbe genitori,
sappiate scrivere ma non leggere, non importa,

By means of that tic-yes well-repaired, so verb-Verb,
I act as bridge and pontifex minimus over
myself and other minimal rock-faults.

The gods' absence, it is written, embroidered, will help us
—will not help us—
after all the absence is not absence the gods not gods
help is not help. And the unknowing silence
ready for everything,
this going beyond this outrage, always, the same
(hardly attributable) (refractory to references)
even more so the reluctance, in its readiness:
and the space-silence, provocative, there it is in diffraction,
it becomes greedy froths with stories, gossip, vignettes
with which one fills that ill-born splendor, never born,
daubed trouvailles, nice-nasty words in slices and mouthfuls, puppets,
cold jokes whistles in the ears.
(Heavy doses of vitamin A to treat them
but not if they're psychosomatic),
and she silence-space
and she spreads her legs and shows it all;
I see the very stretched and libertine splendor
and the charm and the chortle and the ugly fact
and the police running and—in the vacuum in inanity
but radiant—the desire for fresh money becomes more burning
for fresh rule for fresh ideology;
I even see Hölderlin and Tallémant des Réaux arm in arm
superimposition   I superimpose
but yet
but quickly
but anything goes
(let us try, children, to be good
in the good heat, your small brown nipples,
the making pretexts for every movement
in every moment,
warmth never slow to understand
how "certain people" think
on the contrary smart as one of you
when he traps crickets grasses parents.
Learn how to write but not to read, it doesn't matter,

iscrivetevi a, per, pretestuarvi all'istante)
ma: non è vero che tutto fa brodo,
ma: e rinascono i ma: ma
Scardanelli faccio la pagina per Tallemante des Réaux,
Scardanelli sia compilato con passi dell'Histoire d'O.

Ta bon ciatu? Ada ciól e ùna e tée e mana papa.
Te bata cheto, te bata: e po mama e nana.

«Una volta ho interrogato la Musa»

da Profezie o memorie o giornali murali

I
Colline difficilmente profetizzanti,
torturate, torte dalla vostra verità e indicazione fino a qui
per una breve pasteggiatura
per un psss all'orecchio.
Ora: exeresi di una grossa parte
inutile a dir poco; poi vedremo.
Il torturante il verbalizzante del tutto instabile
il proteso a voi o il corrucciato e dietro-front,
ma: protesta o loda e—così—
chiama «vi», si stabilizza in voi.
Favellar tosco, e sculto u-uomo-o, e coonestata beltà.

Oh, solo pochi sguardi qui intorno
a ogni, a tutto, che porti il suo munuscolo
la sua stilla di dono e ammicco.
E ogni ha in sé la sua piccola teodicea;
non mancare allo show, né poi allo show dei piccoli oltraggi.
Anche: profezie memore giornali murali
monogrammi plurigrammi dovunque, sfioranti «   ».
E le interferenze di vite
appena vi, svenute qua e là,
deficienze o mere specularità.

subscribe to, for, find an excuse on the spur of the moment)
but: it's not true anything goes,
but: and the buts are reborn: but
let Scardanelli leave the page blank for Tallémant des Réaux,
let Scardanelli be compiled with excerpts from *L'Histoire d'O.*

Ta bon˙ciatu ? Ada ciòl e úna e tee e mana papa.
Te bata cheto, to bata: e po mama e nana.

"Once I interrogated the Muse"

Translated by Ruth Feldman and Brian Swann

from Prophecies or Memories or Bulletin Boards

I

Trickily predicting hills,
tormented, contorted by your veracity—& indications till here
for a short supping
for a psss in the ear.
Now: excision of an immense part
useless to say little; then we'll see.
The torturer the verbalizer of everything unstable
the leaning to you or the frowning and about-face,
but: protesting or praising and—thus—
calling "to you", steadying in you.
Tuscan uttering, and sculpted h-human-n, and justified beauty.

Oh, only a few glancings near and far
at each, at all, that carries its small offering
its trickle of giving and blinking.
And each has in itself a small theodicy;
don't miss the show, or later the show of the small offenses.
Also: prophecies memories bulletin boards
monograms, plurigrams everywhere, brushing by "   ."
And the interferences of lives
scarcely here, unconscious here and there,
scarcities or mere reflectivities

E, lo stesso, lastre sensibili dossiers registrazioni
per documentare il passaggio
di qua di là dalla forza dalla grazia. «Grazia.»
Gratitudine iniziale—è questo che si vuole capire
e confesserete—o il crimine l'oltranza.
Entri la gloria. Gli avanzi della gloria.

II

Proficuo lavoro del cielo: condìto:
uve dolci e stelle: e l'acino luce
all'avidissimo appetito.
Disinibiti monti caduti disagi
argento quasi dirlo si può
questo fato-arazzo
questo appuntimento e settembrìa lenta
delicatezza di lingua e di dente.
E casta è la suzione, ma acidula l'ape e invidiosa.
Senza posa conosco e riconosco,
un uomo sono un tosco che va
parlando onesto di cose primitivizzate
e primarie anche se niente le allena in eternità.
Perché di eterno non v'è che il diniego
quello là vecchio, fermo davanti a.
(Ehi) vigna minata da fillossera
che s'ostina in un muto bollore d'eloqui
(ehi) alloro oleandro
ori in vigore malandrino

III

Le profezie di Nino.
(Cosa mi fai scrivere, Nino!)
(E non sappiamo se oggi tutto questo
possa ottenere il permesso per un—benché minimo—senso!)
Nino, la più bella profezia
non può mettere boccio che nei clinami di Dolle,
dove tu, duca per diritto divino
e per universa investitura,
frughi gli arcani del tempo e della natura,
e—più conta—dai cieli stessi derivi il tuo vino

And, even so, sensitive sheets dossiers registrations
to document the passing
here and there of the force of grace. "Grace."
Nascent gratitude—it is this that desires to understand
and this that you will confess—or the crime the excess.
Enter glory. The remains of glory.

II

Generative work of the sky: seasoned:
sweet grapes and stars: and the berry glimmering
within sight of the ravenous appetite.
Uninhibited mountains fallen discomfitures
silver one can almost speak it
this tapestry-fate
this slow sharpening and septembering
tenderness of tongue and teeth.
The suction is chaste, but sour the bee and envious.
Without rest I know and recognize,
a man I am a Tuscan who speaks
decorously of things made primitive
and primary even if nothing trains them in eternity.
Because of things eternal there's nothing but denial
that old one there, stopped in front of.
(Ah) vineyard riddled with vermin
that persist in a mute seething of speaking
(ah) laurel oleander
golds in effect miscreant

III

The prophesies of Nino.
(The things you make me write, Nino!)
(And we don't know if today all this
may secure permission for a—however minimal—meaning!)
Nino, the most fetching prophesy
cannot but bloom on the slopes of Dolle,
where you, duke by divine right
and by universal investiture,
rummage through the mysteries of time and of nature,
and—more important—from the skies themselves you draw your
    wine

ché le tue vigne con lo stellato soltanto
confinano e col folto degli stellanti fagiani.
Tu qui le tempeste e le nevi prevedi del domani
qui il percento di latte e di frumento
qui miseria o signoria.
Ma sempre l'onda delle mele depone
il suo meglio nei tuoi cortili,
quadrifogliati foraggi ti gravano i fienili
e le tue uve e i pampani e i tralici non c'è luce
che in vita li vinca né vento né umore di terra:
off limits la sofisticazione, lo stento!
E—come dall'estro tuo si disserra
il raccolto più atteso, più pagato
di tutta la contrada—quando su per le nude
coste mattutine
cui già dicembre pruinoso prude-ude-ude
(ridondanze, ridondanze su strati su
specchi su inesistenze)
sali pedalando verso il feudo stillante
genio e mirabilità,
tu, tra i settanta e gli ottanta anni pedalando quasi volage,
profetizzi che nelle tue cantine
presto ci troveremo in compagnia—che summit!—
sceltissima e con cento e cento «ombre»
conosceremo sempre più profonde
le profondità del tuo valore
tradizionalista a sera all'alba novatore:
questo è lo zenit d'ogni tua profezia.

because your vineyards border only on the starry sky
and on the thicket of glimmering pheasants.
You predict here tomorrow's storms and snows
here the percentage of milk and grain
here misery or seigniory.
But always the wave of apples deposits
its best in your courtyards,
four-leafed fodder weighs down your haylofts,
and no light nor wind nor earth-elixir can
surpass your grapes and vines and shoots:
off-limits the adulteration, the privation!
And—as if by your whim the most awaited,
most valuable harvest of the entire district
is let loose—when above through the naked
morning shores
which hoarfrosted December already stings-ings-ings
(redundancies, redundancies above layers above
mirrors above nonexistences)
you climb pedaling toward the fiefdom dripping
genius and wonderment,
you, between seventy and eighty, pedaling almost volage,
you prophesy that in your cellars
we'll soon find ourselves in the best company—what a summit!—
with hundreds upon hundreds of glasses of wine
we'll know ever more deeper
the depths of your worth
traditionalist at evening innovator at dawn:
this is the zenith of all your prophecies.

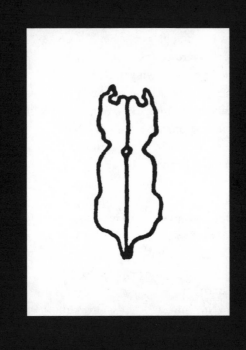

da Gli Squardi i fatti e senhal

---

from Glances, Facts and Senhals
[1969]

da Gli Sguardi i Fatti e Senhal

—«NO BASTA, non farlo non scriverlo te ne prego»

—Doveva accadere laggiù che ti e ti e ti e ti
lo so che ti hanno || presa a coltellate ||
lo gridano i filmcroste in moda i fumetti in ik
i cromatismi acrilici
nulla di più banale   lo sanno i guardoni
da gradini finestre e occhialoni
io guardo || freddo || il freddo

—Sai e non sai vivi e non vivi   ma già dèisangui
già scola da un'incisione sulla neve   neveshocking
rossoshocking   mondoshocking

—Si sfasa discrepa in diplopia

—Temi la vera lingua dei dormienti || è un tuo tema ||
rilutti all'a b c del conservarti
tra il verbo geminato il verbo quiescente
i verbi doppiamente infermi

—Ma ora vengono alle mani   ora saltellano i coltelli
nei luoghi comuni   e t'incide

—Non lo sentivo stando da questo livello || ora sei molti livelli
mi chinavo a osservarti alzavo il capo a osservarti
e apprezzo un po' alla volta questo respiro migliore
rianimazione dell'affanno
questo rianimarsi di tutto in un singulto tuo
tra équipes per rianimare o per animare
disegni e coltellate orgasmi

—«Non sono io e sono-sono, mi conosci
stileimpalatura stilesfondamento stilemaraviglia
mi hai accentuato nei miei pluri-   fanta-   meta-
nei miei impegni (come?) carismatici

from Glances Facts and Senhals

—"NO, ENOUGH, don't do it don't write it I beg you"

—It had to happen down there that you and you and you and you
I know that they || stabbed you over and over ||
the filmscabs scream it in style the comics in ik
the acrylic chromatisms
nothing more banal   the Peeping Toms know
from steps windows and big spyglasses
I watch || cold || the cold

—You know and don't know live and don't live   but already
   godbloods
already it drains by an incision in the snow   snowshocking
redshocking   worldshocking

—It dephases diverges in diplopia

—You fear the true tongue of the sleeping || it is a theme of yours ||
you are reluctant about the ABC's of preserving yourself
among the geminated verb the quiescent verb
the doubly invalid verbs

—But now they come to blows   now the knives jump
in the common places   and it carves you out

—I didn't feel it from this level || now you are many levels
I stooped to observe you I raised my head to observe you
and I appreciate a bit at a time this better breath
reanimation of the dyspnea
this reanimating of all in a hiccup of yours
between teams for reanimating or for animating
sketches and stabs orgasms

—"I am not I and I am-I am, you know me
impalingstyle breakthroughstyle marvelstyle
you accentuated me in my pluri-   fanta-   meta-
in my charismatic (what?) commitments

in empiree univocità o latenze
in un sogno di inerranza di inebriata inerranza»

—E io andavo come in tanti soliti
e abitudini per nevi e per selve
e sapessi il perché di questo mio non essere annoiabile
eri laggiù fuori combattimento e in pugna
eri vicina col vicus villaggio piccina   e lontana
crollavi come una cascata nel lontano

—Che stanchezza doverti ripetere sempre sempre peggio peggio

—Resterò dunque a guardare un pezzo di ramo
su uno specchio ghiacciato
io accosciato accanto a una pozza ghiacciata
ero qui e non attendevo
non ho mai atteso nulla, veramente

—Flash crash splash   down
flash e splash nella pozza nello specchio
introiezione della, crash e splash, introiettata
è la prima tavola la figurina (D centrale)

—Io sto gustando i tuoi sangui i tuoi Es a milioni
sì tesoro, sì tettine-di-lupa in sussulto,
mi va mi sta mi gira che laggiù ti abbiano colpita
le mie || || il non sono mai state abbastanza robuste
non ti hanno mai buttata in causa
non ti hanno mai inquisita né trasfigurata mai

—Io piango, ho saputo del fatto,
nemmeno cronaca nerocinema, fatto ordinario
roba così di scarto   gratis data
mentre stavo guardando
dopopasto dopocorpo dopodopo
avallato da eternità avallato da tempi
mentre stavo mettendo in sublime
la laboriosa neve
l'intrinsecata di equilibri induzioni insegnamenti

in empyrean univocities or latencies
in a dream of inerrancy of inebriated inerrancy"

—And I went as in so many usuals
and habits through snows and through forests
and if you only knew the reason of this not being boreable of mine
you were down there out of action and in battle
you were near with the vicus village tiny   and distant
you collapsing like a waterfall in the distance

—What a bore to have to repeat worse and worse worse and worse

—I will stay then to watch a piece of branch
on a frozen mirror
I, squatted next to a frozen puddle
I was here and wasn't waiting
I never awaited anything, truly

—Flash crash splash   down
flash and splash in the puddle in the mirror
introjection of the, crash and splash, introjected
it is the first table the little figure (center D)

—I am savoring your bloods your Ids a million times
yes darling, yes tremoring she-wolf teatlets,
it suits me it serves me it comes over me that down there they
    struck you
my ‖   ‖ were never strong enough
they never threw you into question
they never investigated nor transfigured you ever

—I cry, I heard about the fact,
not even news filmnoír, ordinary fact
second hand stuff   gratis data
while I was watching
aftermeal afterbody afterafter
guaranteed by eternity guaranteed by times
while I was putting into sublime
the laborious snow
the intrinsicated of balances inductions teachings

—«So che lottavi col fantasma-di-tante-beltà
che mai-verranno-meno-e»

—Qui lotto col fantasma (di una tu?)
che vi s'include con furore e fama
le porta avanti le fa montare in pro in contra

—Ho saputo del tuo ferimento ma tu ne sarai ne sarai
ne sarai complice abbastanza? Ammetti che sei
che sei che sei tu stessa una qualche una qualche
forma di e di e di e di ‖ inflitta ‖
nelle cose i fatti le visioni, dì di punta

—«Ero il trauma in questo immenso corpo di bellezza
corpo di bellezza è la selva in profumo d'autunno
in perdizione d'autunno
in lieve niveo declivio niveo non più renitenza
stelle bacche stille in cori
viola e rosso sul lago di neve»

—Ah quanto ti sei somigliata oggi quanto
sei venuta dal niente sei rimasta niente e col niente
hai fatturato azzeccato giorno,
quanto ti sei giovata di: nevi soli muschio
e sì di querce faggi abeti
come di felciole ebuli aneti,
quanto ti ha giovato oggi il sole il muschio
che ho sparso davanti e dopo i tuoi passi
dal niente, di niente   eri assiderata nella stilla
nella lente nella bacca   desmìssiete
desmìssiete   butta lo slip   dispèllati
datti fuoco alla nella pellicola   e i coltelli

—Ma e i tuoi indugi c bau-sette e (capo)giri?
Da a dove   Per o in?
E non ho confuso il messaggio con un altro? Ho tutto
confuso confuso
nello shocking shocking
non andare ‖ vattene ‖ così avviene
sono ‖ sei ‖ il duale ‖ e in mezzo

—"I know that you wrestled with the phantasm-of-such-beauties
that will-never-fade-and"

—Here I wrestle with the phantasm (one of them you?)
that encloses itself with fury and fame
it carries them forward it makes them mount in pro in contra

—I knew about your wounding but would you be its would you be its
would you be its accomplice enough? Admit that you are
that you are that you are yourself some kind of some kind of
form of and of and of and of ‖ inflicted ‖
in things facts visions, rush day

—"I was the trauma in this immense body of beauty
the forest is a body of beauty in autumn perfume
in autumn perdition
in soft snowy slope snowy no longer reluctant
stars berries drops in choruses
violet and red on the lake of snow"

—Ah how you resembled yourself today how
you came from nothing remained nothing and with nothing
you adulterated right-on-the-mark day,
how you took advantage of: snows suns mosses
and yes of oaks beeches firs
as of ferns elders dill
how the sun the moss that I scattered
in front of and after your steps served you today
from nothing, of nothing   you were frozen within the drop
within the lens within the berry   wake up
wake up   throw away your underwear   peel yourself
set yourself on fire at the in the film   and the knives

—But and your delays and peek-a-boos and (head)spins?
From to where   Through or in?
And didn't I confuse the message with another? I
confused confused
everything in the shocking shocking
don't go ‖ go away ‖ so it goes
I am ‖ you are ‖ the dual ‖ and in the middle

sèi-qua   sei la   dùe
e ùno-qua dùe-là   morra morra

—«No, io non mi sono ancora
no, io non mi sono nata
no, io nido nodoso dei no   diamante di mai
no, io sono stata il glissato a lato
no, io non ero la neve né la selva né il loro oltre
eppure e a dispetto e nonostante»

—Quella volta, scendendo a rompifiato di sbieco dal colle,
ho visto ruotare e andar fuori campo il campo le "La Beltà"
sotto la pioggia   cesure
in maniera particolare
una maniera tua ||
e parestesie diffuse
diffuse per quel mona di mondo per quel mosto di mondo ||
                                   già ottobrato

six-here six there two
and one-here two-there   morra morra

—"No, I am not me yet
no, I was not born me
no, I knotty nest of no's   diamond of never
no, I was the glided beside
no, I was not the snow nor the forest nor their beyond
yet and in spite of and notwithstanding"

—That time, descending gasping askew from the hill,
I saw rolling and going off-field the field of "La beltà"
in the rain   caesurae
in a special way
a way of yours   ‖
and diffuse parasthesias
diffuse through that fool of the world through that must of the
    world   ‖

                             already octobered

Translated by Elizabeth A. Wilkins

26 ottobre 1963
sotto il Vajont

Un de mes rêves: je lisais et après je déchiffrais

(l'iode, corrosion, Unruhe, instabilité, "violet", en grec (rayon violet de ses yeux?) – mais aussi 10 D1O, délire d'apothéose ou choc maximum-minimum (les deux "termini" a quibus?)

Position centrale, équilibre (?)

Le "je-moi", qui se dégage de l'enveloppe (de l'auréole) D1O

nom de Dieu en Dante (Parad. xxvi) pour Adam

symbole de l'iode

le "je" (en anglais)

haine mais aussi O, D1O, manque, amour invoquant (un de mes livres est "Vocativo") Et après: ODIO qui enferme D1O

Zéro mais aussi le cercle total de la réalité

à remarquer : 1. la lecture des deux cathètes et de l'hypoténuse
2. la forme graphique des lettres est toujours un segment de droite ou le cercle ou la droite qui coupe en deux (barre) le cercle (D). Est-ce que D est de quelque manière le "grand signifiant barré", qui a part au nihil (moitié invisible) et au réel (moitié visible)? (Lacan)

etc. u.s.w. κ.τ.λ.

Andrea Z.

da Pasque

---

from Easters
[1973]

da Misteri della pedagogia

Il Centro di Lettura.
Distinguere un poco raccogliere mettere da parte
per dirne bene: in tutto:
rigirando bene tutto sotto la lampada . . .
Qui si somministra la dolcissima linfa del sapere
anche ad ore impensate
e i fanciulli e i vecchi suggono
è certo che apprendono al Centro di Lettura:
e si imparte e comparte la vivanda
si tira l'orecchio al distratto
si premia e castiga con frutto
usando onniveggenza; si offre più d'un documento
a bene pregiare la vita e tutto
(ora che in crepuscolo e dono è tutto:
non forse timbri e toni
nel senso dell'aggiustamento?)

     Meli pieni di pioggia e di fiori
     da sempre, di sempre,
     adoranti, quanti «sempre!»: e dissero:
     in sognolìo e luminìo di primavera
     pioggia a filo a filo a filo
     ribadita e grigie e gridi e forme—
     una sera un crepuscolo ciondola intorno
     mi ciondola la testa e
     sugli habitat é quasi festa
     il profitto qua e là mangiucchia
     qua e là ammucchia e tutto
     rientra in questo ehi! anzi racconto
     di cui vado accennando e poi accentuando
     i trucchi le risorse le voglie d'avvicinamento . . .
     come—se fosse vera—sul bilico di una selva
     di meli in pioggia
     lo scoppiettare di un trattore verso la carraia

Io vengo da abbastanza lontano
salgo in cattedra al Centro di Lettura
ci sono i bambini le ragazze delle medie

from Mysteries of Pedagogy

The Reading Center.
To distinguish somewhat to collect to save
in order to speak well of it: in everything:
turning everything well under the lamp . . .
Here is administered the sweetest lymph of knowing
even at unthought-of hours
and the children and the old people suck
certainly they learn at the Reading Center:
and one imparts and shares the food
tweaks the inattentive ear
rewards and punishes with fruit
using all-seeingness; they offer more than a document
to appreciate life and everything to the full
(now that everything is in twilight and a gift:
not perhaps timbres and tones
in the sense of harmonizing?)

       Apple treesApple-trees full of rain and flowers
       since the beginning of time, forever,
       adoring, how many "forevers!": and they said:
       in dreamering and glimmer of Spring
       rain dripping dripping dripping
       repeated and grays and groans and forms—
       an evening a dusk dangles about us
       my head nods and
       on the habitat it's almost holiday
       profit nibbles here and there
       piles up here and there, and everything
       is contained in this hey! or rather this story
       which I'm indicating and then accentuating
       the tricks the resources the desires to approach . . .
       as—if it were true—on the balancing of a wood full
       of apple-trees in the rain
       the put-put of a tractor toward the cart-road

I come from way off
I climb up to preside over the Reading Center
there are children secondary school girls

la vecchia maestra Morchet,
parlo di Dante: che bravi che attenti,
oh lui, quello sì, Dante!
in cattedra nel luogo dei meli e delle viti
nel pozzo delle delizie grigie.
E la maestra Morchet: «Lume non è se non vien dal sereno
che non si turba mai»
cita, dalla sua sedia a destra della cattedra,
cattedra da cui si parla di Dante,
«Bravissima, signorina:
luce non è che non venga da quella».
Tre bambine un po' lolite certo apprendiste magliaie
nove scolari fra elementari e medie
certo un operaio; nell'armadio ci sono
bei libri qui al Centro di Lettura
niente di marcio niente d'impostura
—anche moderni, si assicura—e
che benefit che gratificazione dà qui
il Ministero della P.I.

«Lume non è che non venga».
Il tizzone l'hai visto, nel brolo ?
Fumava nelle lanugini fumava dal rotto.
E i bachi li hai visti serificare
da tutto il loro immenso ghiotto?
Era il paragone famoso
per me: frivolo e solo
a leccornie attento: ma se questa stessa
fosse quasi didascalia
piena di passi in cammino
piena di stonature accettabili come le
gocce d'acqua di melo
gocce di fiori di melo   piene   . . .
Primavera baco e natura
da troppo in ambage
fuori del Centro di Lettura
vanno al bosco vanno in muda
vanno in vacca dormono della quarta
e noi del Centro invece—oh notte—

the old woman teacher Morchet,
I speak of Dante: how good how attentive,
oh him, that one, sure, Dante!
on the rostrum in the place of apple-trees and vines
in the well of gray delights.
And Signorina Morchet: "There is no illumination unless it comes
    from that serene
which never is disturbed"
she quotes, from her seat on the right of the rostrum,
the rostrum from which we speak of Dante.
"Very good, Signorina:
there is no light unless it comes from there."
Three little Lolitas doubtless knitwear factory apprentices
nine students between elementary and secondary school
and someone a workman for sure; in the cupboard there are
fine books here at the Reading Center
nothing corrupting nothing fraudulent
—modern too, we're assured—and
what benefit what gratification
the Minister of Public Instruction bestows here.

    "There is no illumination unless it comes."
    Have you seen the burning brand in the orchard?
    It was smoking in the ground-mist, it was smoking where it
    broke.
    And have you seen the silkworms making silk
    from their great gluttony?
    The simile was well-known
    to me: frivolous and only
    intent on delicacies: but if this itself
    were almost commentary
    full of marching steps
    full of dissonances acceptable as
    drops of apple-tree water
    drops of apple-blossoms   full   . . .
    Spring silkworm and nature
    for too long in circumlocutions
    outside the Reading Center
    they go to the woods they moult
    they rot they sleep like logs

siamo con Dante e la maestra
e il maestro reggente e gli uditori
alla questua dei valori
siamo tesoro non turbato

[. . .]

La pace di oliva

E nel boccio della mattina quasi estiva
egli non ricorda più.
Non ricorda più la data
della pace di Oliva.
Invano fruga l'è il sarà il fu.
Eh   dopo   mi pare
que   e in   v v v
dunque, nel Riss nel Mindel o nel Würm?
O durante un pluviale?
Sottoporre il docente a un test di accertamento.
Segnalarlo al provveditore.
                «Voi là, in fondo. Fermi!
                La smettete?» Smettiamo
                riponiamo smorziamo
                specularmente fermi nel mattutino dolcore
                in un portento ~ in un
                equilibrio del terrore.

Subnarcosi

Uccelli
crudo infinito cinguettio
su un albero invernale
qualche cosa di crudo

and we of the Center instead—oh night—
we are with Dante and the teacher
and the Principal and the listeners
begging for values
we are undisturbed treasure

[. . .]

Translated by Ruth Feldman and Brian Swann

The Peace of Oliva

And in the bud of the dawn almost summery
he no longer remembers.
He no longer remembers the date
of the peace of Oliva.
In vain he scours the is the will be the was.
Eh   later   I think
que   and in   v v v
so then, in the Riss, the Mindel, or the Würm?
Or during a pluvial?
Subject the teacher to a test of verification.
Point him out to the superintendent.
                 "You over there, in the back. Stop it!
                 Are you going to stop it or not?" We're stopping
                 returning settling down
                 speculatively stopped in the forlorn morning
                 in a portent ~ in an
                 equilibrium of terror.

Subnarcosis

Birds
harsh endless chirping
on a wintry tree
something harsh

forse non vero ma solo
scintillio di un possibile
infantilmente aumano
ma certo da noi che ascoltiamo
             —allarmati—lontano
             —o anche placati—lontano
uccelli tutta una città
pregna   chiusa
                   glorie di glottidi
                   acumi e vischi di dottrine
un chiuso si-si-significare
nemmeno infantile ma
adulto occulto nella sua minimità

                   [disperse specie del mio sonno
                   che mai ritornerà].

Per lumina, per limina

             e quanto m'isnsegnavate.
Tutto è convinto spinto
a dare su un'alba
             come di un altro fatto d'alba
tutto è coinvolto precipite a darsi
             in filiazioni di napalm d'alba
tutto è roso da un fuoco sottile fragile freddo
                   —il tepore—
tutto è impuntato in cristallo fratto in fuoco
è covato e incavato a un fuoco
pruriti aurei di seccume   notturne e
tagliole di luna astrali seccumi-ragni
nel sottile del fuoco   foco
nell'esile del fuoco esile
nel frivolo nel freschissimo del fuoco
                   —il tepore—
mah eh per quanti e quali equilibri
per quale concilio di lumi equilibri
             dell'inavvertito equilibri-ragni

maybe not true but just
a spark of a possible
childishly ahuman
but surely for us listeners
      —alarmed—distant
      —or also calmed—distant
birds a whole city
teeming   closed
           glories of glottises
           acumens and doctrinal snares
a closed me-me-meaning
not even childish but
adult occult in its minimalness

      [scattered species of my sleep
      that will never come back].

By Lights, by Limits

      and all you used to teach me.
Everything's convinced thrust
towards a dawn
      as if of another deed of the dawn
everything's implicated plunging headlong to break
      into filiations of napalm of dawn
everything's pink from a freezing delicate fragile fire.
          —the warmth—
everything's indicted in fire-fractured crystal
harbored and hollowed out by a fire
golden cravings of nocturnal   husks and
snares of lunar astral spider-husks
in the thinness of fire   flame
in the slender of the slender fire
in the frivolous in the freshest of the fire
         —the warmth—
well ah for how many and which equilibriums
for which council of lights equilibriums
      of the unseen spider-equilibriums

rapidità sino alla fine e spazzato via
tutto da spazzare da incelestire in odori e via
in che pause oh no nemmeno effrazioni nemmeno
vado di soglia in soglia—attraversato risaputo—
effrangendo e violando—insegnami—
deliberatamente perdutamente
come se effrangessi a lievi e templati
effrangessi a veti a vie a circoli
circoli aree templifiche in boccio
per limina effrangessi per lumina arachnea
certissimo e come in perdita—oh leciti—
                          —e il tepore—.
qui lo scartare il dirimere   e il venire
all'impatto del levissimo col levissimo
del freschissimo con l'altro astrale
più sconfinata-bramata-mente
          tutto è sotto mani   quasi sotto quiete
     e allora spezzettare e spruzzare spazzare
     lievi sottomano e
francamente-mio deliberato
infusivo di mio brillii egoici scricchiih narcissici
in fiorume—luci—lenissima lumina
francamente ieri domani oggi di noi
                e quanto minato
noi luminoso di noi
fogliame minuto perduto di noi
lische cartocci spade
scrigni lunari di noi-biade
noi secco ma convalidato incontaminato raccolto
e—nel liberamente perduto-effranto—
e il procedere violando intuendo
e l'esitare violando restando violati
in luna e da luna
da sotto l'ombra delle mani scomparse-qui
da sotto la luce protratta-attesa-là
tu nell'intendere nell'accecare nel vellicare più amata
eppure inamabile e   in tua letizia aberrante a diamante
     eccesso di me-eccesso oh più a-perdita-di
     e nulla insufflati di foglie-nulla di luci-nulla
     incardinati incentrati

rapidity till the end and swept away
everything to be swept to be enskied in odors and away
in what lulls oh no not even infractions not even
I go from door to door—traversed well-known—
infractioning and transgressing—teach me—
deliberately passionately
as if I were infractioning templed and light
infractioning in nays ways circles
circles templific areas in bud
by limits I was infractioning by spidery lights
so very certain and seemingly at a loss—oh legalities—
                                    —and the warmth—.
here the jettisoning the remedying   and the impacting
of the buoyant with the buoyant
of the fresh with the other astral
more transgressed-coveted-mind
          everything is in hand almost at rest
      and then fragmenting and spraying sweeping
          light underhandly and
frankly-mine resolved
infusive of my egoish gleaming narcissistic screaking
in flowerage—lights—gentle luminosity
frankly yesterday tomorrow today of us
                              and mined how much
us luminous of us
minute lost foliage of us
lisps wrappings blades
lunar caskets of us-fodder
us dry but legitimized uncontaminated harvest
and—in the freely lost-infractioned—
and the violating intuiting carrying-on
and the violated hesitating remaining violating
in moon and by moon
from under the shadow of the hands disappeared-here
from under the light drawn-out-awaited-there
you in the grasping in the blinding in the titillating loved more
and yet unlovable and   in your diamond-deviant happiness
          excess of me-excess oh more in-loss-of
          and nothing infused with nothing-leaves of nothing-lights
          hinged centered

          —e il tepore—
coi non fattuali equilibri altitudini incavi
             —insegniamoci—
mine di luna in fuga
per lumina per limina
oh più fecondo più verbo più troppo
scarti di luna-noi scaglia in abbaglio sul noi
là nel finalmente nell'ero-uni-ero
nel già esploso nella reticente
e polverio di mine e glossolalìe
in sviluppo   —divincolarsi—
in snudato e offerto
nel fulgido sparso sagrato di segni di luna
               —e l'insegnamento
                mutuo di tutto a tutto—

Lanternina cieca

. . . . (a Epifania, pasquetta, mezz'oretta)
e appena il supplemento di sole s'é consunto
e appena il soffio e l'azzurro cominciano
a produr frutto qua e là di stelle—
qua e là si donano stellari grazie tra i rami
stella-venimmo stella-favo stella-magi
stella in chioccolio ai margini della neve
      si gonfia un po' folle il sogno di queste tante nevi
      letti laghi lastre lenzuola aiole
      difficile e lustro deglutire deambulare bivaccare
      divaricarsi da tanta neve
      da freddi/nevi incaponiti in capricorni e spini
            acronìe atopie
     ma provocare
           fin che provochi   che provochi?
In splitting/specchi che lanternini cieca dondola là?
Lei altissima in nero
         col fazzoletto in testa nero
Lui basso e nero
       ma con gli occhi di fatato ghiaccio

                              —and the warmth—
     with the nonfactual equilibriums hollow heights
                              —teach ourselves—
escaping moon mines
by lights by limits
oh more prolific more words more excess
swervings of us-moon flake over us dazzling
there in the finally in the I-was-one-I-was
in the already exploded in the reticent
and dust-cloud of mines and growing
glossolalias   —wriggling about—
unsheathed and proffered
in the resplendent scattered curse of moon-signs
                         —and the teaching
               lending of everything to everything—

Small Dark Lantern

. . . . (at Epiphany, little Easter, half-hour)
and the supplement of sun is just consumed
and the breath of air and the blue just begin
to produce fruit here and there of stars—
here and there stellar graces show themselves among the boughs
we-came-star honeycomb-star magi-star
star in warbling at the snow's edges
          the dream of these so-many snows swells a bit, mad, beds
          lakes slabs sheets flowerbeds
          difficult and shiny is swallowing strolling bivouacking
          opening wide from so much snow
          from colds/snows stubborn in Capricorns and thorns
                    timelack spacelack
          but provoking
                    until you provoke   what do you provoke?
In splitting/mirrors what small dark-lantern swings there?
She very tall in black
                    with the black kerchief on her head
He short and dark
                    but with eyes of bewitched ice

da domini e viluppi   di candori discendono
lenti di aver tettato il molto e il caldo
dal vino dei Fordàn, stalla e filò,
di fieno e fiati scendono ben fondi,
di stillicidi forze princìpi stelliferi,
da vini e lunghe tettature
tra occhi di vacche e dei tanti Fordàn—
cellule luci dondolano Lui/Lei Lei con Lui
della lanterna il lusso fruga e glissa
per mondi di neve e di stelle
s'illustra il cammino s'immilla di lanternine un po' brille
Neta/assai/ben piú/altissima   in nero
Toni-oci/meno/buio   nerobestemmia
ma vi'tu   ma varda   ma quali
in interminati concili di nevi e geli
in reti di neuroni e sinapsi astrali
in piste riscontri viraggi di nevi su nevi:
Toni, Neta, qui dondolando tra lustri di arbusti
lanterne cieche, domani forse pile!

Codicillo

No, non è vero, più semplice e amico è l'impegno
qui con umani con divinità.
Ombre ≅ luci cieli ≅ terre come in un sogno
                    di fortissimo ozono
anche se talvolta crudeltà. Degno
rapporto di placata amante memoria.
Dulcedini volontà-buone mani
alzate non a prece ma a gloria
            sovradeterminazioni
                  sovrastrati abbattevano
            sgusciati da coltivi e da fabbriche

from dominions and tangles   of dazzling whites they
                                        descend
slow from having suckled the much and the warm
from the Fordàns' wine, stable and nightwatch,
they descend well-fattened by hay and breaths
by drippings strengths starifying principles,
from wines and long sucklings
among the eyes of cows and of the so-numerous Fordàns—
cells lights swing He / She She with Him
the lantern's luxury probes and slides
through worlds of snow and stars
the road shines is multiplied by thousands with dark-lanterns,
    slightly tipsy,
        Neta / quite / much more / very tall   in black
        Toni / oci / less / dark   blackoath
        but you see   but look   but which
        in endless confabulations of snows and frosts
        in networks of neurons and astral synapses
        in tracks comparisons swirlings of snows on snows:
Toni, Neta, dark-lanterns swinging here among shinings of shrubs,
tomorrow—flashlights, perhaps!

Translated by Ruth Feldman and Brian Swann

Codicil

No, it's not true, the commitment is simpler and more friendly
here with humans with divinities.
Shadows ≅ lights skies ≅ earths as in a dream
                                of powerful ozone
even if cruelty at times. Worthy
relationship of soothed and loving memory.
Sacred-sweetness good-wills hands
raised not in prayer but for glory
        superdeterminations
                superstrata they demolished
            issued from the cultivated and from factories

da incensi e da rugiade
operando d'alba in alba si riconobbero.
Biciclette trillarono.—
O stelle viti acque a grappoli, in alba,
quasi disabissate abbondanze d'Emmaus,
conciliazione che in tutto prevarrebbe
congruità embricazione di sanerà
con sanerà.
No nessun nume né umano allontaniamo
grazie sono i certami con lui-ciascuno
perché ciascuno infinitamente
ci avvezzo   ci svezzo
al lucore di questo nostro insieme
e del niente.

∪ ā ∪ ē

Così nel disagio del prato nell'oscuro del bosco
quasi sfrangiato scaduto male
o anche, al tramonto, animale
appello, richiesta di riconoscimento—

da sterilizzanti lunazioni e stonature
ritorno quasi affettuoso nell'oscuro
risarcimento dell'odore, nel lurido
del nido—noi scuotendo il capo—nostro umile:

forse entro abissi di bacche e fogliami superstite
prodursi in voto e profitto umano
d'oscuro da reinvestire in leggi
strappate-in-su, al reversibile, tendini

(e tu fuori mano annuisci povera bastarda folla,
entropie in barcollare riarso/oscuro, infittirsi di spettri
e strette nel bario, tiraemolla
di abitudini somme ed inani, d'invenzioni decrepite.)

from incenses and dews
working from dawn to dawn they recognized each other.
Bicycles trilled.
Oh stars vines waters in clusters, at dawn,
almost disabyssed abundances of Emmaus,
conciliation that would prevail in everything
congruity overlapping of it-will-heal
with it-will-heal.
No, we send away no numen and no human
the contests with him-everyone are graces
because everyone endlessly
trained us   weaned us
to the glimmer of this wholeness of ours
and of nothingness.

Translated by Ruth Feldman and Brian Swann

∪ ā ∪ ē

Thus in the meadow's unease in the woods' dark
almost frayed wasted wrong
or even, at sunset, animal
appeal, request for recognition—

from sterilizing lunations and discords
an almost affectionate return in the dark
recouping of the scent, in the filth
of the nest—we shaking our heads—our humble nest:

perhaps surviving inside abysses of berries and foliage
a production in vow and human profit
of the dark to reinvest in up-wrenched
laws, to the reversible, tendons

(and you—out of reach—nod assent poor bastard crowd,
entropies in parched/dark reeling, thickening with ghosts
and squeezed in the barium, wavering
of sublime inane customs, of decrepit inventions.)

Dove valse cibarsi di fragole e lamponi, citando
citando la verità, dove delle ciliegie emersero i nòccioli
come pietredure nell'alone oscure, evocando dal bando
del nottegiornoniente i più equivoci boccioli—

vedervi con uguale sgomento con uguale assenso
rinnovato in bianco, privo di riserva;
sentirvi, ∪ ā ∪ ē, vicine come l'erba →
oscuro del prato dove perii, dove perirò / sorgerò.

Where it was worth feeding on strawberries and raspberries, quoting
quoting the truth, where from the cherries emerged pits
like semi-precious stones into the dark halo, evoking from the exile
of nightdaynothing the most ambiguous buds—

seeing you with equal dismay with equal assent
renewed from zero, without reserve;
feeling you, ∪ ā ∪ ē, close as the grass →
dark of the meadow where I perished, where I will perish / arise.

2 Dicembre 1931
La famiglia meno papà

da Filò. Per il *Casanova* di Fellini

---

from Peasants Wake for
Fellini's *Casanova*
[1976]

da Filò

Vecio parlar che tu à inte 'l tó saór
un s'cip del lat de la Eva,
vecio parlar che no so pi,
che me se á descuní
dì par dì 'nte la boca (e no tu me basta);
che tu sé canbià co la me fazha
co la me pèl ano par an;
parlar porét, da poreti, ma s'cèt
ma fis, ma tóch cofà 'na branca
de fien 'pena segà dal faldin (parché no bàstetu?)—
noni e pupà i é 'ndati, quei che te cognosséa,
none e marne le é 'ndate, quele che te inventéa,
nóvo petèl par ogni fiól in fase,
intra le strússie, i zhighi dei part, la fan e i afanézh.
Girar me fa fastidi, in médo a 'ste masiére
de ti, de mi. Dal dent cagnin del tenp
inte 'l piat sivanzhi no ghén resta, e manco
de tut i zhimiteri: òe da dine zhimitero?
Élo vero che pi no pól esserghe 'romai
gnessun parlar de néne-none-mame? Che fa mal
ai fiói 'l petèl e i gran mestri lo sconsilia?
Élo vero che scriverte,
parlar vecio, l'é massa un sforzh, l'é un mal
anca par mi, cofà ciór par revèrs,
par straòlt, far 'ndar fora le corde de le man?

Ma intant, qua par atomo, a girar pa'i marcà,
o mèjo a 'ndar par canp e rive e zhópe
là onde che 'l gal de cristal canta senpre tre òlte,
da juste boche se te sent. Mi ò pers la trazha,
lontan massa son 'ndat pur stando qua
invidà, inbulonà, deventà squasi un zhóch de piombo,
e la poesia no l'é in gnessuna lengua
in gnessun logo—fursi—o l'é 'l busnar del fógo
che 'l fa screcolar tute le fonde
inte la gran laguna, inte la gran lacuna—
la é 'l pien e 'l vódo dela testa-tera
che tas, o zhigna e usura un pas pi in là
de quel che mai se podaràe dirse, far nostro.

from Peasants Wake

Old dialect, a drop of Eve's milk
lingers in your flavor,
old dialect that I can't remember,
you've worn yourself out
day after day in my mouth (and you're not enough for me);
you've changed with my face
with my skin year after year;
poor speech, of the poor, but pure
thick and dense as a handful
of freshly scythed hay (why aren't you enough?)—
grandpas and dads have passed away, who used to know you,
grandmas and moms have passed away, who used to invent for you
new babblings for every baby in diapers,
in the suffering, the screams of labor, the hunger, the nausea.
It bothers me to roam through these ruins
of me, of you. Time's relentless teeth
have left nothing on the plate, and even less
in the graveyards: should I call you graveyard?
Is it true that there can no longer be
a speech for nursemaids-grandmas-moms? Does baby talk
harm children and do the big experts advise against it?
Is it true that writing you,
old tongue, is too tiring, is it a pain
even for me, the way picking up something the wrong way,
at the wrong angle, wrenches the hand's tendons?

But meanwhile, hereabouts, wandering the markets,
or even better, walking the fields, hillocks, and crags
there where the glittering rooster always crows three times,
you're heard spoken by honest mouths. I've lost track,
I've gone too far while remaining here
screwed down, bolted in place, becoming almost a lump of lead
and poetry's not in any language
in any place—perhaps—or it's the roaring of fire
that makes all the foundations creak
in the great lagoon, in the great lacuna—
it's the fullness and the emptiness of the earth-head
who remains silent, or winks or sniffs out a path beyond
what we'll never be able to tell each other, to make our own.

Ma ti, vedo parlar, resisti. E si anca i òmi
te desmentegarà senzha inacòrderse,
ghén sarà osèi—
do tre osèi sói magari
dai sbari e dal mazhelo zoladi via—:
doman su l'ultima rama là in cao
in cao de zhiése e pra,
osèi che te à inparà da tant
te parlarà inte 'l sol, inte l'onbría.

★ ★ ★

L'ora se slanguoris inte 'l zhendre del scaldin,
l'é l'ora de des'ciorse, de assar al calduzh, al coàt.
Ma da 'ste póche brónzhe de qua dó,
dai fià dei filò de qua dó,
si i fii, si i fii
del insoniarse e rajonar tra lori se filarà,
là sù, là par atomo del ventar de le stele
se inpizharà i nostri mili parlar e pensar nóvi
inte 'n parlar che sarà un par tuti,
fondo come un basar,
vèrt sul ciaro, sul scur,
davanti la manèra inpiantada inte 'l scur
col só taj ciaro, 'pena guà da senpre.

    (Disèe manèra, disèe taj,
e l'era sol che 'na sguinzhada
    un jozholar de débol miei
de lustri mèsteghi de bròse e guazh).
    (Disèe fii, disèe fià,
    e co le ónge intive sol che in
    s'césene—noi—de calcossa
    desconpagnà   sparpagnà
    inte la lópa de un posterno   eterno)
(Disèe, disèe   )

〜 𝖪𝖨b·ﬡ·ﬡ𝖴𝖷𝖑·ﬁ·D𝖑·ﬁ·𝖷‖𝖃·ﬁ· 〜

('Note, 'note; 'l filó l'é finí)

luglio-ottobre 1976

But you, old tongue, hold fast! And even if people
end up forgetting you without noticing it,
there'll be birds—
maybe only two or three
flown away from the shooting and slaughter—:
tomorrow on the last branch off in the distance
at the edge of hedges and meadows,
birds that learned you long ago,
will speak you in the sun, in the shadows.

★ ★ ★

The hour is drooping away in the ashes of the brazier,
it's time to go, to leave the warmth of the nest.
But from the few embers down here,
from the breaths of the filò down here,
if the threads, if the threads
of dreaming and thinking spin themselves together,
up there, where the starry wind blows
our thousand tongues and new thoughts will ignite
in a dialect that will be one for everyone,
deep as kissing,
open to the light, to the dark,
in front of the axe stationed in the darkness
with its glimmering blade, forever newly sharpened.

    (I said axe, I said blade
and it was only a sprinkling
    a dribbling of watery honey
of faint lights of frosts and dews).
      (I said threads, breaths,
      and with my fingernails I meet
      only splinters—us—of something
      disarrayed   scattered
      in the moss of an eternal   postern)
(I was saying, I started to say   )

Kl bʰ|.lɴ ʊ X |ɛ ·|ˌ D Ɛ ·|ˌX ||bˠ ·|ˌ

(Goodnight, goodnight; the filò is over)

July–October 1976

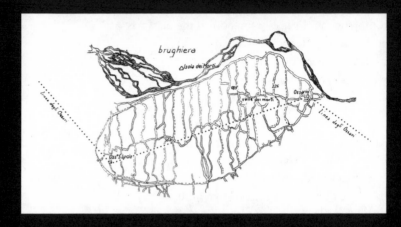

da Il Galateo in Bosco

from The Woodland Book of Manners
[1978]

Dolcezza. Carezza. Piccoli schiaffi in quiete.
                    Diteggiata fredda sul vetro.
Bandiere piccoli intensi venti/ve tri.
                    Bandiere, interessi giusti e palesi.
Esse accarezzano libere inquiete. Legate leggiere.
Esse bandiere, come-mai? Come-qui?
Battaglie lontane. Battaglie in album, nel madagliere.
Paesi. Antichissimi. Giovani scavi, scavare nel cielo, bandiere.
Cupole circo. Bandiere che saltano, saltano su.
Frusta alzata per me, frustano il celeste ed il blu.
Tensioattive canzoni/schiuma gonfiano impauriscono il vento.
    Bandiere.
Botteghino paradisiaco. Vendita biglietti. Ingresso vero.
Chiavistelli, chiavistelle a grande offerta.
Chiave di circo-colori-cocchio circo. Bandiere.
Nel giocattolato fresco paese, giocattolo circo.
Piccolissimo circo. Linguine che lambono. Inguini. Bifide
trifide bandiere, battaglie. Biglie. Bottiglie.
Oh che come un fiotto di fiotti bandiere balza tutto il circo-cocò.
Biglie bowling slot-machine trin trin stanno prese
nella lucente [   ] folla tagliola del marzo—
come sempre mortale
come sempre in tortura-ridente
come sempre in arsura-ridente ridente
E lui va in motoretta sulla corda tesa su verso la vetta
del campanile, dell'anilinato mancamento azzurro.
E butta all'aria. Bandiere. Ma anche fa bare, o fa il baro.
Bara nell'umido nel secco. Carillon di bandiere e bandi.
S'innamora, fa circhi delle sere.
Sforbicia, marzo. Tagliole. Bandi taglienti. Befehle come raggi e
    squarti.

Partiva il circo la mattina presto—
furtivo, con un trepestio di pecorelle.
Io perché (fatti miei), stavo già desto.

Sweetness. Dearness. Little muffled slaps.
                              Fingered cold on the glass.
Flags little intense winds/windows.
                              Flags, evident and just interests.
Free and unquiet, they caress. Bound and buoyant.
Flags, how-so? How-here?
Distant battles. Battles in albums, in the medal case.
Towns. Extremely old. Fresh excavations, excavating the sky, flags.
Circus Cupolas. Flags that leap, leap up.
Whip upraised for me, they whip the celestial and the blue.
Tensioactive songs/foam swell up frighten the wind. Flags.
Paradisiacal ticket office. Tickets on sale. True entrance.
Latches, bolts at cut-rate prices.
Key to circus-colors-carriage circus. Flags.
In the toyed fresh land, toy circus.
Tiniest circus. Tonguelings that lick. Groins. Bifid
trifid flags, battles. Balls. Bottles.
Oh that like a gush of gushes flags it bounces all the circus-ruckus
    about.
Balls bowling alleys slot machines clink-clank are caught
in the gleaming [   ] throng trap of March—
as ever mortal
as ever in torture-laughing
as ever in parched-laughing laughing
And there he goes on a motorbike along the cord stretched taut to
    the top
of the steeple, of anilined azure scarcity.
And flinging into the air. Flags. But also making caskets, or being a
    cheat.
Casket in the damp of the dry. Music-box of flags and decrees.
Falling in love, making circuses of the evenings.
Snipping away, March. Traps. Cutting decrees Behests like rays and
    quarterings.

The circus left early in the morning—
furtive, with a trampling of sheeplings.
Since (that's my business) I was already awake.

Io sapevo dell'alba in partenza, delle
pecorelle del circo sotto le stelle.
Partenza il 19, S. Giuseppe,
a raso a raso il bosco, la brinata, le crepe.

Gnessulógo

Tra tutta la gloria
messa a disposizione
del succhiante e succhiellato verde
di radura tipicamente montelliana
circhi in ascese e discese e—come gale—
arboscelli vitigni stradine là e qui
affastellate e poi sciorinate
in una soavissima impraticità   ah
ah veri sospiri appena accennati eppur più che completi
lietezza ma non troppa
come un vino assaggiato e lasciato—zich—a metà
dall'intenditore che subito via sgroppa
vaghezza ma certo intrecciata
di imbastiture e triangolazione,
di arpeggi   e poi amplessi boschivi
(è così che bosco e non-bosco in quieta pazzia tu coltivi)

Ed è così che ti senti nessunluogo, gnessulógo (avverbio)
mentre senza sottintesi
di niente in niente distilla se stesso (diverbio)
e invano perché   gnessulógo
mai a gnessulógo è equivalente e
perché qui propriamente
c'è solo invito-a-luogo c'è catenina
di ricchezze e carenze   qua e lì   lì e là
—e chi vivrà vedrà—
invito non privo di divine moine
in cui ognuno dovrà
trovarsi
come a mani (pampini) giunte inserito
e altrettanto disinserito

I knew of the dawn's departure, of the
   circus sheeplings under the stars.
   They left on the 19th, Saint Joseph's Day,
   hugging the woods, the hoarfrost, the fissures.

Noplace

Amidst all the glory
put at the disposition
of the sucking and suckled green
 of typical Montellian glades
  expanding and contracting corries, and—like ribbons—
   saplings vines lanes there and here
   bundled and then hung out
    in the mildest impracticality ah
ah true sighs just breathed and yet more than finished
   happiness but not too much
    like a wine tasted and left—zich—half-finished
    by a connoisseur who at once bucks off
   vagueness no doubt intertwined
       with tackings and
 triangulations,
   of arpeggios   then woody embraces
  (it is thus in silent madness you cultivate woods and non-woods)

And it is thus that you feel nowhere, noplace (adverb)
 while without allusions
  from nothing to nothing distills itself (in dispute)
   and in vain because noplace
    is never the same as noplace and
    because exactly here
    there is only invitation-to-place there is a chain
    of riches and scarcities here and there there and
     here
        —and who will live will see—
    invitation not without divine wheedlings
    in which everyone must
    find oneself
    as in hands (vine leaves) joined inserted

per potersi fare, in ultimo test di succhio
e di succhiello,
farsi yalina caccola, gocciolo di punto-di-vista
tipico dell'infinito quando è così umilmente irretito . . .

Gale, stradine, gloriole, primaverili virtù . . .
Ammessa conversione a U
ovunque.

Diffrazioni, eritemi

Eritemi ovunque, causati da fortissimi diffrazioni e riverberi relativi
a una / partita non-giocata con Carte Trevisane da non esistenti né
meglio identificabili giocatori e / ripresa col grandangolare / quasi
a fish-eye, / quasi rimorsi a mazzetto / vuoti di memoria a pac-
chetto / di schede bianche. / Dicerie, sbattere di sedie, vini foschi
sul tavolo.
   Osteria della Malanotte. In bosco fosco di tossica
      intensissima luce. Partita a tenia, a ossiuro, ad anchilostoma?
     Risalendo la tenia
        che / perde / dietro a sé / l'organizzazione
        sviante / delle proglottidi /
     Accompagnamento di chitarre erotodemagogiche
     Pretesa di narrazione e di ripresa, rubata
                a grandangolo.
   Detto.
   Quel che è detto è maledetto.
     Rimescolamento, Vrrrrrrrr di carte in mani esperte.
     Sbatterle sul tavolo, a pacchetto.

. . . .
     NON TI FIDAR DI ME SE

I gravissimi Provveditori
EMO GRITTI RENIER

as much uninserted
so as to become, at the end test of sucking
and of suckling,
become mucus, a drop of point-of-view
typical of the infinite when it is thus humbly ensnared . . .

Ribbons, lanes, glories, springs, virtues . . .
Granted conversion to U
everywhere.

Diffractions, Erythemas

Erythemas everywhere, caused by very strong diffractions and re-
verberations related to a / game unplayed with Trevisan Cards by
neither existent nor better identifiable players and / captured by
wide-angle lens / almost fish-eye, / almost remorseful in a bunch /
empty of memory in a deck / of blank cards. / Hearsay, banging of
chairs, murky wines on the table.
  Tavern of the Malanotte. In the woods murky with toxic
    extremely intense light. Game of tapeworms, pinworms,
      hookworms?
  The tapeworm climbs up
    and / loses / behind itself / the deviating
    organization / of the proglottids
Accompaniment of erotodemagogic guitars
Demand for narration and filming, stolen
                    by wide-angle lens.
Said.
That which is said is accursed.
      Shuffling, Vrrrrrrrr of cards in expert hands.
      Banging them on the table, in a deck.

. . . .
            DON'T TRUST ME IF

The very grave Providers
EMO GRITTI RENIER

i famosissimi banditi e predatori
i lupi pagati cari agli uccisori
se fuor del telletorio uscivano del bosco
a mangiarsi interi casolari
con gente piangente alle finestre •••·•••`..·.•..·..,,•^`..·•••••·•••·. //D^{ne}
.............//D^{ne}, quo fugiam?

.........E, dietro quello sprone losco
di roccia, abitava il sàntolo più sadico
e più tonto e più orco, il
Barba Zhucón oggetto di burla atroce,
che al posto di frittelle ebbe dalle figliocce
una fazzolettata di caccotte di mulo;
ma non riuscì a vendicarsi penetrando dal buco
dell'acquaio e ingozzò inoltre un intero agoraio . . .

···•••`..•`..••·•••·•••·•••• E // † Mane nobiscum D^{ne} //

NON VAL SAPER A CHI HA FORTUNA CONTRA
(Teodomiro Dal Negro succ. Prezioso)
la vecchia danarosa che aveva chissà come
avuto licenza a farsi una villa in bosco
circuendo le più solide norme
e che trescò coi ladri del baule
del conte Renaldin, trovato vuoto
sul greto del gran fiume—non si sa—
vuoto d'un bendidìo di franchi ori e valute:
la mutuante Cian: mistero
che non son mai riuscito a diradare
(in che veste apparisse nell'affare:
ricattatrice, complice, comare?)
(« Gavemo sbalà la vecia »): strozzata
e gettata come la vecchia di spade
via dal mazzo consumatosi a giocare
non una sola partita ma infinite
partite farabutte tutte esemplari •••·•••`..`..•••·•••·•••·•••·

the infamous bandits and predators
the wolves who carried a high price for hunters
if out they crept from their realm, the woods
to devour entire cottages
with people weeping at the windows •••• ••...•..•..••...•..••.•...••...//Dne
............//Dne, quo fugiam?

MARTIN BY A POINT

.... And, behind that sinister spur
of rock, lived the most sadistic, most gormless
and most hideous sàntolo, the
Barba Zhucón butt of an atrocious prank,
who in place of fritters got from his goddaughters
a handkerchief full of mule crap;
but he couldn't get even by poking up from the hole
of the sink and even gulped down an entire needle-case . . .

••• ••..•.•.••.• .••. •••• ••••• And // † Mane nobiscum Dne //

KNOWING DOESN'T HELP IF YOU'VE GOT BAD LUCK
(Teodomiro Dal Negro succ. Prezioso)
the rich old woman who had who knows how
obtained the right to build a villa in the woods
getting round the strictest regulations
and who plotted with the thieves of Count Renaldin's
trunk, found empty
on the gravely riverbank—one can't tell—
emptied of a pile of gold francs and other coins:
the money-lending Cian: mystery
that I've never been able to untangle
(in what guise did she appear in the affair:
blackmailer, accomplice, godmother?)
("We killed the hag"): strangled
and tossed like the knave of spades
out of the deck worn out from playing
not just one game but infinite
villainous games all exemplary ••• ••••.••.•.•..••••...••....•

Sparsi joni, elettroni di fati
che qui cercano di riaccozzarsi—
impudenza, demenza del ricordare • • • ⋮ • ⋮ • • • • // E

SE TI PERDI TUO DANNO

. . . . . . precipitando nella più infima feccia
|| Noli, D^{ne}, iudicare ||
del tempo,   dare   nella breccia
nel brecciame della vetrata / vortice
dell'Abbazia, poi reimpostarne i seghettati
frammenti di portenti,
L'Arcipriore demonologo   [autore, forse, di un
che faceva faville   trattatello « Della Prepotenza »]
di parricidio, incesto, stupro e altre mille
favolose perversioni e che quel santo luogo
avea reso ritrovo
di eretici di maghi e di zhisanpe
di zombies di sciamani e di assassini
sino a far saltare le relazioni
tra la Repubblica e la Chiesa
che una grandissima contesa
fra loro misero in piedi su chi dovesse giudicarlo—
la davvero saturnina e surreale
Questione Giurisdizionale.
Noli, D^{ne}, quaeso, iudicare.

— • — • •• — — — — — ⌒ ～ ～ ℰ꒐ (taenia)

Di questi e d'altri eventi
—se sono eventi—
[E non facciano ressa allo sportello. Batticuore. Collisioni, collages di
malintesi. Partita sospesa. Tatti schifosi. Galateo spiaccicato. Fuggi
—fuggi. Torna.]
eventi
degni comunque di minuziosissimo riguardo
se si collocheranno   nella giusta costellazione
nel mandala   allo sportello   se cadrà la rimozione
si potrà, col tempo, appurare: —cose del tempo
quando il Montello era un frondoso mare . . .

Scattered ions, electrons of fates
that here attempt to re-gather—
impudence, dementia of remembering · ··:· :··· // And

IF YOU GET LOST IT'S YOUR PROBLEM

...... pitching down into the lowest dregs
|| Noli, D^{ne}, iudicare ||
of time,   falling   into the breach
into the frame of the window/vortex
of the Abbey, then repositioning the jagged
fragments of portents,
    The Archprior demonologue   [author, perhaps, of a little
who made sparks   treatise "Of Arrogance"]
of parricide, incest, rape and a thousand other
fabled perversions and who at that sacred place
had formed a coven
of heretics, wizards and slatterns
of zombies, witch doctors and assassins
until relations exploded
between the Republic and the Church
and a huge quarrel
among them erupted over who should judge him—
    the truly saturnine and surreal
    Jurisdictional Question.
    Noli, D^{ne}, quaeso, iudicare.

—·——··———— ⁓⌁⁓ 𝄐 (taenia)

Of these and other events
        —if they are events—
[And they shouldn't crowd at the counter. Heartbeats. Collisions, col-
lages of misunderstandings. Suspended game. Disgusting touches.
Squashed manners. Escape—escape. Come back.]
events
worthy nonetheless of the most meticulous care
if they fall into place   in the right constellation
in the mandala   at the ticket counter   if the removal fails
one will be able, in time, to ascertain: —things of time
        when the Montello was a leafy sea . . .

E intanto si cerca di adagiarvi quanto
                    fuori per il mondo resta
(testa e croce, croce e testa)
di sestosenso/terzoochio
rendendolo adeguatamente
tremolo e selvaggio nel soppesare e valutare—
ma come di troppo dolce e infrollita selvaggina—
                    nel massimo di grandangolare:

          ecco è tranciata la bobina
della scorretta endoscopia per entro il dentro-tenia dei tempi
     e delle materie grigio-boscive
     tranciata   dalle prime baionettate
                        dalle prime smitragliate
                        sul fondo del cupo   cupo tambureggiare
     delle migliaia e migliaia di cannoni

          dallo Stelvio al Mare

(Certe forre circolari colme di piante—
e poi buchi senza fondo)

Dovrebbero gli assaggi essere cauti e rabdomantici
     come mosse di biopsie o di liturgie—
     e per questo fecondi, come tu li accordi per tua natura
     anche quando pare tu li ricalci,
          quando tu falci   all'
improvviso ogni cammino—

                                   tabù
          di piante invorticate e rintanate giù giù:

. . . .

e nessuno nessuno nessuno
divinerà   toccherà   eviterà
con bastante allarme bastante amore
—o bosco ancora e sempre rapinatore

And meanwhile one attempts to find a place for how much
                    scattered across the world remains
(head and tails, tails and head)
of sixthsense/thirdeye
adequately rendering it
trembling and wild in the weighing and evaluating—
but as if it were too sweet and tender game—
                    in the extreme of wideangling:

        here the reel is hacked off
of the mistaken endoscopy from within the inner tapeworm of the
    times
    and the woody gray matter
    hacked off   by the first bayonets
                    by the first machinegun fusillades
                    backed by the deep   deep hammering
    of the thousands and thousands of cannons

        from the Stelvio to the Sea

(Certain circular chasms brimming with plants— and then holes without bottom)

The tastings should be cautious and dowsing
        like the motions of biopsies or liturgies—
        and for this also fecund, as you reconcile them with your nature
            even when it seems you knock them back,
                when you cut   all
of a sudden every path—

                                taboo
            of enswirled plants burrowing down down:
. . . .

and no one no one no one
will divine   will touch   will avoid
with sufficient alarm sufficient affection
—O woods still and always a robber

entro il tuo stesso vantarti fantasma—
nessuno rasenterà con adeguato rapimento
e pallore di morte e di speranza
il tuo irriccirti in divieti/avvitamenti,
    i tuoi grumi di latitanza,
    i crolli rabbiosi nei buchi delle tue tenebre
    che sono scrolli graziosi entro gli scrigni delle tue tenebre—
    finte fosse comuni di potentissime essenze,
        miniaturizzate foreste di incognite che
        nessuna iattanza o farsa umana sconvolse del tutto:
        nidi, allora, di resistenze,
        di pericolosi mitraglianti rametti-raggio

Ma a tanta grazia senza limitazione incrudelita
    che s'inserpenta sotto
    come per uno scatto
    o, soltanto, crucciata e sfregiata
    in chivalà rattratti si demarca,
        è riservato
    appena dare segnalazioni a stelle di passaggio
        a cavalieri erranti
        obliquamente usciti dal teleobiettivo
a don Abbondi in cerca
        dell'erboristeria del coraggio
a dèi carcami e feti scagliati nel motocross
        di rabbia in rabbia
        verso l'ebbrezza dell'ultima faglia

O gangli glomi verdi di paure,
paure-Pizie, incriptati piziaci sbavaggi e fonemi—
    con passi liturgici, con andirivieni liturgici
    imposti dalle vostre
    topografie note soltanto a Comandi Supremi,
    guidateci ai santi ossari
    dove in cassettini minuscoli
    han ricetto le schegge dei giovinetti fatti fuori

Con passi liturgici con andirivieni liturgici
distratti rabdomantici   come entro al coma solitari
calcoleremo a un press'a poco il disavanzo
verso quelle scheggine, stuzzicadenti

you boast a phantom within—
no one will come near with adequate rapture
and pallor of death and of hope
your hedgehog-bristlings in prohibitions/twists,
    your clots of hiding,
    the rabid collapsings in the holes of your shadows
    that are gracious shakings within the caskets of your shadows—
    false communal graves of the most potent essences,
        miniaturized forests of enigmas never entirely
    unsettled by arrogance or human farce:
            nests, then, of resistance
                of dangerous fusillading beam-branches

But with much grace without limitation made cruel
    that snakes itself under
    as if a clicking
    or, only, distressed and disfigured
    on the lookout benumbed demarcating,
        it is reserved
    to give subtle signs to passing stars
        to errant knights
            obliquely departed from the telephoto lens
to Don Abbondios in search
            of the herbalist of courage
to gods carcasses and fetuses flung into the motocross track
        of rage in rage
            toward the intoxication of the final fault

O ganglions glomera green with fear,
Pythian-fears, cryptic pythian foamings and phonemes—
    with liturgical steps, with liturgical comings and goings
    begun from your
    topographies known only to Supreme Orders,
    guide us to the sacred ossuaries
    where in miniscule little boxes
    they've collected the splinters of the young men done in

With liturgical steps with liturgical comings and goings
distracted dowsing as if within the coma alone
we'll calculate more or less the distance
to those little splinters, toothpicks

alla mensa della Vecchia di Spade—
       qua e là sotto importune   disperse date di comete e lune
       tra infezioni e iatture   o sobbalzi di moto ruggenti
       tra feste intestinali   e zone militare

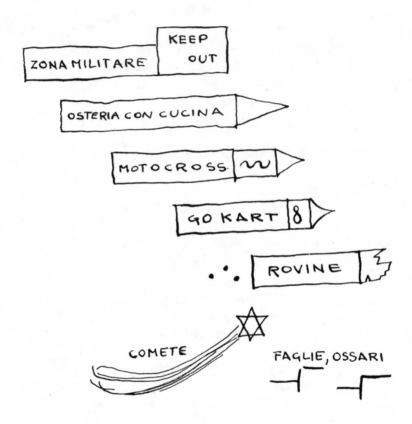

Passare alla morsura

            ★

Rivolgersi agli ossari. Non occorre biglietto.
Rivolgersi ai cippi. Con il più disperato rispetto.
Rivolgersi alle osterie. Dove elementi paradisiaci aspettano.
Rivolgersi alle case. Dove l'infinitudine del desìo
           (vedila ad ogni chiusa finestra) sta in affitto.

at the dinner table of the Knave of Spades—
    here and there insistent   scattered dates of comets and moons
    amidst infections and calamities   or the joltings of roaring
       motorcycles
    amidst intestinal festivals   and military zones

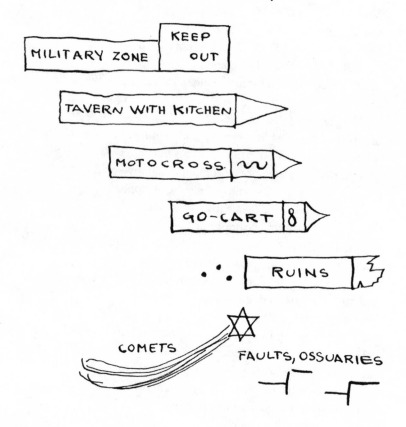

Passing to the etching

                ★

Apply to the ossuaries. No ticket is needed.
Apply to the headstones. With the most desperate respect.
Apply to the taverns. Where heavenly elements await.
Apply to the houses. Where the infinitude of desire
            (see it at every closed window) is for rent.

E la radura ha accettato più d'un frondoso colloquio
ormai, dove, ahi,
si esibì la più varia mostra dei sangui
   il più mistico circo dei sangui. Oh quanti numeri, e rancio speciale.
   Urrah.
Vorrei bucarmi di ogni chimica rovina
per accogliere tutti, in anteprima,
nello specchio medicato d'infinitudini e desii
di quel circo i fermenti gli enzimi
dentro i succhi più sublimi dell'alba, dell'azione, in piena diana.
   E si va.
E si va per ossari. Essi attendono
gremiti di mortalità lievi ormai, quai gemme di primavera,
gremiti di bravura e di paura. A ruota libera, e si va.
Buoni, ossari—tante morti fuori del qualitativo divario
                onde si sale a sicurezze di cippo,
fuori del gran bidone (e la patria bidonista,
che promette casetta e campicello
e non li diede mai, qui santità mendica, acquista).
Hanno come un fervore di fabbrica gli ossari.
Vi si ricevono ordini, ordinazioni eterne. Vi si smista.
All'asilo, certi pazzi-di-guerra, ancora vivi
allevano maiali; traffici con gli ossari.
Mi avete investito, lordato tutto, eternizzato tutto, un fiotto di sangue.
Arteria aperta il Piave, né calmo né placido
ma soltanto gaiamente sollecito oltre i beni i mali e simili
                e tutto solletichìo di argenti, nei suoi intenti, a dismisura.
Padre e madre, in quel nume forse uniti
          tra quell'incoercibile sanguinare
          ed il verde e l'argenteizzare altrettanto incoercibili,
in quel grandore dove tutti i silenzi sono possibili
voi mi combinaste, sotto quelle caterve di
os-ossa, ben catalogate, nemmeno geroglifici, ostie
          rivomitate ma come in un più alto, in un aldilà d'erbe e d'enzimi
                erbosi assunte,
          in un fuori-luogo che su me s'inclina e domina
                un poco creandomi, facendomi assurgere a
Così che   suono a parlamento
per le balbuzie e le più ardue rime,
quelle si addestrano e rincorrono a vicenda,

And the glade has accepted more than one leafy talk
by now, where, ah,
there is offered the most varied show of bloods
the most mystical circus of bloods. Oh how many, and a special mess.
   Hurrah.
I'd like to shoot up with every ruining chemical
so to receive them all, in preview,
in the medicated mirror of infinitudes and desires
of that circus the ferments the enzymes
inside the most sublime suckings of dawn, of the action, in full
   reveille. And off we go.
And off we go to the ossuaries. They await
overcrowded with mortality, lightened by now, almost springtime
   buds,
overcrowded with bravura and fear. Freewheeling, and off we go.
Calm, ossuaries—so many dead outside the qualitative difference
                whence one rises to headstone safeties,
outside the great swindle (and swindler nation,
that promises a humble home and garden
and never grants them, here holiness begs, acquires).
The ossuaries have a factory-like fervor.
There one receives orders, eternal ordinations. There one is sorted.
At the asylum, certain war-crazed veterans still alive
raise pigs; trafficking with the ossuaries.
You knocked me down, dirtied all, eternalized all, in a gush of blood.
The Piave an open artery , neither calm nor placid
but only gaily solicitous beyond the good the bad and similar
            and all pricked with silvery glimmers, in its intents, out of
                all proportion.
Father and mother, perhaps united in that numen
            amidst that incoercible bleeding
            the green and the glimmering equally incoercible,
in that grandeur where all silences are possible
you entangled me, under those heaps of
bo-bones, well catalogued, not even hieroglyphics, hosts
      revomited but how in a higher-up, in an other-world of
         assumed grasses
                  and grassy enzymes,
               in an outer-place that leans over me and
                  dominates

io mi avvicendo, vado per ossari, e cari stinchi e teschi
mi trascino dietro dolcissimamente, senza o con flauto magico
    Sempre più con essi, dolcissimamente, nella brughiera
io mi avvicendo a me, tra pezzi di guerra sporgenti da terra,
si avvicenda un fiore a un cielo
dentro le primavere delle ossa in sfacelo,
si avvicenda un sì a un no, ma di poco
differenziati, nel fioco
negli steli esili di questa pioggia, da circo, da gioco.

Stati maggiori contrapposti, loro piani

Ed ero come riflesso
o meglio fratto in ognuna delle facce
di un cubo a quattro dimensioni
    di un lunapark formato a tesseract
        mai mai nella stessa positura
            mai mai nella stessa pastura mentale

  E quelli, folli, ridevano
  senza ridere, era il puro fatto di vivere
  fin dentro il rogo in cui dolori e dolori
      intonano i loro cori divenuti corolle d'alberi
  in disamore   disagio malevolenza
  fin dentro un madore tossico di acquaforte
  nell'andatura furiosa ma
  militarmente precisa nell'andatura di
lluvias ||)|||||| chuvas   a
          bacini bacinelle
          in cui primavera si scioglie   HCl
          con demoni ventosi, ventriloque
          promesse e minacce   HCl

a bit creating me, making me rise up
So that   I summon words
for stutterings and the hardest rhymes,
which train and pursue one another,
I take turns with myself, I wander through ossuaries, and dear
    shinbones and skulls
I drag myself along so gently, with or without magic flute
                        Always more with them, so gently, into the heath
I take turns with myself, amidst pieces of war protruding from the
    earth,
a flower takes turns with a sky
inside the springtimes of the decomposing bones,
a yes takes turns with a no, but little
differentiated, in the faint
in the slender stems of this rain, of the circus, of the game.

Conflicting Dominant States, Their Designs

And I was like a reflection
divided into each of the faces
of a four-dimensional cube
        of an amusement park in the shape of a tesseract
            never never in the same position
                    never never in the same mental pasture

And those lunatics laughed
without laughing, it was the simple fact of living
inside the pyre in which sufferings upon sufferings
            attune their choirs turned corollas of trees
in estrangement   unease malevolence
inside a toxic light sweat of etching
in the gait furious yet
militarily precise in the gait of
lluvias ||||||||||| chuvas   in
        basins bowls
        in which springtime dissolves   HCl
        with windy demons, ventriloquous
        promises and threats   HCl

di cremazioni lasciate a metà e così interramenti—
e la bacinella con verdure e verzure aizzate in HCL

. . . .

Oh potenze di potenze
di numeri d'alberi di dolori di piogge:
pentimenti e protervie istruiscono controversie certo giuridiche
 e i Galatei di formula in tratto
 hanno codificato—è un peso smisurato—
 le mafiose connivenze di boschi e piogge:
  là, tutto che traluce
  dalla superficie del vetriolo (in guardia! lluvias ||||||||
             HCl, minute
   così che sia   a morti minutanti cadute
    poesia   di mano, in lluvias, filze,
            archivi, archivi
         per burocrazie boschive)—
 Galatei-Poesie quali pure scomparizioni
   che mi lasciano
   solo come una meta i mai raggiunta, mai girata
    dalla biga infuocata

Ora è stato tastato tutto il bassorilievo il manufatto
 di quella cubità estrapolata dalla
 Selva Incantata   Gerusalemme Liberata, XIII
 manufatto quale tomba
 che è per certi aspetti rampa di lancio HCl in faccia
 (considerala meglio in notte / fotogramma accecato
 se appena il gufo
 giusto si tuffa, becca e trangugia lucciole e
    gioie sfolgoranti di UFO
 e lo stesso apparecchis che lo riproduce)
 rampa o zampa o mascella di / che affiora
 crepa e divora
 ogni sosta ogni dimora |||||| ε < > ʌ
  Coup de dés tétradimensionnels
  Hcliques arc-en-ciel

of cremations left half-done and thus interments—
and the basin with vegetation and verdure stirred up by HCl

. . . .

Oh powers of powers
of numbers of trees of sufferings of rainfalls:
repentances and obstinacies instruct controversies certainly juridical
   and the formulated Manners in treaties
   they've codified—it's an immeasurable weight—
   the mafia-like connivances of woods and rainfalls:
      there, all shines through
      from the surfaces of the sulfates   (on guard! lluvias ||\||||\
                                HCl, minutes
     thus it is   of dead minute-takers fallen
       that poetry exists   from hands, in lluvias, files,
                                 archives archives
                                 for woody bureaucracies)—
Manners-Poems those pure vanishings
     that leave me
     alone like a goal i never reached, never spun about
        by the flaming chariot

Now the entire bas-relief has been tasted, the artifact
    of that cubism extrapolated by the
    Enchanted Forest   Jerusalem Delivered, xiii
    artifact crafted as a tomb
    which for certain aspects is a catapult: HCl in your face
    (consider it better   at night / blinded freeze-frame
    if suddenly the owl
    justly swoops down, nabs, and gobbles down glowworms
                the blazing joys of ufos
    and the same apparatus which reproduces it)
    paw or claw or jaw of/   which emerges
    cracks and devours
    every rest every respite ||\|||\ ε < > ʌ
       Coup de dés tétradimensionnels
         HCliques arc-en-ciel

★

Tentando e poi tagliuzzando a fette
con un bisturi boschereccio (di nascosto perfino a me stesso)
questo simulacro da Selva Incantata
         della Gerusalemme Liberata

ho messo a nudo e crudo un corpiciattolo strambo e durissimo
       con miliardi di acuzie
       di ogni guisa penetranza sadizie dovizia
       una statuina miliardaria
       pronta là—orribilmente immobile e morta, nel suo essere
          in agguato,
       pronta a far saltare il bisturi pronta—
       e poi—ad essere ficcata in bocca a fare da mordacchia!
       Lei, mordacchia, signora di tutta la realtà . . .

E fosse stata almeno
un lavoro del Solutreano del Magdaleniano
di qualche preistoria che qui ha fatto di tutto con selci etc
       (a gara con le cavillose intenzioni carsiche della natura
       che nasconde ammennicoli e ghingheri da selva Incantata
       della Gerusalemme Liberata
         ben truccati di felci etc)

       non preistoria, che qui ha fatto del suo meglio e chiude
         in pareggio
       ma cosa mia, mia deprecata scelta/scoperta, orrido vanto!
       Mordacchia di tutta la realtà!
       Un certo modo-mostro dei cari bramati accettati silenzi
         una loro lunatica cancerizzazione, cah!
       Nessuna chimica nessuna logica
       nessuna pentecoste la dissolverà.

★

Touching and then chopping into slices
with a sylvan scalpel (hidden even to myself)
this simulacrum of the Enchanted Forest
       of Jerusalem Delivered

I bluntly laid bare a strange and very hard object
       with millions of spines
       in every way penetration sadisms abundance
       a millionaire figurine
       there ready—horribly immobile and dead, in its
         lying-in-ambush,
       ready to overthrow the scalpel ready—
       and then—to be thrust like a muzzle over the mouth!
       You, muzzle, mistress of all reality . . .

And it was at least
a work of the Solutrean of the Magdalenian
of some prehistory that here made everything with flintstones etc
   (vying with the captious karstic intentions of nature
   who hides trinkets and frills from the Enchanted forest
   of Jerusalem Delivered
       well disguised with ferns etc)

   not prehistory, that here has done its best and breaks even
   but my thing, my deprecated choice/discovery, horrid boast!
   Muzzle of all reality!
   A certain mode-monster of the dear coveted accepted silences
       one of their moody cancerizations, cah!
   No chemistry no logic
   no pentecost will dissolve it.

(Indizi di guerre civili)

Sospesa nella febbre   sfuocata nella febbre
    quella brughiera che mai non trassi abbastanza
Nei vuoti di memoria   nelle spinte e nei flussi
    della memoria   quasi danza—
    quasi sfocata, brughiera da brughiera,/ in febbre
E nel chimico buio sto pensando volgere
    l'abile vomero   indirizzare il talento della ruota
La brughiera risponde   ahi no   ahi sì   per mille vie remota
È troppo ⌢ avanzare ⌣ impossibile ⌢ nulla ⌣ regredire
(brughiera) (e fiume nella ramaglia leggera)   (e uccelli):
    così che a grate di ramaglia leggera e uccelli
    e cancelli di puro/morto legno
appoggio il capo come atteggiando un riposo.

Nel pozzo del mio corpo, corpo affondato,
alle sue indimostrabili potenze collegato
ai suoi pus alle sue verdi/vermi reazioni con disagio adeguato

con solerzia con sguardo occhialeggiato, lemure
e volpe di quella brughiera mai-stata-del-tutto,
ti fo cenno, mi aspetti intanto (o no?)—
e come degno di ogni buon dimando
sulla tranche azzurra/svolta]   [sullo stock glaciale delle cose—
sul nudo del cancello e del legno—
appoggiato—oh sostegno—
del puro azzurro ardo meditando.

(Sono gli stessi)

Ora posso carpire—e poi—strampolare con gambe/raggi
verso i più lontani indecidibili angoli/raggi
Non si dica che è chiusa o aperta
se è nel più bosco del bosco a fianco del bosco

(Indications of Civil Wars)

Suspended in the fever   blurred in the fever
     that moor that I never internalized enough
In the gaps of memory   in the thrusts and fluxes
     of the memory,   almost dance—
     almost blurred, moor from moor, / in fever
And in the chemical darkness I am thinking of turning
     the able ploughshare   steering the wheel's talent
The moor responds   ah no   ah yes   distant by a thousand
     paths
It's too much ⌒ advancing ‿ impossible ⌒ nothing ‿
     regressing
(moor) (and river in the light branches)   (and birds):
     thus at the lattice of light brush and birds
     and gates of pure / dead wood
I rest my head as if faking a nap.

In the well of my body, sunken body,
to its undemonstrable powers joined
to its pus to its green / worms reactions with adequate unease

with diligence with bespectacled glancing, lemur
and fox of that moor, never-been-of-everything,
I nod to you, will you wait for me (or no?)—
and as if worthy of every good question
on the azure / bending slice]   [on the glacial stock of things—
on the nudity of the gate and the wood—
rested—oh support—
of the pure azure arduous meditating.

(*They're the same*)

Now I can worm out—and then—wobble with legs / rays
towards the most distant undecidable corners / rays
Nobody should say if it is closed or open
if it's in the more-woods of the woods next to the woods

se è dentro il fiato il morbido l'arduo sparire della gola in gola
        di torbido di ricco di luminescente

e ora posso col regolo calcolatore col contagocce
    infiltrarmi tra le compagnie di virus di idiozie di settimicieli
    in una pencolata sbilanciata sbilenca libertà (sull'altro):
        questi versamenti di sogno   ⎞   colli   a torso d'orso
        questi spargimenti di sogni   ⎟   poteri della bile dell'orso
        nella bocca pelliccia dell'orso   ⎨   virus a navetta
        sfilarsi da sogno-lupo-orso   ⎠   per genesi trasverse
    questo ammonticchiarsi di tratti del sogno

Oh come riarmo con selezione e contiguità   —pertinente
    glossario
oh come sfoglio il catalogo delle novità di armi —prezzi per ogni
    borsa
            available here   astonishing, acquolina in borsa
  .   attonito davvero come sotto scatto di ghigliottina
                                    e poi testa in paniere

pur dormendo stravolto su spine
pure rattratto nei più sottili e mistici brogli di bosco
per traverse trói tramiti bisettrici
        aracneanti a dondolo a sfioro-oro   (broli)
        sull'invincibile produzione di produzione

                    Chele   chele di transferasi
                    ancora pressanti   oranti   sù   sù

                    e testa che rotola   giù giù

202

if it's within the breath the mushiness the tricky vanishing from
   gullet to gullet
               of murky of rich of luminescent

and now I can with ruler calculator with eyedropper
   infiltrate the company of viruses of idiocies of seventhheavens
   in a wavered unbalanced cockeyed liberty (on the other):
      these dreamy spillages　　　　　⎞　hills　like a bear's torso
      these scatterings of dreams　　⎬　powers of bear bile
      in the maw fur of the bear　　　⎰　shuttle-like viruses
      unraveling by dream-wolf-bear　⎭　for transverse origins
   this heaping up of the dream's fragments

Oh how do I rearm with selection and proximity　　　—relevant
   glossary
oh how do I flip through the catalogue of new arms　—prices for
   every budget
        available here　　　　　astonishing, drooling wallets
     truly dumbfounded as if under the trigger of the guillotine
                 and then head in the basket

even distraught sleeping on spines
and yet shrunken in the thinnest and most mystic woody intrigues
along sideroads paths tracks crosswise trails
    rocking arachnids on withering gold　　(orchards)
    on the invincible production of production

                 Claws　　claws of transferase
                 still pressing　　　prayers　　up up

                 and head that tumbles　　down down

da Ipersonetto

I

(Sonetto di grifi ife e fili)

Traessi dalla terra io in mille grifi
minimi e in unghie birbe le ife e i fili
di nervi spenti, i sedimenti vili
del rito, voglie così come schifi;

manovrando l'invitto occhial scientifico
e al di là d'esso in viste più sottili,
da lincee linee traessi gli stili
per congegnare il galateo mirifico

onde, minuzie rïarse d morte
—corimbi a greggia, ombre dive, erme fronde—,
risorgeste per dirci e nomi e forme:

rovesciati gli stomaci, le immonde
fauci divaricate, la coorte
dei denti diroccata: ecco le norme.

III

(Sonetto di stragi e di belle maniere)

Moti e modi così soavemente
ed infinitamente lievi / sadici,
dondolii, fibre e febbri, troppo radi
o fitti per qualunque fede o mente,

stasi tra nulla e quasi, imprese lente o
più rapide che ovunque rai s'irradino,
per inciampi stretture varchi guadi
un reticolo già vi stringe argenteo,

un codice per cui vento e bufera,
estremo ciel, braciere, cataclisma
cederanno furor per altre regole . . .

from Hypersonnet

I

(Sonnet of snouts hyphae and filaments)

Were I with clever claws and a thousand tiny
snouts to unearth the hyphae and filaments
of spent nerves, the vile sediments
of rite, longings and loathings alike;

maneuvering the unbowed scientific lens
and beyond that even, in subtler sightings
were I, lynxlike, to unearth the styles
needed to assemble the marvelous book of manners

whence you, minutiae scorched by death
—corymbs in swarms, divine shades, lone fronds—,
were reborn to tell us the names and the forms:

the outturned stomachs, the foul
gaping gullets, the rotten
legion of teeth: these are the norms.

III

(Sonnet of massacres and good manners)

Motions and modes so mellifluously
and infinitely slight / sadistic,
rockings, fibers and fevers, too scattered
or dense for any such mind or faith,

stasis amid nothing and almost, slow or swifter
exploits everywhere irradiating rays,
meeting obstacles narrow gaps fordings pathways
already a matrix squeezes you silvery,

a code for which wind and storm,
farthest sky, brazier, cataclysm
will surrender fury for other rules . . .

Ma quali mai «distinguo», e in qual maniera,
quali belle maniere, qual sofisma
le stragi vostre aggireranno, prego?

IV

(Sonetto del decremento e dell'alimento)

Ahi sottil pena ahi ago ahi rovo e spina,
ahi frangersi di stelo, ahi della foglia
esaurirsi allo sguardo, ahi sparsa doglia
di tutto il bosco che all'autunno inclina . . .

Ahi languore che in strami si trascina:
e sì: ma d'alimento cresce voglia,
e sì: ma tutto al trogolo convoglia
la gran voglia, appetiti figlia, affina.

Catene alimentari vanno al trogolo,
in miriadi s'impennano mandibole
a vuoto o a pieno, salivati stimoli.

Disciolta furia e cura dentro il fimo
aureo, macello senza sangui, rogo
senza fiamme, pia lex: per te peribo.

(Che sotto l'alta guida)

O boschi non defoliati
delle guerre di tanti anni fa,
quando il ciliegio ai disperati
urli ed al sangue opponeva un salto di qualità.

Nell'ora che più intenta al suo banco squartava ala battaglia,
quando come a pidocchi si sentenziavano destini,
neutrali a sé stavano le bestiepiante della boscaglia
e a divine fogliate pause portavano i cammini.

But by whichever "distinction," and in what manner,
which good manners, with what sophism,
may I please ask, will your massacres elude?

IV

(Sonnet of decrement and nourishment)

Ah subtle torment ah needle ah briar and spine,
ah collapsing of stems, ah of leaves
burning up in a glance, ah sparse throes
of the whole woods that in autumn inclines . . .

Ah languor that drags itself along in cut grass:
and yes: but the desire for nourishment grows,
and yes: but everything flows towards the trough
whetting the great desire, from appetites spawned.

Food chains go to the trough,
mandibles rear up in multitudes
missing or catching, salivated stimuli.

Dissolved fury and cure within golden
dung, bloodless butchery, flameless
blaze, pia lex: per te peribo.

(That under the noble guidance)

O undeforested woods
of wars distant in the past,
when against screams and blood there stood
the cherry tree with a qualitative leap.

At the hour when the battle reached its fiercest pitch
when as if to lice fates were decreed,
the animalplants remained neutral in their thickets
and the paths led to divine leafy peace.

Stava il ciliegio con le sue gocce rosse
privilegiatamente dimenticato e dimentico
tra piante qua e là per sbaglio ferite, tra fosse
di granate e il bruum delle artiglierie ardenti.

Giovanni Comisso saliva sul ciliegio,
l'ilare sangue ne gustava a sazietà:
di Giovanni e del ciliegio il privilegio
lascia ad ogni vivente, o umanità.

( )   ) (

Alberi vari e valghi / nemmeno latinizzati / senza diritti / senza
religioni / privi di destini / e di zecchini / privi di vocazioni

L'Arborescenza, nella sua fase attuale,
intravista sovente nelle arborescenze
del Bosco attuale

Varo e Valgo
) (
con le tue gambe
( )
di nano
avvelenandomi
ballami sulla mano

) (( )

E mi addentro ora
mi tuffo nel tuo oro
luna mio unico capolavoro

Bosco di te sola
luna fiorito

The cherry tree stood with its red drops
in privilege forgotten and forgetful
among plants here and there wounded by mistake, among
bombed-out ditches and the boom of burning artillery.

Giovanni Comisso climbed the cherry tree,
eating his fill of the cheerful blood:
give the privilege of Giovanni and the cherry tree
to every living being, O humanity.

( )   ) (

Knock-kneed and bowlegged trees / not even latinized / without
rights / without religions / devoid of destinies / and of dollars /
devoid of vocations

      Arborescence, in its present phase
glimpsed often in the arborescences
of the present Woods

Knock-kneed and bowlegged
)   (
with your dwarf
(   )
legs
poisoning me
dance on my hand

) (( )

And now I plunge in
I dive into your gold
moon my only masterwork

Woods—by you alone
moon—made to bloom

nera orda d'oro
bosco capolavoro

Pupilla pronta   (in vetrina)
e sforzo pronto
ma la guardia smonta
e di orizzonte
cade in orizzonte   (in vetrino)

Fiore di cui tutto infioro
inezia che tramonta
inezia unico capolavoro.

(Lattiginoso)

Lattiginoso e mielato bruco
che avesti un'intervista speciale
uno scoop—oggetto il Della Casa—
ripugni ripungi tutto
a tutti e tu a tutto
Nella sempre rinviata essenza
appena mimetizzato tubo digerente
          la sigla del tuo grifo onnipresente
          smorfie-volti di smorfia
          ammicchi di ripicca   uncina
          e atterrisce dal giù della ruina
                    donde tubo per tubo è venuta
          la grifità del grifo
          che è poi la voltità del volto
                    secondo quello schema
                    che si è coerentemente svolto
                    e finalmente è giunto al sodo
                    nel cranio nettato allo shampoo, residuato,
                              fuori da ogni modo
                              maglia d'alimentazione
                              catena di sant'Antonio
                              battaglia   —sputato
                              sputato fuori dalla brodaglia

dark horde of gold
masterwork woods

Pupil ready   (in the showcase)
and effort ready
but the sentry leaves
and from the horizon
falls into the horizon   (under the microscope)

Flower with which I adorn everything
trifle that is fading into dusk
trifle—the only masterwork.

(Milky)

Milky, honeyed worm
who had a special interview,
a scoop—on Della Casa—
you repel and repulse everything
sickening to everyone and everything
You, a barely camouflaged digesting tube
in the always deferred essence,
      the seal of your omnipresent snout
      grimaces-faces of grimace
      winks of spite   snares
      and terrifies from beneath the ruin
         whence tube by tube it came
      the snoutness of the snout
      which is also the faceness of the face
         according to the pattern
            that coherently unfolded
            and finally got to the point
            in the shampoo-scrubbed cranium, a surplus
               beyond any norm
               stitch of alimentation
               chain letter
               battle—spat
               spat out of the brew

Bah, qualcosa d'altro che te cranietà voltità
da te grifo per grifo, bruchio per bruchìo, squisc a squisc,
   si scrampi fin lassù sui trampoli e sulle liane più eteree del bosco
        fino alle sue più alte e ridenti raggiere di piova
        alle sue più fini lettere algebriche ed algoritmi
        in prova
     sempre più sbilanciati in avanti in fuori
     e senza pudori: frangersi
     di cartilagini in iridi di ritmi
         ire viticci spire—
                  nero autoscatto
       di spore   sopori.

Refta in pafe , ò bel ɒuʀ̄ ,
  Niaro dè bontè , de pafe vera,
  Tornerò preſt'à verte, c voļentiera ;
  Per què dà ti è sbandì lite , e piminti,
  L'odio l'adulacion , e i tradiminti.

I L   F I N E.

1683 1683 1683 1683

Oh well, may something other than you, craniumness faceness,
come out from you snout by snout, munch by munch, squish by squish,
    and scuttle way up there on the wood's stilts and most ethereal vines
            up to its highest, smiling rays of rain
            to its finest algebraic letters and its algorithms
            on trial
        ever more off balance forward and outward
        and shameless: a crashing
        of cartilage in irises of rhythms
            ires vinetendrils spires—
                        black camera click
            of spores   torpors.

Refta in pafe , ó bei ᴅᴜɪᴄᴇ,
    Niaro dè bontè, de pafe vera,
    Tornerò preft'à verte, c volentiera ;
    Per què dà ti è sbandì lite, e piminti,
    L'odio l'adulacion , e itradiminti.

            I L   F I N E.

        1683 1683 1683 1683

[Rest in peace, fair wood
    Nest of goodness, of true peace,
    I shall soon come back to see you, and gladly,
    For from you are banned quarrels and torments,
    Hatred, flattery, and betrayals.]

                THE END.

da Fosfeni

---

from Phospenes
[1983]

Come ultime cene

Sete notturna di marzo,
arse campagne   rasoiate a freddo
          come rasa la barba
          rasa ogni volontà di levitazione
e tutto e lievitato eppure compreso   nel gelo,
                    comprimario del gelo
la polvere e gel,   tanto arse di sete, nei fari,
che nella rasoiata troviamo   non abbaiare
la strada la svolta—sternuto—
sconvolte gibbose crescenti a carico di vuoto
cariche strade e poi erbette da campo e palato svuotato
          e troppo responsabili d'invenzione   non abbaiare
ma non notte, ma sobbalzare nella notte,
strade cui ogni più minima cosa accorse a morire
per essere più casta più degna un istante
          per essere un faro
          o un luccichio di niente-vetro   non abbaiare

Come entrando dalla porta di servizio
nel dolcissimo componimento di un'ultima cena
più quadro—sbalzo a sbalzo di fuori—di quanto
mai si potesse affannatamente sognare, invidiare—
come nel dovuto di una sublimazione
senza raggi senza rilievi senza pretese
tutto comunque eccelsamente contento nel suo abessere
anzi una specie di N.N.N. sotto gel sotto alcool gel
Cena nel gelo difesa solo da se stessa
cena dove e' sempre opportuno insinuare il piede
dove meats viande vivande e latte e cappuccino
dove dorata droga di cena s'affonda
          s'effonde in un'emersione di se di volti di con-figure
          servi di nulla e di sé, composizione abboccabile,
          abbordabile iniziazione   miniorgasmo in etcì
calduccio poi d'iniziazione in in zzz di sonni   rasoio
calda pertugia   (insinuazioni) (indiziarii)
                    coagulo sacro (dicerie)
d'iniziazione, di paupertà, di rassegnata al poco
pupi

Like Last Suppers

Nocturnal thirst of March,
parched countrysides   razor-cuts in the cold
      as the beard is shaven
      shaven each wish for levitation
and everything is leavened but still comprised   in the chill,
                              supporting actor of chill
the dust is gel,   so parched with thirst, in the headlights,
that we find in the razor-cut   don't bark
the road the turn—sneeze—
flustered hunched growing laden with emptiness
laden roads and then field-grass and an emptied palate
      and too responsible for invention   don't bark
but not night, but jolting in the night,
roads of which each slightest thing hastened to die
to be more chaste more worthy an instant
      to be a headlight
      or a glitter of nothing-glass   don't bark

As if entering by the service door
in the most gentle composition of a last supper
more of a painting—jolt by jolt outside—than
one could ever anxiously dream, envy—
as in what's due to a sublimation
without rays without reliefs without any pretence
everything in any case celestially content in its out-being
indeed a type of N.N.N. under gel under alcohol gel
Supper in the chill defended by itself alone
supper where it is always fruitful to insinuate one's foot
where carne viande viands and milk and cappuccino
where a golden drug of supper infuses
      effuses in an emersion of self of faces of con-figurations
      servants of nothing and of self, palatable composition
      approachable initiation   miniorgasm in ahchoo
a cozy warmth then of initiation in in zzz of sleeps   razor
warm inlette   (insinuations) (suspicions)
                              sacred coagulation (hearsay)
of initiation, of pauperage, of resigned to little
tots

di bellissima-al-poco
turgore da poco, sguardo incappato nei lacci
di vivande e giri di frutti di tavolo, nemmeno mensa
    Qui non ci sono mense   rasoio
ma solo sangui-cibi e gelatini irritabili
e ragazza-osteria che sgonna via
    e circuiti círcei, giocattoli in ansia altissima
Se rendessi teoria di un volto se mi
    arrendessi alla dissimmetria (se mi)
di un convolvolarsi di volto nel proprio biondore, secca piova,
di un coccolarsi di beltà-ine-bel-gel   rasoio
fili d'oro dentro una lampada, sotto un violento ricordo:
    scarse parole e scarse linee, tutta confidenze,
    viaggiare, posata la testa,
    dormire, posato il riposo su tutto,
    concrescere a tutto dormendo,
    sobbalzando per strade divinamente sconquassate

    Da tanto non vedevo nulla nei paraggi
    del delicato, del dopo-viso,
    da tanto non scartocciavo alcun viso dal viso,
    da tanto non sottraevo, non facevo man bassa
    da tanto non sobbalzavo nell'auto
    equilibri di grovigli e campagna, tavolo-di-biliardo falso
    tintinno inganno e vero ahi di chiome per ultime cene
«Che cachet preferisce per i capelli?»
chiometta da parrucchiera per ultima
cena sull'orlo dei campi, per osteria
«Che lacca per unghie?»
ragazza, osteria (sotto polvere)
(tralice) (traoro) (tracapelli e poi chi sa)
«Che detergente che assorbente per le intimità, quelle fuori
sotto le stelle   o quelle?»
e quante dolci cerimonie
         ΘΕΩΡΙΑ ΚΡΥΟΣ

of most beautiful-to-little
turgidity for little, glance ensnared in the laces
of viands and rounds of table fruit, not even a table
    Here there are no tables   razor
but only blood-foods and irritable icecreamlets
and girl-tavern who ungowns away
    and circean circuits, playthings in deepest despair
If I rendered a theory of a face if I
    surrendered to the dissymmetry (if I)
of a convolvulating of face in its own blondness, dry rainfall,
of a cuddling of beauty-let-bel-gel   razor
gold wires within a lamp, under a violent memory:
    scarce words and scarce lines, all confiding,
    to travel, head laid,
    to sleep, rest laid on everything,
    to grow together with everything by sleeping,
    jolting along roads divinely devastated

    For a long time I had seen nothing in the surroundings
    of the delicate, of the after-face,
    for a long time I had unwrapped no face from the face,
    for a long time I had not subtracted, not robbed
    for a long time I had not jolted in a car
    balances of knots and countryside, false billiard table
    jingling deception and true alas of tresses for last suppers
"What dye would you like for your hair?"
a hairdo of a hairdresser for last
supper on the edge of the fields, for tavern
"What polish for your nails?"
girl, tavern (under dust)
(midglance) (midgold) (midhair and then who knows)
"What detergent what absorbent for your intimacies, the outer ones
under the stars   or the?"
and how many sweet ceremonies

ΘΕΩΡΙΑ ΚΡΥΟΣ

Translated by Thomas J. Harrison

Amori impossibili come
sono effettivamente impossibili le colline
Non è possibile che tanto amore
in esse venga apertamente
dato
e al tempo stesso dissimulato, anzi
    reso inaccessibile

    Serie senza requie di inaccessibilità
    che pur fa da accattivante
    ingradante tappeto sulla
    più grande breccia demenza desuetudine
    Colline ricche di mille pericoli di morte
        per   quietamente
        per   avventato soccorrere
                    tra cielitudini
        per   insufficienza di attenzione a sé—
    di sorte in sorte
    «intralcerà»   «si defilerà»

da Silicio, carbonio, castellieri

Oh se per tutti un legame
un eros vago lontano
come una stretta di mano
perenta in un'alba grigia . . .
        (Silicio, carbonio)

Da un'osteria all'altra, su sommità
nemmeno aguzze, ma comunque
eccelse, nella pallida oh
non più oscenità non più purificazione,
pallida nascenza, sulla scia di esempi
    di pietre da acciarino, chicchi
    di melograno, insettini, era tranquillo
    e bello mettere a dimora

Loves impossible as
effectively impossible are the hills
It's not possible that so much love
in them is openly
given
and at the same time dissimulated, even
        made inaccessible

    Series without rest of inaccessibility
    which yet acts as a reaching
    spreading carpet on the
    largest breach dementia desuetude
    Hills rich with thousands of fatal dangers
        for   quietude
        for   reckless succor given
                           amidst skyhoods
        for   insufficient self attention—
        bit by bit
        "will intertwine"   "will spread forth"

from Silicon, Carbon, Fortified Villages

Oh if for everyone a connexion
a vague distant eros
like a handshake
vanished in a gray dawn . . .
                (Silicon, carbon)

From one tavern to another, on summits
not even pointed, but nonetheless
lofty, in the pale oh
no more obscenity no more purification,
pale nascency, on the trail of examples
        of steely rocks, pomegranate
        grains, tiny insects, it was easy
        and good to lay to rest

le più attenuate non-scissioni e intergamie
quasi in abissale sonno albale consumate
oppure un colpo di lucente selce durate—
per noi furtivi in un tempo
comodo, comodo di grigi e chiusure grigie

O nel viola esausto, come di febbre che va disperdendosi,
pareva giusto coltivare
logos in carbonio   logos in silicio
come smarginati smarriti qui a generare presente
    a educare
    sogni del giorno-per-giorno
    simpatie di simpatie
    nervine, alquanto ritrose sintonie
[...]

Squadrare il foglio

Così accade, così pedalando—
pedala tu sul crine sul ciglio sullo spigolo
    mentre ghiaie intervengono e anche ombre
    sfarfallate dal pioppo e pregiate verde per verde
Pedala, piede contro piede
    e gamba contro gamba,
    osseggia, pedalando, intrica tarsi e stinchi
Cascate di farfalle ti sponsorizzano,
all'incontro all'incontrario si procede
pedala e premi e ansima peggio che in un parto
tra lucenti figliate di soli come farfalle
e tra figliate di farfalle commenti lievi
Pedala e pigia come entro grande uva
e curvati su tutta l'uva
che hai davanti, mondana, truccagna, fedeltà
Ricupera ricupera e fa
    premio, fa aggio oltre i sudori e le carnalità;
    osseamente pigia   dolcezze da acerbezze da forti lucri
Pedala senza trillare ché nessuno
la volata saltante sulla ghiaia tra le farfalle
    impedirà a nessuno

the thinnest non-fissures and interbirthings
almost, in abyssal dawn-slumber, consumed
otherwise a burst of glistening enduring flintstone—
for furtive us in an easy
time, easy with grays and gray closings

Oh in the exhausted violet, as with a fever that fades out,
it seemed right to cultivate
logos in carbon   logos in silicon
like cropped confused here to generate this
          to educate
          day-by-day dreams
          nervine likings of likings
          a certain amount of reluctant tunings
[...]

Squaring the sheet

It happens like this, it happens pedaling—
pedal on the crest on the curb on the edge
     while gravel intervenes and also shadows
     birthed from poplars' pupal sacks esteemed green by green
Pedal, foot against foot
     and leg against leg,
     skeletize, pedaling, tangle tarsals and tibias
Cascades of butterflies back you,
onward to the convergence to the divergence
pedal and push and pant as if in labor
through gleaming litters of sunbeams like butterflies
litters of butterflies subtle comments
Pedal and press as if crushing giant grapes
wrap yourself around all the grapes
before you, mundane, mutable, loyal
Catch up catch up and push the
     limit, overcome the sweat and carnality;
     skeletally press   felicities and acerbities from what you gain
Pedal without trilling since no one
—the leaping flight over gravel amid butterflies—
          will prevent any one

La squadratura del foglio è cominciata—
a pedate   ben pedalata.

Impossibile accedere alla dolce ruina
dell'osteria immota sull'angolo
delle due vie volte alla pruina
di autunnali vecchiezze e ghiaie acquiescenti,
immota come incanta vignetta
        nel giornalino degli gnomi
        nel giornalino degli eroi
        nel giornalino dei sommi suoni—
Nessuna temporalità nei
muri che ancora
tengono la traccia di un comodo, pronfondo sé,
e si adeguano e vanno incontro
sbrecciati a un tenerissimo, intenso perché.
Intravedonsi pannelli e pareti sfondate
reggonsi travi e coppi a far tetto
        così che l'imperfetto
        del tutto vi si sposta, ma accentuato,
        esaltato oltre ogni assuefazione
        al di là di ogni sicurezza—
        lievissima sipariette o porta inferi
        o porta di limbo-vignetta
        Quiete e certezza nel tuo infinito sbrecciarti
        nei travi che tengonsi
        tra loro a fatica nei forati
        da me già apportati o strappati uno a uno
        nei mattoni che a malta affidansi
        ancora, stina, sintesi d'ogni colorazione
        d'ogni perdonazione, d'ogni ristoro
Perlustransi i tuoi neri incavi
talvolta da chi passa dinanzi,
      ma non v'è mistero che duri
      che in calcine e malte sfritte non si purifichi
      per occhi appena divaganti

The squaring of the sheet has begun—
by kicks   well pedaled.

(At Ghène's)

Impossible to enter the dear ruins
of the tavern motionless on the corner
of the two lanes leading to the hoarfrost
of autumnal old ages and acquiescent gravel,
motionless as an enchanted vignette
            in the storybook of gnomes
            in the storybook of heroes
            in the storybook of sublime sounds—
No temporality in the
walls that still
hold the trace of a comfortable cavernous self,
that breached, comply and approach
a most tender, intense because.
They discern smashed boards and inner walls
hold beams and roofing tiles
            so that the imperfect
            of everything shifts, but accentuated,
            exalted over every habit
            beyond every measure of safety—
            lightest drop curtain or underworld door
            or limbo-vignette door
            Stillness and certainty in your infinite self-breaching
            in the beams that together scarcely bear up
            in your blocks
            by myself already carried off or torn down one by one
            in bricks that still trust
            in mortar, faded synthesis of every coloration
            of every absolution, of every consolation
Now and then those who pass by
scan your black hollows,
        but there is no mystery that endures
        that in crumbling lime and mortar does not become pure
        for eyes barely straying

o buttati giù col ruscello
o nidificanti peggio che ogni uccello là dentro
ancora—o cara ruina—
da te ospitato insieme con le panoplie
delle scritte invitanti—sempre quelle—
VINO E BIRRA quasi minacciosamente
o sottilissimamente
o dementemente asseverando.
Chi mai oserà contraddire?
Chi non s'arresterà su quest'orlo?
Chi non gusterà, passando, di questo tuorlo
d'ordini e spazi
invano contestati:
      non ci sono qui forse tutti i dati??

        *

Ben disposti silenzi
indisseppellibili
ma pur sparsi in scintillamento
nudo
o in nebbiuscole cieche
ordinati
Silenzi sempre innovati
e pur sempre in fedeltà protrusi
entro innumerabili estrazioni di tempo
Silenzi sottratti
ad ogni speculazione, in sé intenta
non soccorrevole—e pur tanto
aggregata all'amore—folla
Nelle contingenze onnipresente
e nei continui disparati provenire:
dove fu giusto e senza sottintesi il soffrire
dove l'offerta fu senz'altro μηδέν ἀπελπίζουσα

or cast down into the stream
or nesting worse than every bird still there
within—oh dear ruins—
hosted by you together with the panoplies
of the inviting inscriptions—always those—
WINE AND BEER almost threateningly
or extremely delicately
or dementedly affirming.
Who will ever dare contradict?
Who will not halt upon this edge?
Who will not taste, in passing, this yolk
of orders and spaces
contested in vain:
  are there not here perhaps all the facts??

*

Well-disposed silences
unexhumable
yet scattered in nude
scintillation
or in blind haziness
ordered
Silences always innovated
and yet always in faithfulness protruding
within innumerable extractions of time
Silences removed
from each speculation, intent on itself
not helpful—and yet so
bound to love—crowd
Omnipresent in the contingencies
and in the continuous disparate comings:
where to suffer was just and without allusions
where the offer was without doubt μηδέν ἀπελπίζουσα

da Periscopi

I

Accumulati anni, come pietre
     tirate a caso laggiù
oh ma quanto blu dentro il blu
da quei lanci indensito
anche se è purulento di eternità—
     in quel laggiù
E io che sto qui purulento nel tempo
e le mani intirizzisco in conciare e lanciare anni,
battendo, ora, le mani
preparo il terreno a liquidi cristalli
vibrantissimi, trascoloranti, trasecolanti
verso tutte le tinte e i limiti:
circostanza da non perdersi, suprema.
Oh purulento di eternità blu
cumulo, allora, di entità
fuoruscite al sole
per singoli appelli che mi hanno,
veramente, anno per anno,
reso incomprensibile questo mio sperato comprendere

Stomacato di persone verbali, di prime-persone
ma non di ammucchiare ammucchiare laggiù
     anni colori e altre finte virtù
     definitivamente, senza scampo,
     assestato nel proprio nello stampo,
     pur stravedo per un frizzantino di soli che scolano
     feccia di miele, appiccicoso nel far dire di sì
     al crudelissimo imperversare di
          mondani beni fosfeni

Soprammobili e gel

E sono due nel cristallo della stanza
che ad altri gradi di cristalli
scoscende, accede, s'infianca, s'incastra

from Periscopes

I

Accumulated years, like stones
         thrown randomly down there
oh but how much blue within the blue
compacted by those flingings
even if festering with eternity—
         in those depths
And I who remain here festering in time
benumb my hands pickling and flinging years,
now, clapping my hands,
prepare the earth with liquid crystals
—wildly vibrating, hue-mutating, bewildering—
towards all tints and limits:
supreme, not-to-be-missed circumstance
Oh festering of eternal blue
heap, then, of entities
seeped from the sun
for single appeals that have,
truly, year by year, rendered for me this,
my hoped-for understanding, incomprehensible

Sickened by verbal persons, by first-persons
but not by heaping heaping down there
         years colors and other false virtues
         definitively, with no escape,
         arranged on one's own in the mould,
         thrown off by a sparkling of suns that drain
         the dregs of honey, ensnared in accepting
         the cruel raging of
                  phosphenic worldly goods

Trinkets and Gel

And they are two in the crystal of the room
which at other grades of crystal
splits, accedes, enflanks, is embedded

E sono due   due vecchi o anche no—& amici—
per nulla e di nulla in lieve accordo parlando
hanno già povere arterie grassocce e i visceri
chissà come smacchinando stentano
E se avessero profili, essi, gli amici, sarebbero
nel taglio di quell'infinito cristallo in che
novembre osa sempre divaricarsi e poi dopo embricarsi
                    avido cristallo
                    assassinante cristallo
prémito   preme all'essenza-colori-dell'essenza
Due che non hanno certo la sapienza dei bonzi,
non zen, ma l'occhio sul cortile dove
          trottano verso i colori scatole di latta e penombre
                    Jijo è il nome di uno   e dell'altro
E in un mezzo-sogno essi tale realtà intravedono
          tra coppi e foglie stravolti dal cristallo
Due da nulla congiunti se non dal senso di un certo nulla
ma come valgono le inezie che vanno dicendosi
nemmeno «i lontani amori evocano
                    men che meno i ricordi
          essi sono i ricordi
          essi sono un bel niente
          e si scaldano al bel niente
Ma è fatale   è sfasciato
          in vasti e variabili cristalli   è novembre
O noi nel dittico crepuscolare intrusi come un fruscio
          Noi-essi frusciamo parole
          così scorrenti nel loro luccichio così stagnanti
                    da divenire sapienti
Essi-noi stanno comunque nel vivo anche se al decoro
delle ombre fini e fredde un po' alla volta
                    s'adeguano—oscuri—tonti
Asignificante e forse monda è la loro vita
          rattrappita o gonfia l'arteria l'entragna
          essi sono ricordi
          essi stanno seduti ma inciamperanno
          essi sono queste faccende di finestre cortili ed interni
          essi cercano di riaccodarsi—e non fa niente—
          a una indivisibile fila folla—anzi la lasciano a parte
          si ritrovano a valle adorarono si distrassero

And they are two   two old folks or even not—& friends—
talking for nothing and of nothing in light accord
they already have poor plump arteries and those intestines
who knows how unengineering they struggle
And had they profiles, they, the friends, would
be in the cut of that infinite crystal in which
November dares always divaricate and then later be shingled
                    avid crystal
                    assasinating crystal
contraction   contracts to the essence-colors-of-the-essence
Two who surely don't have the wisdom of bonzes,
not Zen, but their eye on the courtyard where
            cans of tin and twilight trot toward colors
                    Jijo is the name of one   and of the other
And in a half-dream they spy such reality
            through tiles and leaves troubled by the crystal
Two conjoined by nothing but a sense of a certain nothing
yet how do those trifles matter that they go on telling each other
don't even "evoke distant loves"
                    memories even less
            they are the memories
            they are a good nothing
            and they warm up beside a good nothing
But it's fatal   it's dismantled
            in vast and variable crystals it's November
O we intruded into the crepuscular dyptich like a rustling
            We-they rustle words
            so flowing in their glitter so stagnant
                    as to become wise
They-we nevertheless stand in the living even if among the dignity
of the delicate and cold shadows a bit at a time
                    they adapt—obscure—dull
Their life is asignificant and maybe clean
            the arteries entrails shrunken or swollen
            they are memories
            they are seated but will stumble
            they are these affairs of windows courtyards and interiors
            they try to reaccord—and it doesn't matter—
            with an indivisible line crowd—indeed they leave it aside
            they meet again downstream they adored were distracted

nell'onnipotente irrespirabile levità
distanti sono come due soprammobili
e vicini comee radicate convenzioni figurative
nella sempre-più-ombra più-cristallo
Parlottano e non è che questo luccichi gran che
ma, ahi naso chiuso, ma c'è.

Tigre novembre intanto e sempre si aggira
ci versa tutto ai piedi l'astrale felice disastro
usa come armi il falcialune e il falciasoli
fa che il salto dei colori che il disaccordo o coro—
fa versamento pleurico per pelli e strati yalini e gel
travasa cristalli smarrisce un dito di vino
sul tavolino per due

Due di noi si convincono,
nell'ombra di una stanza s'infittiscono,
due di noi perlustrano con chiacchiere e bisbigli

Eh eh! Zio novembre, così ci stellasti
alla primizia del gelo
così ci estraesti
in propizi ma inaccessibili «là»
di finestra in finestra—noi/postremi
ci intrecci in tintinni in clivi in estraneità
—dall'interno all'esterno sempre più interno
—dagli interni con mobili made in paradise
—con tendine farfalline in mutazione
e direi soprammobili e direi noi
è/a conoscersi come non visti non raccontati   né accertati
e ricoverarsi in dicerie in rumeurs
in spenti barattoli da cortile
mentre infierisce il silenzio
e dà di volta all'infinito   il cristallo
mentre s'infianca la stanza   la bella mente
mentre due c'infianchiamo, muniti,
ai pellegrini muschi-colori-topi
tra scatti di falcialune, di falciasoli
Rossícchiare, verzicare, sfalciare
rosicchiare giallicare oltre i tonfi e le serenità,

in the omnipotent unbreathable levity
they are distant as two trinkets
and close as rooted figurative conventions
in the ever-more-shade more-crystal
They jabber and it's not as if it glitters much
                    but, o stuffed nose, but it is there.

Tiger November meanwhile and always roams
pours all at our feet the fortunate astral disaster
                    uses a mow-moons and mow-suns as weapons
makes it that the leap of colors that the disaccord or chorus—
makes a pleural discharge for skins and translucent strata and gel
decants crystals mislays a thimbleful of wine
                    on the table set for two

Two of us convince themselves
thicken in the shade of a room
two of us scout with chatter and whispers

Hey hey! Uncle November, that's how you starred us
                    at the first fruit of chill
                    that's how you extracted us
              in propitious but inaccessible "theres"
              from window to window—we/ultimates
              you weave us into jingles into hillocks into
                    extraneousness
—from the interior to the exterior ever more interior
—from interiors with furniture "made in paradise
—with curtains small butterflies in mutation
and I'd say trinkets and I'd say us
it is/in order to know ourselves as not seen not recounted   nor
    ascertained
              and to recover ourselves in hearsay in rumeurs
              in wornout courtyard tin cans
while silence grows fierce
              and goes out of its infinite   crystal
while the room enflanks   the beautiful mind
while two of us enflank, in arms,
         the pilgrim mosses-colors-mice
         between strokes of mow-moons, of mow-suns

azzurricare di lunghissime modulazioni ottiche
alligna e perlustrando si affila (al nero)
si affida — ciack — cieco.

(Anticicloni, inverni)

I

Vedi tutto che—viola e oro e molle—
    direi quasi rigurgita rigurgita
  non si trattiene è contento è maturo
  nel dar figure strappare figure   altre figure
in viola e ori   A spuntare ori considera, poni mano,
  affàcciati, prendi nota, a cuore, a carico,
  sii una qualche violenza per tenere a cuore

      Sii nel prossimo a-tu-per-tu col remoto del viola
      sì, violenza in questa gola
ascolto nuotando tutta questa violenza
così prima e increata da essere innocente
      ma non meno assassina—nell'oro e nel viola
C'è il vocio o il tocco o lo sfascio
  viola di no no no   lo scampanio del predicente
      Viola è il mio carpire interleggere
      fa carico fa massa va in massa oro e viola
tutta per te questa trasparente
mania di destrutturazione   ma issi là sopra la tavola
il sopravvissi

    e la macchia di sangue Gewalt
    mi allevava come letame viola
    mi torceva in sé, mi aveva perso a sé, letame.

II

E tu nell'intimo del mio oro mi attendi
e io nell'intimo del tuo oro mi vagheggio

Reddening, greening, unmowing
nibbling yellowing beyond the plunges and serenities,
bluening of terribly long optic modulations
takes root and scouting sharpens   (to blackness)
entrusts itself — action! — blind.

Translated by Thomas J. Harrison

(Anticyclones, Winters)

I

See all that which—violet and gold and soft—
   I would say nearly regurgitates regurgitates
does not linger is happy is mature
in offering images tearing images   other images
in violet and golds   To blunt golds consider, undertake,
step forth, take note, to heart, as a load,
be a kind of violence for holding to heart

       Be in the near *téte à téte* with the remoteness of violet
          yes, violence in this throat
I hear swimming all this violence
so primal and uncreated as to be innocent
       but no less assassin—in gold and in violet
There is a din or touch or ruin
   violet of no no no   the bell-peal of foretelling
       Violet is my seizing my reading-between
       is under loading is a ground runs aground gold and violet
all for you this transparent
mania of destructuration   but hoist there over the table
the I-had-lived

   and the *Gewalt* bloodstain
   reared me as violet dung
   wrung me to itself, had lost me to itself, dung.

   II

And you in the depths of my gold await me
and I in the depths of your gold do charm myself

è troppo lieve, ambrosiacamente versato com'etere
    per essere oro   è troppo lontano per essere nostro
    eppure nulla è più nido di questo infinito
    perfuso in oro, zappettato via per il campo d'ozono
          (anticicloni, inverni)
sostanza in cui eternità circolerebbe
    godrebbe farebbe
    tutt'uno con lo spaventapasseri
    solo ma ma abilitato abitante del colle
    in tutti gli ori gli azzurri,
    le incistate astinenze   viola
         l'incontinenza senza pari   viola
    le erratiche verità gli sgranocchianti e le rampicanti
      Attento a chi impugna il tomahawk
      a chi s'attesta a malapena sul guado
        e—senza pari—a turbazioni
        scadute dai lunari terreni
           di gola in gola.

    III
Raccolgo, è certo, nel bello dello stordimento,
    col più granulato impetrare
    quanto v'è di silenzio—ed è tanto
    Dove si forma l'intorno e s'acclima
    ad altri sottili doveri e diritti

O nelle sperperate del greto tesaurizzazioni
    cui vitreocupo s'avvena
    quanto v'è d'acqua—ed è tanto

    Orientata da folli fierezze e deficienze
    e cupi idiomi
    precipitata entro l'idioma
    a moltiplicarne le spine i ghiaccioli

Pare che rarità fischi tra i vischi del vento e
staffilano, tutti quei vinchi piegati nel greto,
    ma misteriosissimamente ribelli

Qualunque e dovunque cosa in vecchiezze s'allevia
    davanti a ciò che vecchio non sarà mai né mai,

it is too light, ambrosiacally poured like ether
    to be gold   it is too distant to be ours
    yet nothing is more nestlike than this infinite
    perfused in gold, hoed away through the ozone field
            (anticyclones, winters)
    a substance in which eternity might circulate
    might relish might make
    entirely one with the scarecrow
    alone but but competent occupant of the hill
    in each of the golds the blues,
    the involuchred abstinences   violet
            the unparalleled incontinences   violet
    the erratic truths the kernel-crunchers and climbers
        Beware of who grips the tomahawk
        of who barely makes the bridgehead on the ford
            and—unparalleled—of turbations
            expired from earthly almanacs
                        from gorge to gorge.

        III

I harvest, without question, in the beauty of stunnedness,
        with most granular beseeching
        however much silence there is—and there is much
        Where the surrounding takes shape and acclimates
        to other subtle duties and rights

O hoardings in the shingle squandered
        in which gloomyglassy runs veinlike
        however much water there is—and there is much

        Oriented by crazy prides and deficiencies
        and gloomy idioms
        hastened within the idiom
        to proliferate its thorns its icicles

It seems that rarity whistles through mistletoes of the wind and
they flail, all those willows bent in the shingle,
        yet most mysteriously rebellious

Whichever and whatever thing is allayed in oldnesses
        before that which will never and never be old,

è meno insecchita di quel che tutto all'intorno si creda;
sterile, non perde brio
feconda, in esempli si stempera

E la luna facella frine e galaverna
nell'abbassarsi del sì
di passata   inopinata
con opposizione come facendosi animo
da dove più digiuna è la montagna
                    sorti guadagna
immobile scia sul pendio
                    [più addio]

Vocabilità, fotoni

Dispersa entro una vocabilità dolcissima
                    Eurosia, genio dei chicchi
di grandine, dispersa ivi Barbara
fotoricettiva delle radicolarità del fulmine

emerge ora Lùcia dal terremotato
cristallo delle diafanità
collinari   Diva e niña del Freddo
forse con un certo sèguito di cupi pretuscoli
che m'invitano a pranzo, a mensa, a caldo rancio
Ha in mano una scheggia di raggi
          che forano qualsiasi ubiquità
nell'altra mano i 9 gradi sottozero
          di lieve garza-neve,
          piuma d'uccello-già-neve,
Non può proteggere non può guidare
ma non sarà in secondi ordini giammai
L'ustione le ha scorticato
tanta parte del volto e fatto fumare via gli occhi
—e non se ne sa più il percome il percosa—
Essa fu buio e viene dal buio del suo eccesso

it is less shriveled than what is thought in the whole surrounding
  sterile, it loses no briskness
  fecund, dissolves in examples

And the moon phryne dim beacon and hoarfrost
  in the self-lowering of yes
  in passing   unforeseen
  in opposition as if mustering up courage
  from where the mountain is more famished
     wins lots
  motionless trail on the slope
     [more farewell]

Translated by Thomas J. Harrison

Vocability, photons

  Dispersed within a honeyed vocability
     Eurosia, genius
of hailstones, Barbara scattered there
photoreceptive to the radicularities of lighting

  now Lucia emerges from the earthshaken
  crystal of the hilly
  limpidities   Diva and niña of the Cold
perhaps with a certain following of somber priestlings
  who invite me to lunch, to table, to warm rations
  She carries in her hands a sliver of rays
    that pierce whatever ubiquity
  in the other hand 9 degrees below zero
    of light gauze-snow
    bird's feather-once-snow,
  She cannot protect cannot guide
  but she will never be of second rank
  The burn has scorched
  much of her face and smoked out her eyes
  —and no one knows any more the whys and wherefores—
  She was darkness and comes from the darkness of her excess

        tutta trinata di raggi
in nome del ΛΟΓΟΣ veniente e di tutti i freddi venturi
ma ben schierati, schedabili in nevi,
ma tutti pupilla e ricca lacrima d'attenzioni
ma in fregola di numeri e tracce
        oh come s'infittisce il dialogo a soffi a spiscii
                            hints glimpses!

Lùcia: né madre tu sei, né doni-in-tenebra o in cristallo,
    ma sei tu che aggiorni su quel che ti restava
    alle spalle scarso dirupo d'anno,
    svenimento giù giù di collina in collina
    svenimento sù sù per le celestialità
    Entro la riaffamata tagliola del freddo
    proprio davanti a te
    ci si dibatte
    e si ha voglia di rancio
    e di spicciar fuori sudar fuori dimettere zappettando,
    sì, di lasciar andare tutto, le stie vuote, spalancate
    È andato, niente rimpianto,
    secchezze soltanto qua e là o brandelli,
    carnicino nel selvatico dei palati—
    proprio nell'occhio il secco n
        (voglia di numeri, del conto, al dopo-rancio)

(Vien drìote adès anca la Lùzhia
pi granda e pi scarma de la só istessa imensa bontà)

Ammetti, diva Lùcia, ai tuoi piedi—dove so io
posati, così che ne sono ben cieco di tutti
i gradi della luce—
questa sbandante per forre—dove ben tu sai—
umile voglia di panegirico.

                Rimbalzo di pianto agli occhi. Blow up di
                un solo fotone. Ω

all enlaced with rays
in the name of ΛΟΓΟΣ and of all the coming colds
but neatly arranged, classifiable in snows,
but all pupil and rich tear of attentions
but in a craze of numbers and traces
        oh how the dialogue thickens with puffs with trickles
                hints glimpses!

Lucia: you're neither mother nor gifts-in-darkness or in crystal,
    but it is you who adjourn on what remained to you
    at your back the meager crag of the year
    swooning down down from hill to hill
    swooning up up through celestialities
    Within the recurring ravening cold's snare
    right in front of you
    one is embattled
    and dreams of rations
    and to burst out to sweat out to quit while hoeing,
    yes, to let everything go, the coops empty, thrown open
    It's gone, no regret,
    only dryness here and there or tatters,
    the color of flesh in the wilds of palates—
    right in the eye the dry n
        (desire for numbers, for counting, after mess)

(Lùzhia follows like a shadow
tall, slender, and of immense goodwill)

Allow, diva Lucia, at your feet—where I know
so that I am the most blind of all
the grades of light—
this swerving among ravines—where you know well—
humble desire for eulogy.

            Tears springing to the eyes. Blow up of
            a single photon. Ω

da Tavoli, giornali, alba pratalia

I

Che «è vento da neve», che «stagna, anzi»
e «la padrona ha una cugina, anzi due»
«gemelle, che assomigliano a lei» «e in tre fanno
confondere tutti»
    «sbatte le porte e viene freddissimo dentro»
    (27 dicembre 1976
    osteria vicina alla Porta con l'Orologio). Dentro:
nulla di più vasto di quei tavoli
dove ogni possibilità storica e metafisica
esce, scivola fuor dalla guaina e certamente (sost.) e derivati
                sta-e-stanno tra macchie
di vino e segni di piattini   e lustro e fragili pattumi.
Un lustro appena indiziario—
da certi tavoli—
che sbanda e se ne va per conto suo così di sbircio
che va al lontanante
following nothing nothing
getting up getting on
un lustro qui venuto, ai tavoli, e ormai sfuggente
        da una ben nota Emmaus dai fari anabbaglianti
    Qualcosa si altera stupendamente nel suo aderire
    al punto più basso della realtà del tavolo
    low sunshine   «suo» lucido e sguancio
Hanno poi confermato i due
    pensionati che—qui—è—
    dolcissimo esser chiusi nell'ovo della pensione
    e dell'osteria
e che: i riflessi del vino-ombretta nel calice
    bevuto «in modo che, se la moglie entra,
    sembri il primo calice», i contorni
    di tale vino i segni indiziarii
    di tale resto di vino—
        fanno un cerchiolino imprigionato nel calice—
        tutto vi si lascia
    cogliere e sciogliere
    comprese alcune domande che si sporgono, soltanto, così,

from Tables, Newspapers, Snow-Covered Fields

I

That "it's a frigid wind," that "isn't actually going anywhere"
and "the owner has a cousin, two actually"
"twins, that look just like her" "and all together they
fool everybody"
      "slam the doors and it gets freezing cold inside"
      (December 27, 1976
      tavern near the Gate with the Clock). Inside:
nothing vaster than those tables
where every historical and metaphysical possibility
leaks, slips out of the sheath and certainly (nouns) and derivatives
            lo-&-loom among the wine
stains and signs of saucers   and luster and delicate litter.
A luster scarcely circumstantial—
from certain tables—
that disintegrates and takes off on its own squinting
that goes drawing away
following nothing nothing
getting up getting on
a luster here arrived, on the tables, and by now elusive
            from a renown Emmaus with dipped headlights
      Something stupendously alters in its adhering
      to the lowest point of the table's reality
      low sunshine   "its" luster and splay
The two pensioners have thus
      confirmed that—here—it is—
      so sweet to be wrapped in the egg of the pension
            and the tavern
and that: the reflections of the wine-shadow in the glass
      drunk "so that, if your wife comes in,
      it seems the first glass," the contours
      of that wine the circumstantial evidence
      of that residue of wine—
            make a little ring imprisoned in the glass—
            everything disappears
      to gather and unravel
      including a few questions that pop up, only, this way,

E il vento scopa via la morte che non ci sente per niente
o la persuade a recarsi a ritirare la pensione
giù all'ufficio, se mai fosse aperto
E il freddo scopa via l'orrido millepiedi
                e il '76 con i suoi 366 peduncoli di sventure
E verrà Epifania che tutte le feste scopa via
meno che i vecchi eterni di pensioncine
        e mogli sorvegliatiche,
        e men che mai padroncine gemelle 1+1+1 cugine

Davvero gronda di fato il giornale
di qui che, appunto, non reca nessuna notizia
ma è come se ne recasse—oh—
        quai vive stelle, notizie che fate noto il niente,
        notizia suppergiù, emanante, gazzetta abrasa, ad angolo radente
        che accenna perfino talvolta a un rametto
        che il vento (quello di cui sopra) ha spezzato nel bosco—
        a dieci fili d'erba calpestati da un ragazzino
        a «si ferisce con una lamiera»
        alla cena di tutti quelli che si chiamano Mario
        alla neve del '76 che forse
        forse, qui in osteria, sul giornale, supererà quella
        degli ultimi cinque, anni o secoli, che fa?—
Osteria e voglia di giornale vuoto
Osteria: sbattetevi i piedi per bene, entrando:
                dalle nudità delle nevi sbattetevi,
del gemmeo grumo sotto le scarpe camminanti
fate mucchio sulla porta,
sbattete via i piedi
già altissimi di nevi
                se vorrete sul piede giusto ripartire

Futuri semplici—o anteriori?

Logos, in ogni cristallo di brina di neve glorioso
anche se forse non sei più che un'ipotesi
        che un Witz un moto di stizza sottile

And the wind sweeps away completely deafened death
or persuades it to go and draw its pension
down at the office, if it were ever open
And the cold sweeps away the hideous millipede
                and '76 with its 366 pedicels of bad luck
And the Epiphany will come and sweep away all the holidays
unless the eternal old people of meager pensions
        and watchdog wives,
        and even unless smalltime bosses twins 1+1+1 cousins

Gutter of fate indeed the local
newspaper that, precisely, contains no news
but as if it contained—oh—
        almost living stars, news that makes note of nothing,
        approximately, emanative news, rough gazette, at an abrasive angle
        that at times even alludes to a twig
        snapped off in the woods by the wind (the one here above)—
        to ten blades of grass trampled by a little boy
        to "injuring himself with a metal plate"
        to the dinner of all those named Mario
        to the snow of '76 that perhaps
        perhaps, here in the tavern, in the newspaper, will top that
        of the last five, years or centuries, what does it matter?—
Tavern and longing for empty newspapers
Tavern: stomp your feet well, entering:
                from the nudity of the snow, stomp them,
make a heap by the door
with the gem-like lumps under your walking shoes,
stomp your feet away
already sublime with snow
            if you want to leave on the right foot

Futures—Simple or Anterior?

Logos, in each hoarfrost crystal of glorious snow
even if perhaps you are no more than a hypothesis
        than a Witz, a movement of subtle vexation

Inverificabile nesso tra geli e geli
    punte di lume e punte di lume

Non pentirsi   non dire troppo   non affastellare
    troppo   essere stelo e sterpo
        scintillato da immobilità in gocce
        a inventare   a incavare   a irretire

L'albata e variata nudezza dell'essere
    mimerò presto, e il tocco infimo, la vibratile nota,
    negato io nel gelo
    contaminazione e chiarore ciliato appena al di qua

Logos—non importano mutismi né dicerie
    —non   stonature né colori-nani sgambettanti assiepati
    non   l'altra tua possibile importanza
            né la tua morte
            né la tua perdita
    che assunsi a profusione
Perfusione di gelo e febbricole abbacinanti
                e immicrobirsi infinito
perfusione di vena in vena—di povertà in povertà

    Ogni passo   sposta e attenaglia come un giro di vite
    ogni voce   si soffoca dolcissima inutile
    ogni sguardo si disocchia

ma per riscuoterti il più del compenso e la
più terribile stellarità, come
                di neve sul ciglio della   dell'indicato
                                movimento
                                Ma umiliato.

Unverifiable nexus between frosts and frosts
    points of light and points of light

Don't repent   don't say too much   don't muddle
    too much   to be stem and twig
                agleam with immobility in drops
                to invent   to hollow out   to ensnare

The dawned and varied nudity of being
    I will soon mime, the lowest touch, the vibratory note,
    myself negated in the frost
    contamination and eyelashed glimmer just this side

Logos—neither rumors nor mutisms matter
    —neither   discordant notes nor shuffling crowded
        dwarf-colors
        neither   your other possible importance
                    nor your death
                    nor your loss
        that I took on in profusion
Perfusion of frost and dazzling fevers
                        and infinite enmicrobing
perfusion from vein to vein—from poverty to poverty

    Each step   shifts and grips like the turn of a screw
    each voice   is smothered sweetly uselessly
    each glance uneyes itself

but to gather for you most of the reward and the
most terrible stellarity, as if
                    of snow on the verge of the   of the indicated
                                                        movement
                                                        But humbled.

MI STIEROI

AL JUSTAONBRELE

Se justa onbrele, po' va
che nol pioǵ mai che basta
parché se pose impignirse la panha
Ma che man che ghe vól,
che soramanego che zhata
par far un onbrelia squasi da sposa
de na onbrelata veǵa e meda in toch:
e ve parelo poch?

Andrea Z. 83

da Idioma

---

from Idiom
[1986]

Gente—come tante altre genti—

. . . .

    Forse è per questo che ho sempre stentato
    e malvoluto partire,
    per l'invadenza beata di una certa tua virtù
    che in nonviolenza tesse
    e ritesse quotidianità—
    essa di per sé dona tanti altri beni
    di accoglienza e dolcezza
    reciproca, né esclude la fermezza—
        pur se tra lievi distrazioni
        reciproche, indifferenze incrociate
        coaguli di minimi affari e mafie—
        e poi una piccola appiccicosa
        volontà di non guardar troppo lontano
        una bonarietà qualche volta sonnolenta

Mi scopro tavolta del tutto solo
pensando a tali cose, sento di
omettere molto, di non poter
né saper dire di più,
ma poi mi libero,
con un po' di sgomento un po' di gioia
che ‖   e mi adagio nel giusto
essere uno coi tanti di qui.
Mi libero: e vedo una carta che va
verso nord, nel vento, verso la notte.

E talvolta mi abbacina un prato
dimenticato dietro una casa antica,
solitario, che finge indifferenza o
lieve o smunta distrazione

    ma forse soffre, forse è soltanto
        un paradiso

People—like many other peoples—

. . . .

    Perhaps for this I always found it difficult
    and never really wanted to leave,
    for the blessed meddlesomeness of a certain virtue of yours
    that in nonviolence weaves
    and reweaves everyday life—
    this in itself carries many other rewards
    of acceptance and mutual
    affection, nor does it exclude firmness—
        even if amidst modest mutual
        distractions, intersecting indifferences
        coagulums of minimal affairs and mafias—
        and then a little clingy
        determination to not look too far away
        a sometimes sleepy mildness

Now and then I find myself all alone
thinking of these things, I feel as if I'm
leaving out so much, as if I'm unable
to come up with anything more to say,
but then I free myself,
with a bit of dismay a bit of joy
that ‖   and I settle into the fitting
being one with the many from this place.
I free myself: and I see a bit of paper that takes off
towards north, in the wind, towards night.

And every so often a meadow dazzles me
forgotten behind an old house,
solitary, feigning indifference or
slight or waxen distraction

    but perhaps it's suffering, perhaps it's only
        a paradise

Come di là dai mari
grida grida l'innocenza—
bambini non più solitari
su litorali infiniti
rincorrono rincorrono e vincono
di abbaglio in abbaglio rapiti

E che si saprà mai di tanta innocenza?
Che di questo spicciarsi di bambini?
Feroci come l'afa
come i divini
loro doni che fuggono, sfere
su tutto il mondo, oltre ogni potere?

Folla che troppo distratto e assonnato
raggiungo ad una svolta
a un dirupo dove crollò improvviso
ogni confine in un soprassaltante riso,
    folla dolcissima, vero
    disumano, perfetto aldilà
    in elisie tivù, fosfeni a cascate,
    acufeni di gloria gloria e gloria
            per questa bella estate.

Orizzonti

Stanco di non allinearmi
verso l'orizzontalità—e con odio
dell'irrequietezza dei colli,
stanco forse di avervi insultati
accettando che diveniste fantasmi,
o genitori:
che pressoché dissonate, che state fuori
da ogni contaminazione o sospetto
o lecca-lecca di tempo,
fuori dagli effetti speciali

Spheres

As if beyond the seas
innocence shouts out—
children no longer solitary
on endless shores
chase down and prevail
carried from glimmer to glimmer

And what we will ever know of so much innocence
Of this upwelling of children?
Fierce as sweltering heat
as their divine
gifts that steal away, spheres
across the entire world, beyond every power?

Too troubled and sleepy crowd
that I reach at a curve
at a precipice where every boundary
suddenly crashes into startling laughter
     sweet crowd, truly
     inhuman, perfect other-world
     in TV elysiums, cascading phosphenes,
     acouphenes of unending glory
          for this beautiful summer.

Horizons

Tired of not aligning myself
towards horizontality—and with loathing
of the hills' restlessness,
tired perhaps of having insulted you
accepting your transformation into specters,
oh parents:
who are nearly jarring, looming beyond
every taint or suspicion
or time's incessant licking,
beyond the special effects

e dai metabolismi erratici
del Tutto. Non avete bisogno
del mio sostegno, del mio
ricordo.
Non esiste bisogno né critica del bisogno.
Siamo, anche se io stento, fatti di orizzonte,
disadattati a questo tipo di mondo.
Ma in linea di massima convinti
       (costituendo chissà quale frase)
       di essere,
       di meritarci di essere, un bell'essere,
       di avere in pugno, chissà come,
       ogni carenza e rastrematura
       infida e terrificante
              dell'essere.

         ★

Pericolose—un giorno—bellezze
che in tanti e tanti anni mai più
da alcuna parte
siete state viste,
avete letto, chissà dove, una sola pagina,
avete coltivato, ciò che parve crudele,
una gentile monomania.
Futile, questo nascondervi? Oggi
dovunque è accettato.
Non siete ombre non luci
Ma solo un atto della solita
      non comprensibile giustizia.

Nino negli anni ottanta

25 gennaio 1983, S. Paolo

Durante l'estate sotto l'equivoco sudore
del solstizio arrancavi
Nino, come reggendoti a malapena
sulla sponda dell'aldiquà,

and erratic metabolisms
of the All. You have no need
of my support, of my
memory.
There exists no need nor criticism of need.
We are, even if I find it hard, made of horizon,
unfitted for this sort of world.
But for the most part convinced
        (constituting who knows what expression)
        of being,
        of deserving to be, a splendid being,
        of having in hand, who knows how,
        every deprivation and diminishment
        treacherous and terrifying
                of being.

             ★

Dangerous—once—splendors
who never in many, many years
in any place
have been seen,
who have read, who knows where, a single page,
who have cultivated, a seemingly heartless,
genial monomania.
Is this self-concealment futile? Today
it is everywhere accepted.
You are neither shadows nor lights
But only an act of the usual
        incomprehensible justice.

Nino in the Eighties

January 25, 1983, S. Paolo

During the summer under the solstice's
equivocal sweat you were slogging along,
Nino, scarcely holding yourself up
on the bank of the here & now,

salivi le chine incretinite
del tuo feudo ormai scalpato
d'ogni vite,
dai grevi tacchini sbeccuzzato
vedovo di lepri e fagiani, strampalato.
Tu faticavi, vestito di nero, ansimavi
la tua già irreale presenza
anche se egregiamente
raccordato a fermezze finezze
imprinting elementi
per ogni dove a noi da sempre sfuggenti.
Ora no: splende ora gennaio
e la gloria di gennaio ti assume
a sé—
immune da malattie
svelto del tuo costume,   privo
dei defedanti soprabiti.
E certo la tua fronte può di ghiaccioli
farsi scintillante com'è di quotidianità
e di furbizia contro l'aldilà,
quando, pedalando
tra i novanta e i cento anni quasi volage,
ti addentri nel mistero delle colline
per te ricanticchiato, riacutizzato senza fine.

da Andar a cucire

A la Maria Carpèla
(che la 'ndéa a pontar par le case)

Si no 'l te fèsse 'n paradiso
aposta par ti, anca si paradisi no ghe n'é,
al saràe da méter a l'inferno
l'istesso Padreterno—
la saràe da méter a l'inferno
tuta, tuta quanta «la realtà»,
si par ti no la fèsse 'n paradiso
pien de bontà come la tó bontà,

256

you were climbing the stultified slopes
of your fiefdom now scalped
                    of every vine,
pecked at by plump turkeys,
widower of hares and pheasants, eccentric.
          You labored, dressed in black, panting
your already unreal presence
even if singularly
connected to fixities subtleties
imprinting elements
everywhere always eluding us.
          Not now: January shines now
          and the glory of January enfolds you
                    in itself—
immune from illnesses
nimble as usual,   lacking
protective overcoats.
And doubtless your forehead, made of everyday
reality, can make itself gleam with icicles,
          and with wiliness against the beyond,
when, pedaling
between ninety and one hundred, almost volage,
you delve into the mystery of the hills
for you softly sung again, rekindled without end.

from Going Out to Sew

For Maria Carpèla
(who went out to sew for families)

If he didn't make a paradise
just for you, even if paradises don't exist,
the Eternal Father himself
should be sent to hell
all, all of reality
should be sent to hell too,
if he didn't make a paradise for you,
full of goodness like your goodness,

gnentaltro che 'l paradiso
come che ti tu l'à pensà.

La contrada. Zauberkraft.
Come è esistita la contrada? Si può
davvero assumerla come un dato—
o almeno un fattore di contestualità?
Lei con le casette male allineate
sbocconcellate ma talvolta
messe a nuovo dal vento
o da soldi arrivati col vento . . .
Sì, la tua esistenza
chiede, si attira lettere patenti, attestati
del resto superflui,
sta, a picco, su ciò che di per sé sprofonda
nella propria sovrana potenza
(potenza intesa come spessore del ghiaccio
        in una valle ampia, fatta a U
        ghiaccio mai sciolto, nonostante il parere dei più)
Occorre tutta la Zauberkraft
di cui parlava Hegel
come di cosa di cui lui sapeva qualcosa
per credere che la contrada senza posa
si rinnovi in face mentale, vibri
notte e dì stravolta da irti inesprimibili
soli, saggezze, tenebre, riposi e gridi-cigolii:
tela in cui
le stanzette in cui
le funzioni i grafemi in cui
i lucignoli gli smoccolii in cui
noi-io   ci risolvemmo
o magari in finissimo etra
Come si può pretendere
che qualcuno sopravviva con piccoli commerci
in precarietà più delicate che vapori sui vetri
che orgogli di fili d'erba, di aghi di brina:
a te due castagne, io ti lavoro una sedia,
tu un materasso, io ti cucio un abitino
e io che faccio il contadino

nothing but the paradise
pictured by you.

The quarter. Zauberkraft
How did the quarter exist? Can we
really assume it as a given—
or at least a contextual fact?
She with her badly aligned little houses
nibbled at but sometimes
renewed by the wind
or by money blown in by the wind . . .
Yes, your existence
asks for, attracts patent letters, testimonials
however superfluous,
it rises, upright, over all that which sinks by itself
into its own sovereign power
(power understood as the thickness of ice
      in a broad, U-shaped valley
      ice that never melted, despite popular opinion)
The entire Zauberkraft is needed
of which Hegel spoke
as of something he was familiar with
so as to believe that the quarter might unceasingly
renew itself in mental light, vibrating
night and day distraught with inexpressible bristling
suns, wisdoms, shadows, rests and shouts-squeaks:
web in which
the little rooms in which
the functions the graphemes in which
the wicks the snuffings in which
we-I   unraveled
or perhaps into very fine ether
How can we presume
that someone survives on small dealings
in precariousness more fragile than vapor on window-panes
than glorious leaves of grass, or needles of frost:
for you two chestnuts, I'm at work on a chair for you,
for you a mattress, I'm sewing you a little suit
and I'm the one playing the peasant

Occorre una Zauberkraft senza pari
per sperare di arrivare a domani, a dopodomani
così commerciando e dandosi a manipolare—
senza precipitar giù tra le nebulose
senza scivolare in un unico passo falso, di sette leghe
Tu non tornare alla decenza dello stato minerale
    Zauberkraft è la mia contrada
    l'edificio della mente non lo sento possibile
    l'illuminazione ottico-mentale
    funziona con orari incerti—mi sta imbrogliando
    Ma avallo, firmo cambiali
    su sentieri di Zauberkraft
    in stanzette di Zauberkraft
    pur senza picciòlo cordone tubetto di flebo;
    e per qualche arteriola—vedi—si riattiva il circolo
    balugina sempre l'anagrafe
Quanto   vi costò trattenervi
qua su in contrada a manipolare
e, per me già spinto a spallate dove   invade
quanta mania ci fu, contrada, per
reggerti, sola in tutta la tua siderale
forza, inattualità, demoralizzazione costituzionale
e sovrumana inerzia di presenza
sempre più immagicata in colori linee piani—
forse a farli volare basterà un battito di mani.

Onde éli

Onde éla mai la pi cara de le mé jèje
che la scrivéa par carnevai e feste
i «dialoghi» in puisia e fin
co drento parole in latin
che tanti i se li recorda ancora;
«la se 'véa trat al béver», i diséa,
par passarghe sora a la malora.
Chi sa. Ma sol che éla la sa quant
che finte 'sto scribinciar mi ghe soméje.

A matchless Zauberkraft is needed
in order to hope that we'll make it to tomorrow, the day after
    tomorrow
dealing in this way and devoting yourself to maneuvering—
without plunging down through the nebulae
without slipping into a single seven-league false step
Don't return to the decency of the mineral state
        Zauberkraft is my quarter
        the edifice of the mind I don't feel possible
        the optic-mental illumination
        works with uncertain schedules—is muddling my mind
        But I guarantee, I sign promissory notes
        on Zauberkraft paths
        in little Zauberkraft rooms
        even without the stalk-like string phelbo tube;
        and through some small artery—see—the circle reactivates
        the registry office always glimmers
How much   it cost you to stay
up here in the quarter pulling strings
and, for me already shoved and shouldered where   it invades
there was such mania, quarter, to
keep you going, alone in all of your starry
power, inactuality, constitutional demoralization
and superhuman inertia of presence
ever more alchemized in colors lines planes—
a clap of the hands might suffice to make them fly.

Where Are They?

Wherever is the dearest of my aunts
who used to write skits in verse
for carnivals and festivities, even
dropping in a few words in Latin:
many still remember them;
"she started to drink," they said,
to drown her sorrows.
Who knows. But only she knows how much
in this scribbling I resemble her.

Onde éla la Pina dei giornai
e la só botegheta drio la piazha
coi color che lustréa come ferai . . .
«Rivendita carbone e giornali»:
negra pedo de 'n camin, co' i grun
de garbon, e in medo—che canpanele e sonai!—
al ros e 'l blu e 'l verdo dei giornai
al se destiréa e 'l cresséa
'fa 'n pradusel de mareveje—
ma 'l garbon ne rivéa fin su le zhéje.

Onde éla infra le amighe de me jèia
cussita bone tute e cussì stranbe
quela vedova Bres che vegnéa da Belun
e al loto la vinzhéa senpre i so anbi
e in pì la 'véa redità da so òn
otanta carte da milí, un balon
de schei, ma pò la 'véa magnà-su tut
a frajar, far savoia co 'ste amighe:
no l'era altro che sopete coade, graspin, govet,
onbrete e compagnia bela,
anca si zherti no lo cret.

Onde éla la Urora e i buzholà
e le caròbole e i sòrboi che la ghe vendéa
ai cèi par diese schei: che marcà
ala festa, drio vespro, che i ghe féa!
Su 'l fornelet Bora 'l balcon podà
intant la só zheneta la bojéa:
ma i tosatan un dì drento finte 'l brodo
un zhochet de morer i ghe 'véa mes—
e ela col piron catando dur co la inpiréa—
«A che tenp, la diséa, che son tiradi ades».

Where is Pina of the newspapers
and her little shop behind the piazza
with its colors bright as headlights . . .
"Coal and newspapers for sale":
blacker than a chimney, with heaps
of coal, and in the middle—what bells and rattles!—
the red and blue and green of the newspapers
expanded and grew
like a little wondrous meadow
but the coal came up to our eyebrows.

Where among my aunts' friends
all so good and strange
is that widow Bres who came from Belluno
and always won at lottery
and what's more had inherited from her husband
eighty thousand lire, a heap
of money, but then squandered it all
having fun, letting her hair down with her friends:
nothing but chicken soup, a bit of grappa, eggs,
glasses of wine and good company,
even if certain people don't believe it.

Where is Aurora and the sweets
and the carob beans and crab apples that she sold
to children for a few cents: what great business
they made for her at festivals after vespers!
On a little stove resting on the windowsill,
her little dinner would boil away:
But once a bunch of naughty kids
put a little hunk of mulberry in her soup—
and when she tasted it with a fork found it hard to bite—
"What a sorry state of affairs we're in, she used to say."

No te pias véder pióver sul bagnà
(ma ades scravazha), né che zhuite i porte
dó par Atene, o legne e roe 'nte 'l bòsch.
Par questo, asséi difizhil no basta che stranbo
me par mandarte, Eusebio, par casa versi—
co no fusse un de quei sonet tajadi fusti come stèle,
che se uséa meter dó al ciaro de 'n mòcol,
co la gabana ados finte 'l fret dei gran tènp del passà.
Ris'ce cussì 'sta òlta de intrigarne
e de inverigolarme pèdo che par al solito;
quant mèjo un taser fondo, taser e lèderte.
    Ma par quei sbari de s'ciòp o de mine
finte 'l pi raro vodo dei canp, dei mondi,
e pi ancora par quei racolar de rochéte
sufiade su in s'ciantis de sagra
e in sghirli de ventade fin dentro le nèole,—
che senpre i sbocia da la tó poesia,—
che senpre i me desmissia
e che tanti ani fa me 'véa segnà 'na strada
sofà tra mèdo de 'na calivèra,—
bisogna pur che te salude, ancó.
    No so si drét son 'ndat, si ò scantinà,
si de farse capir 'ste righe merite
che da zhope e da rive lontane te mande.
Ma son sfiguro che ti tu vét quant lanpido
l'é l'agurar che mi—co tanti altri—te fae
par i tó otanta de 'sta umana vita
e fursi mili de sgorlarne-incantarne
col tó scur col tó lustro
col tó serarte in rizh e col tó pànderte:
rari e radis de l'istessa boscaja
onde che fazhil, difizhil, tra lori ingatiadi,
i é senpre lori e senpre 'l só contrari.

For Eugenio Montale on His Eightieth Birthday

You don't like to see coals carried to Newcastle,
(although that's what I'm doing)
owls brought to Athens or firewood and brambles to the forest.
That's why it seems so difficult, and bizarre too,
to send you a poem, Eusebius—
unless it were one of those sonnets cut, like chips of kindling, just right,
like the ones they used to draft by candlelight
bundled up in a heavy cloak against the cold in the great days gone by.
This time I risk making a mess of things
and I'm mixed up worse than usual;
how much better a deep silence, keeping quiet and reading your poems.
    And yet, because of those rifle shots,
    those mine explosions in the rarest void
    of the countrysides, of the worlds,
    and even more for that crackle of squibs
    blown upward in festival flashes
    in the vortices of wind
    in the very heart of storm clouds,—
    that always bud and bloom from your poetry,—
    and always rouse me
    and which, many years ago, showed me a road
    as in the middle of a fog bank—
    that's why I must greet you today.
    I don't know if I have gone straight or if I have deviated,
    if these lines, sent from distant cliffs and slopes,
    merit understanding.
    But I'm sure that you see how clear
    is the wish that I (along with many others)
    make for your eighty years of this human life,
    and perhaps a thousand more as well of your
        jolting-entrancing us
    with your darkness, your sparkle,
    your hedgehog obscurity and self-disclosure:
    branches and roots of the same forest
    where the easy and the difficult tangled up together
    are always themselves and always their opposites.

Translated by John P. Welle and Ruth Feldman

In ricordo de Pasolini

Ti tu magnéa la tó ciòpa de pan
sul treno par andar a scola
tra Sazhil e Conejan;
mi ere póch lontan, ma a quei tènp là
diese chilometri i era 'na imensità.
Cussita é stat che 'lora
do tosatèi no i se à mai cognossést.
Ma quande mai se 'varàelo podést
catarse sote 'l stesso pòrtego
de 'na stazhioneta in medo ai canp
co 'l só canpanelet che 'l fa ten ten ten ten
disèndone quant fondo che é 'l seren—
  e intant ore dornade e stajon
  le va via co l'onbrìa che la serif,
  par case e vieri par muret e pra
  par bus zhiése e canton,
  radis e scarabizh?
Ma quande mai, prima che 'l treno l' rive,
se 'varàelo fat ora
par quele do tre ciàcole,
le sole che pól dar Bora 'sta tera
de cognosserne 'n póch, póch ma devera?
  Se se à parlà, pi avanti, se se à ledést;
  zherte òlte 'von tasést o se à sticà,
  la vita ne à parà sole straségne
  e ciapà-dentro par tamài diversi,
  mi fermo, inpetolà 'nte i versi,
  ti dapartut co la tó passion de tut;
  ma pur ghe n'era 'n fil che 'l ne tegnéa:
  de quel che val se 'véa l'istessa idea.

Mi te spetèe qua sù, 'ndove che ancora
coi só lustrin i suspira i alba pratalia
ma senpre pi marzhi de sole e parsora;
ti tu sé restà là col tó corajo,
'ndove che pi la zhavària l'Italia.

  Ah, scùseme, se adès no so darle
  altro che 'sto muzhigamènt, 'ramai da vecio . . .

In Memory of Pasolini

You used to eat your bread on the way to school
riding the train
between Sacile and Conegliano;
I lived close by, but in those days
ten kilometers was a huge distance.
And so it happened that at the time
two boys didn't get to know each other.
But when could we have met
under the same roof
of a little station in the middle of fields
with its bell going ding ding ding ding
telling us how deep the clear sky is—
      and meanwhile hours days and seasons
      vanish with the shadow that through windows,
      through houses, low walls, meadows,
      through hedges, and everywhere in hidden places,
      writes roots and illegible signs?
But when, ever, before the train pulled in,
would we have found time,
for that bit of chatter,
the only thing you can exchange on this earth,
so that you get to know another person slightly, slightly but truly?
      Later we talked, we read each other's work;
      sometimes we kept silent or we argued,
      life pushed us under drippings of cold water (blows)
      and caught us in different traps,
      me, motionless, mired in poetry,
      you, everywhere, with your passion for everything;
      but there was always a thread that linked us:
      we had the same idea of what really matters.

I was waiting for you up here, where the dawn meadows
(white expanses of snow) still sigh with their sparkling
but always more spoiled above and down below;
you, with your courage, remained fixed,
where Italy is most delirious.

      Ah forgive me if all I can give you now
      is this old man's mumbling . . .

L é sol che 'n pore sforzh, tremor,
par pontar-sù, justar-sù in qualche modo
—par un momento sol, par saludarte—
quel che i à fat dei tó os e del tó cor.

da Mistieròi

Come élo che posse 'ver corajo
de ciamarve qua, de farve segno co la man.
'Na man che no l'é pi de la só onbría
cagnina e caía,
anzhi 'na sgrifa, ma tèndra 'fa molena.
Epuro ades calcossa la tien sú,
no so se 'n sgranf o se 'na forzha;
par quel che l'é, la é tuta vostra,
e voi dèghe l' polso par ciamarve.
Dèghe 'na pena che no la se schinche,
fè che la ponta sul sfój no la se inciónpe.
Me par de no 'ver gnent da méter-dó
par scuminzhiar 'sto telex
che tut al gnent bisogna che 'l traverse
(tut al gran seramènt
che 'l bruca come solfer
che l'incaróla e l'intrunis).
Ma proarò la trazha, almanco, de 'n amor—
fora par là finte 'l scur
orbo dei pra del passà.
Cussì

. . . .

[   ]

Cussì, sote 'l camin squasi stusà
se 'n tosatèl vardéa
par quela finestrela cèa
che su la sera la féa 'ncora lustro

268

It's only a tremor, a poor effort
to stitch together again, patch up somehow
—for just a moment, to say farewell—
what they did with your bones and with your heart.

Translated by John P. Welle and Ruth Feldman

from Small and Humble Occupations

How shall I find the courage
to summon you here, to beckon to you with my hand.
A hand divorced from its shadow,
greedy and mean,
a claw, rather, but soft as breadcrumbs.
And yet something holds it up now,
I don't know if it's a cramp or a force;
for whatever it's worth, it's all yours,
give it the power to summon you.
Give it a pen that won't bend,
don't let the point catch on the page.
I seem to have nothing to put down
to start this telex
that must cross the whole void
(the blazing passageway
that burns like sulfur
that corrodes and stuns).
But I will try for a trace, at least, of a love—
outside there in the pitch dark
of long-ago meadows.
And so

. . . .

[   ]

And so, under the nearly extinguished fireplace
if a small boy were looking
through that tiny window
that still appeared clear in the evening

in medo ala fulisca
(ah che bel blu, che arjento,
che grísoi de l'inverno inbarlumidi
de ciaro e neve finte la finestrela):
chi èrelo, pò, che passéa, che batéa
su quel viero, e sparía
no so se zhotegando o se 'nte 'n bal;
èreli tuti lori, none, del vostro tènp,
cola só fan de radici la só sé
de vin pìzhol, cole só fadighe che
le ghe 'vea ingropà tuta la figura
fin squasi a canbiarghe natura?
Ma co mi, tosatèl, quant maturloni
e quant de bona vója, senpre, e boni . . .
E mi i vede, me par, farme 'n póch marameo,
zhignarme, ridolar, pò farme ciao . . .

. . . .

Pastor

I pastor, che 'na òlta i ghe ciaméa
«pastre» e che i val in poesia
de pi de ogn'altra categoria
parché in Arcadia lori i comandéa,
i pararàe bestie, se un li vede
inpetoladi senpre intra le fede l
e càvere i can e i cavai.
E no l'é vera: òmi i resta e poeti
e re de Arcadie che gnessun
savarà mai.

Femene che le fila

Filar co corlo e fus
finte i dì bassi e curti che i mór in filò . . .
Filar par tante ore
che no le vien pagade gnent
parché le femene—se sa—no conta gnent.

in the middle of the grime
(oh what lovely blue, what silver,
what dazzling winter chills
of light and snow in the small window):
whoever could it have been that passed, that rapped
on the windowpane, and disappeared
limping or dancing I don't know;
were they all people from your day, grandmothers,
with their hunger for wild chicory,
their thirst for young wine,
with the labors that twisted their shapes
and almost changed their natures?
But with me, a little boy, what scatterbrains,
how merry they always were and how good . . .
I seem to see them now, thumbing their noses at me,
winking at me, laughing softly, then saying "so long". . .

. . . .

Herdsmen

Herdsmen, who once were called
sheep herders and who occupy more space in poetry
than any other category
because in Arcadia they ruled,
would seem like animals to someone
who always sees them mud-smeared among the ewes
goats dogs and horses.
It's not true: they're still men and poets
and kings of Arcadias
no one will ever know.

Spinners

Spinning with wheel and spindle
in the short dark days
that end with vigils in the stables . . .
Spinning for endless hours
for which we're never paid

Cànevo lana e lin
tele grosse e tele in fin
par tuta la dènt del colmèl:
ore nostre che no le val gnent
gnent cofà le ciàcole a filò . . .

Femene che le lava

Tute le femene le va dó al lavador:
no l'é 'n mistier 'sto qua
ma l'é 'n destin, cofà l'amor
o 'n fiól, o la só ora co la vien.
La va dó l'ora e la lava
co l'acqua che la fila via,
l'acqua che anca de 'sta vita
e no sol de 'ste póche nostre robe
la ne fa pulizhia.

Alto, altro linguaggio, fuori idioma?

Lingue fioriscono affascinano
inselvano e tradiscono in mille
      aghi di mutismi e sordità
sprofondano e aguzzano in tanti e tantissimi idioti
Lingue tra i cui baratri invano
si crede passare—fioriti, fioriti, in altissimi
      sapore e odori, ma sono idiozia
Idioma, non altro, è ciò che mi attraversa
in persecuzioni e aneliti h j k ch ch ch
      idioma
      è quel gesto ingessato
      che accumula
      sere sforbiciate via verso il niente. Ma

because—everyone knows—women
aren't worth a thing.
Hemp, wool, and linen
rough weave and fine
for all the people who live nearby:
like the idle evening chatter,
our long hours don't seem to matter . . .

Washerwomen

All the women go to the wash-house:
this isn't really work,
it's a "destiny," like love,
a child, or the hour when our time is up.
Time passes and washes
with water that trickles away,
the water that cleanses us
not only of our few belongings
but of our very lives.

Translated by John P. Welle and Ruth Feldman

High, Other Language, beyond Idiom?

Tongues blossom beguile
run wild and betray in a thousand
        needles of muteness and deafness
they sink and are sharpened in so very many idiots
Tongues amidst whose abysses in vain
we believe we pass—blooming, blooming, in the highest
        flavors and smells, but they are idiocy
Idiom, none other, is what runs through me
in persecutions and panting h j k ch ch ch
        idiom
        is that ossified gesture
        that accumulates
        evenings snipped away towards nothingness. But

pare che da rocks crudelmente franti tra
i denti diamantiferi, in
ebbri liquori vengano gl'idiomi!
Pare, ognuno, residuo di sé, di
io-lingua, ridotto a seduzione!
Ma vedi come—in idioma—corra i più orribili rischi
la stessa nebbia fatata del mondo, stock
di ogni estatico scegliere, di ogni devozione
       E là mi trascino, all'intraducibile perché
       fuori-idioma, al qui, al sùbito,
       al circuito chiuso che pulsa,
       al grumo, al giro di guizzi in un monitor
Non vi siano idiomi, né traduzioni, ora
       entro il disperso
       il multivirato sperperarsi in sé
       di questo ritornate attacco dell'autunno.
«Attacco», «traduzioni», che dissi? O
altri sinonimi h j k ch ch ch
sempre più nervosamente adatti, in altri idiomi?
Ma che m'interessa ormai degli idiomi?
Ma sì, invece, di qualche
piccola poesia, che non vorrebbe saperne
ma pur vive e muore in essi—di ciò m'interessa
e del foglio di carta
per sempre rapinato dall'oscurità
ventosa di una ValPiave
davvero definitivamente
canadese o australiana
             o aldilà.

          ★

Il cielo è limpido sino ad
essere sconosciuto
Tutto è intossicato dal sole
Io tossisco sotto questo, in questo
brusire di entificazioni
e sono distratto

it seems that from rocks cruelly crushed between
diamontiferous teeth, in
drunken liquors come idioms!
Each seems the residue of itself, of
me-tongue, reduced to seduction!
But see how—in idiom—the same bewitched
mist of the world runs the most horrible risks, stock
of every ecstatic choosing, of every devotion
       And I drag myself there, to the untranslatable why
       beyond-idiom, to the here and now,
       to the pulsating closed circuit,
       to the clot, to the spin of flickerings in a monitor
Let there be no idioms, or translations, now
       within the scattered
       the multihued squandering in itself
       of this recurring onslaught of autumn
"Onslaught," "translations," what did I say? Or
other synonyms h j k ch ch ch
ever more nervously adapted, in other idioms?
But what do I care about idioms now?
But yes, on the other hand, some
small poem, that doesn't want anything to do with it
yet lives and dies in idioms—I do care about that
and about the piece of paper
carried off forever from the windy
darkness of a Piave Valley
truly definitely
Canadian or Australian
           or other-worldly.

          ★

The sky is transparent until
it becomes unfamiliar
Everything is intoxicated by the sun
Myself coughing under this, in this
whirring of entifications
and distracted

molto distratto dalla violenza
                    di un freddo
che pur non fa nulla di male

Adocchio solitudini
già mie   ora di se stesse
                    unicamente
Tutti i rimproveri pare si calmino
                    riverberando
Tutto è distrazione e
                    forse meno, un
poco meno del previsto, pena

Docile, riluttante

    1

Docile e qua e là riluttante assai
feudo di Nino—ti mantieni
con la tua stessa immensità
con la tua stessa intensità
per tante valli e dossi posati qui in te
da chissà quante e quali eternità.
Mi sorridono le tue vertigini
m'accarezzano i buffi dei tuoi rovi
che sono i fior-fiori dell'invernale universo,
un che di brina spuma e ore
cui non spetta, nemmeno lontanamente, morire—
          segno di, in mille e mille respiri, preservare
e regno di—alitando—sopravanzare—

    Feudo che emani emani emani
da te, che esprimi accogli
e nascondi
ma soprattutto spalanchi te e noi
e ciò che mai
potrà essere in noi
ma che è qui, se-lo-vuoi,
sterpo betulla croco

very distracted by the violence
of a chill
that is yet harmless

I glance at solitudes
already mine   now of themselves
solely
All the scoldings it seems are subsiding
reverberating
All is distraction and
perhaps less, a
bit less than expected, pain

Docile, reluctant

1

Docile and, here and there, very reluctant
Nino's fiefdom—you maintain yourself
with your same immensity
your very same intensity
through so many valleys and hilltops placed here in you
from who knows how many and which eternities.
Your dizzying heights smile at me
I'm caressed by the puffs of your brambles
that are the flower-flowers of the winter universe,
a bit of hoar-frost foam and hours
which one doesn't expect, not even remotely, to die—
sign of, in thousands and thousands of breaths, preserving
and realm of—panting—overcoming

Fiefdom that you emanate emanate emanate
from yourself, that you express gather together
and hide
but above all you lay open yourself and us
and that which can never
be in us
but is here, should-you-wish-it,
dry branch, birch tree, crocus,

culla di dovizia primizia e foco
applicato da uccelli d'ogni più preziosa estrazione
   Silenzio troppo poco umano così
   che dà, per scale di confronti ciò
   che è umano—e che sta nell'amore, amerà

   2

Nessuna tristezza per i me stessi
che non vi ho ritrovati
né per gli altri, i cari amici, che sempre ho ritrovati,
anche se talvolta più vaghi,
più paghi
degli ultimi arboscelli nei fondi o sui crinali—
Nulla che parli davvero
di cose effimere o finali
bensì della pertinenza,
bensì del fatto, della mai
mai fattuale presenza,
che pur qui si dà giustamente straripando
da tutti gli altrove e singolarità
            alla nostra quasi-indolenza
Quanto quanto qui distilla
e si distillò quale paradiso
perfino dolorosamente nel suo insistere muto
ora è soltanto lieto, e non distrattamente,
ma i suoi valori li compie e li ritira
e li riacconsente un posto più in là
comodi e umili anche se dalle nostre mani
alquanto strani e stralontani
E nei grigiori assopiti, appena specchianti
con gridii di dipinte piume e sbeccuzzati silenzi
(è) come se noi e i nostri ricordi
ma più i nostri presenti
si unissero senza appello, ma non sotto imperio,
ma induzioni di ragionamenti
che non lo saranno mai più, per aver raggiunto
pacatamente (e insegnandolo) gli elementi

cradle of plenty, first fruits and focus
applied by birds of every most precious extraction
    Silence too little human so that
      it gives, through steps of confrontations, that
      which is human-and that remains in love, it will love

   2

No sadness for those selves of mine
which I have not found
nor for the others, the dear friends, whom I have always found again,
though sometimes less intent,
more content
with the last twigs in the depths or on the crests—
Nothing that really speaks
about fleeting or final things
but about the relevance,
but about the fact, of the never
ever factual presence,
that even here gives itself rightly overflowing
from all the elsewheres and singularities
        to our near-indolence
How very much distills here
and was distilled as paradise
downright sadly in its mute insistence
and is now only happy, not distractedly,
but it achieves its values and withdraws them
and again grants them a place farther on,
useful and humble even if from our hands
somewhat strange and very far off
And in the drowsy darkness, scarcely mirroring
with cries of painted plumes and debeaked silences
(it is) as though we and our memories
but even more our here and nows
were to unite without appeal, but not under compulsion,
but inductions of reasonings
that will never be such again, because they have peacefully
reached (and by teaching reasoning) the elements

Translated by John P. Welle and Ruth Feldman

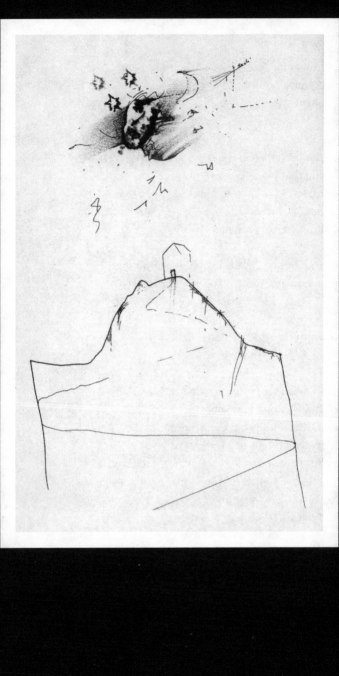

da Meteo

---

from Meteo
[1996]

*Sangue e pus, e dovunque le superflue
superfluenti vitalbe che parassitano gli occhi;
un teleschermo, fuori tempo massimo,
Dirette erutta e Balocchi*

Morèr Sachèr

1

O fedeli
o immoti ma conversati
restando ognuno là nella rarità—
o attivissimi col nulla
dei prati dal febbraio
      dissufflati in mille
mai viste secche   mai visti appostamenti

Residuali e stinchi   MORÈR SACHÈR
liberati per gli habitat
più manifesti del grigiore
ma nella
lietezza di-pur-essere,
consistenza con l'essere,
derisione
infine, derisione / amore
         dell'essere?

. . . .

2

Morèr, sachèr
  nudi, dementi
  resti di storie-eventi
  fedeli fino alla demenza
    amorosa silenzio / demenza

Live

Blood and pus, and everywhere the superfluous
superfluent clematises that parasitize the eyes;
a videodisplay, run over the time limit,
erupting Live Broadcasts and Gewgaws

Morèr Sachèr

1

Oh faithful
oh motionless but conversed
each lingering there in the scarcity—
oh engrossed with the nothingness
of February meadows
        emanated in a thousand
never-seen shoals   never-seen ambushes

Remnant skeletons   MORÈR SACHÈR
released in habitats
more evident than the grayness
but in the
rapture of-yet-being,
consistency with being,
derision
at last, derision / love
        of being?

. . . .

2

Morèr, sachèr
  naked, demented
  relicts of stories-events
  faithful until dementia
    amorous silence / dementia

Alberi in   proporzioni
   e sacre / sfatte
proposizioni inseminati
nella violenta grigità dei prati—
     e no, templa non fanno
non vogliono, non dànno

MORÈR SACHÈR,
   vittime e padri
   e figli dei prati / tradimenti,
   februarietà pura
   ostile ad ogni
   tratto   avida d'ogni immisura

Ma a voi, erme, ermi,
questo brusio tra i denti
      non basta
assai di più bisogna, assai
che più
   vi si consenta amando   vi si oblii

Lanugini

   I
Prato di globi di pappi laggiù smarrito
avanzare sempre più profondo
di concezioni dell'infinito

     ★

Lanugini di lai leni lontananze
vibratili trappole in cui cadde la luce
soffi, tocchi   su immense aree sostati

     ★

Luce e gloria delle composite,
globi incerti del loro stesso esistere—
ma in alta mutezza, in dedizione attonita

Trees in   proportions
  and sacred/flaccid
  proportions inseminated
  in the violent greyity of the meadows—
          and no, templa don't make
  don't want, don't give

MORÈR SACHÈR,
  victims and fathers
  and sons of meadows/betrayals,
  pure Februarity
  hostile to every
  trait   eager for every immeasure

But to you, limits, eremitic,
this buzzing between teeth
              isn't enough
much more is needed, much
more than
      consenting to you loving forgetting you

Lanugos

I

Meadow of globes of pappi down there bewildered
progression ever deeper
of conceptions of the infinite

*

Lanugos of faint laments faraway
vibratile traps capturing the falling light
puffs, touches   over immense suspended areas

*

Light and glory of the composites
globes uncertain of their self-same actuality—
but in high muteness, in dazzled dedication

*

Armoniche, colme grammatiche,
ologrammi di estreme matesi,
o voi, da tutti i soffi, amati

*

Delicati e imbambolati
quali purissime dissoluzioni
gli eserciti-soffioni offrono ai prati?

II

Nome bislacco, taràssaco
per tanto eleganti metamorfosi
di giallori taglienti in bianchi soffi

*

Radicchiette seghettanti, gremito
appetito di soffi, di ipotesi—
stasi o tremito, mai si saprà

*

Verde per cupezza quasi rabbioso
giallime di solicini in sé perfetti
                poi candori appena accennati
affidati affidati agli equilibri dei prati

*

Globi di includenti ricami
esclusioni improvvise e totali
evoluzioni verso invisibili
                        prove finali

*

Le belle cadenze le rapidità
dei pappi librati verso aldilà
impossibili eppure immediati

(incerti frammenti 1993–94)

*

Sonorous, teeming grammars
holograms of extreme acuity
oh you, by all the gusts, loved

*

Delicate and bedazed
what immaculate disintigrations
do the dandelion-armies offer the meadows?

II

Strange name, dandelion
for such elegant metamorphoses
of keen yellows in white gusts

*

Rending rootlets, packed
appetite for puffs, for hypotheses—
stasis or shiver, we'll never know

*

Green edging gloom almost rabid
sallowness of little suns in themselves perfect
         then gleaming candors scarcely hinted at
entrusted entrusted to the equilibriums of the meadows

*

Globes of enclosing embroideries
sudden exclusions and total
evolutions towards invisible
                    ultimate tests

*

The beautiful cadences the swiftnesses
of the pappi soaring towards other-worlds
impossible and yet immediate

(uncertain fragments 1993–94)

★

I

Non si sa quanto verde
sia sepolto sotto questo verde
né quanta pioggia sotto questa pioggia
molti sono gli infiniti
che qui convergono
che di qui s'allontanano
       dimentichi, intontiti
Non-si-sa   Questo è il relitto
di tale   relitto piovoso
il verde in cui sta reticendo
       l'estremo del verde
Forse non-si-sa per un
sordo movimento di luce si
distilla in un suono effimero, e sa
    Forse si lascia sfiorare, si sporge,
    congiunge
    membra a membra, ritorce

II

Quanto mai verde dorme
sotto questo verde
e quanto nihil sotto
    questo ricchissimo nihil?
Ti sottrai, ahi, ai nomi
pur avendo forse un nome
    e pur sapendone qualcosa?
Ma chissà quanta pioggia
dorme sotto questa debolissima
    sovraconfidente pioggia

chissà quanto lustro
    del grigiore, quanto
invito a scivolìo del verde
    fanno altro caso altro genere
    consumano le ultime
    lanugini degli occhi e
    degli orecchi e

★

I

There's no telling how much green
is buried under this green
nor how much rain under this rain
many are the infinities
that here converge
that from here wander off
                    oblivious, stupefied
There's-no-telling   This is the relict
of that   rainy relict
the green in which the extreme of the green
                          is weaving
Perhaps there's-no-telling for a
deaf movement of light distilling
itself in an ephemeral sound, and knowing
          Perhaps allowing blooming, extending
          combining
          member to member, rejoining

II

How much green sleeps
under this green
and how much nihil under
          this richest nihil?
You escape, ah, from names
yet having perhaps a name
          and yet knowing something of it?
But who knows how much rain
sleeps under this most delicate
          superconfident rain

who knows how much luster
          of the grayness, how
drawn to the ever-sliding green
          they become another case another genus
          consume the last
          lanugos of the eyes and
          of the ears and

«Stenti ma inorecchiti . . .»
«Qui approvai la più rapita carta»
«Prova su prova-verde
ricchi fittissimi-pioggia»
«Qui dove   pensai di pensare
e di afferrare e   sbilanciare
              come Da un'altezza nuova»

Leggende

Nel compleanno del maggio
«Tu non sei onnipotente»
dice la pallida bambina

*

Polveri di ultime, perse
battaglie tra blu e verde
dove orizzonti pesano sulle erbe

*

Lievi voci, api inselvatichite—
tutto sogna altri viaggi
tutto ritorna in minimi fitti tagli

*

Forse api di gelo in sottili
invisibili sciami dietro nuvole—
Non convinto il ramoscello annuisce

*

Voglie ed auguri malcaduti,
viole del pensiero
sotto occhi ed occhi
           quando maggio nega

*

Il bimbo-grandine, gelido ma
risorgente maggio,

"Hardships but with ears cupped . . ."
"Here I approved the most rapt paper"
"Test on green-test
rich thickest-rain"
"Here where   I thought of thinking
and of grasping   and   unbalancing
                as From a New Height"

Legends

On May's birthday
"You are not omnipotent"
says the pallid little girl

*

Dusts of final, lost
battles between blue and green
where horizons loom over grasses

*

Light voices, feral bees—
everything dreams of other voyages
everything returns in minimal thick cuttings

*

Perhaps icy bees in thin
invisible swarms behind clouds—
Unconvinced the twig nods in assent

*

Desires and wishes badly fallen
wild pansies
under eyes and eyes
                when May negates

*

The infant-hail, chilly but
resurgent May,

«Non sono onnipotente»
batte e ribatte sui tetti

★

«Mai più maggio» dicono
in grigi e blu
segreti insetti grandini segrete

★

Mai mancante neve di metà maggio
chi vuoi salvare?
Chi ti ostini a salvare?

★

Come, perché, il più cupo
maggio del secolo—cento
anni d'oscurità in un mese?

★

Acido spray del tramonto
Acide radici all'orizzonte
Acido: subitamente inventati linguaggi

1985

Stagione delle piogge

16 buiogiugno 199 . . .

«Scusatemi, sono qui ancora
coi miei piedini di gocce come ogni sera»
dice, di soppiatto arrivata
la compulsionale ventata di buiogiugno

★

Tic tic tic, non di più: goccerelle rade
e dolci che stanno arrivando stasera
nella sera di buiogiugno: sgradite

"I am not omnipotent"
it beats and beats again upon the roofs

★

"Never again May" they say
in grays and blues
secret insects secret hails

★

Never missing snow of middle May
who do you want to save?
Who do you insist on saving?

★

How, why, the darkest
May of the century—one hundred
years of darkness in a month?

★

Acid spray of the sunset
Acid roots on the horizon
Acid: immediately invented languages

1985

Season of the Rains

16 gloomyjune 199 . . .

"Excuse me, I'm here again
with my little feet of drops like every evening"
says the compulsional gust of gloomyjune
by stealth arrived

★

Tick tick tick, no more: scattered and sweet little
drops that are arriving this evening
in the gloomyjune evening: unwelcome

Falsa è quella sua gentilezza l'
espressione bambola, tra finte
e tracotanze sottilissime. Taglia corto
        un ultimo far-del-sole.

*

«Sono qui ancora, deh, vi prego, non odiatemi»
fa la prima pioggina del sonno di buiogiugno—
che dietro si trascina
poi tutta una Caina
ogni dì, fino a qui

*

Sia pure in bisbigli, confessa e poi TUONA—
Anche tu, allora,
sprizzi dal vermo reo che il mondo fora?

Tu sai che

    La città dei papaveri
     così concorde e gloriosa
     così di pudori generosa
così limpidamente inimmaginabile
      nel suo crescere,
   così furtiva fino a ieri e così,
  oggi, follemente invasiva . . .

Voi cresciuti in monte su un monticello
   di terra malamente smossa
  ma ora pronta alla vostra voglia rossa
  di farvi in grande-insieme vedere
    insieme notare in pura
     partecipazione e
naturalmente, naturalmente adorare

Che ridere che gentilezze che squisitezze
di squilli e vanti per la sorpresa infusa

*

False is that gentleness of yours the
childish expression, amidst pretence
and the subtlest conceit. Cut short
          a final gleaming-of-the-sun

*

"I'm still here, eh, please don't hate me"
says the first sprinkling of gloomyjune's sleep—
that at the back drags itself
then all a Cain
every day, until here

*

Even if in whispers, it confesses and then THUNDERS—
You too, then,
spray from the evil worm that bores through the world?

You know that

City of poppies
so harmonious and glorious
so overflowing with modesties
so limpidly unimaginable
in its growing,
so secretive till yesterday and
today, so foolishly invasive . . .

You grown in the hills on a hillock
of badly tilled earth
but ready now for your red craving
to craft yourselves in enormous collective seeing
together observing in pure
participation and
naturally, naturally, adoring

What joy what gentleness what exquisiteness
of peals and boasts for the infused surprise

a chi nella notte ottusa
non poté vedervi aggredire-blandire
il monticello che fu le vostre mire!

E sembra che là installati
solo ardiate di sfidare a sangue
per un nanosecondo il niente, ma
deridendoci, noi e voi stessi,
nella nostra corsiva corriva instabilità e
meschina nanosecondità—
sì quel vostro millantarvi
e immillarvi in persiflages
butta tutto ciò che è innominabile
fuori dal colore
del vostro monticello seduttore . . .

Un saluto ora non bizzoso, tutto per voi-noi,
sternuto

(1989)

Altri papaveri

Fieri di una fierezza e foia barbara
sovrabbondanti con ogni petalo
rosso + rosso + rosso + rosso
    coup de dés maledetto
    sanguinose potenze dilaganti,
    quasi ognuno di voi a coprire un prato intero—
da che
da che mondi stragiferi
stragiferi papaveri
    qui vi accampaste avvampando,
    sfacciato forno del rosso
    che in misteriche chiazze
    non cessa di accedere sgorgar su
    straventando i soliti maggi grigioblù?

to those in the dim night who
couldn't see you assail-soothe
the hillock that was your goal!

And it seems that there ensconced
you only burn with daring and blood
nothing for a nanosecond, but
mocking us, us and you,
in our reckless spiraling instability and
scanty nanosecondity—
yes, that boasting and extemporizing
of yours in persiflage
throws all that which is unnamable
out of the color
of your seductive hillock . . .

A salute now not sulky, all for you-us,
sneezed

(1989)

Other Poppies

Proud of a savage pride and lust
superabundant with every petal
red + red + red + red
accursed toss of the dice
bloody powers overflowing
each of you nearly covering an entire field—
from what
from what murderous worlds
murderous poppies
did you encamp here ablaze,
brazen oven of the red
that in mysterious stains
never stops acceding gushing over
blasting the usual gray-blue Mays?

Come i calabroni si fanno sempre più enormi
CRABRO CRABRO
e quasi difformi da ogni destino
e le limacce budella a stravento su verzure:
via! via! è tempo di togliere via questa primavera
di pozze di sangue da tiri di cecchino
Correre correre
coprendosi in affanno teste e braccia e corpi orbi
correre correre per chi
corre e corre sotto calabroni e cecchini
e in orridi papaveri finì

(1993–95)

Currunt

Papaveri ovunque, oggi, ossessivamente essudati,
sudori di sangui di un
assolutamente
eroinizzato   slombato   paesaggio,
sudore spia
di chissà quale irrotta malattia
—mala mala bah bah tempora currunt   bah bah—
                    o stramazzata epilessia
Ora non strati a strati accordati
in fervidi iati o contatti o spartiti
ma fole di confusamente
e no, no, mai
intercettabili da menti   currunt
Prati-sfatte-fucine
    di nuovissime zanzare-tigri
        di zecche-Lyme
            di matrie stuprie
                di patrie rebus-pus
sotto cieli franati nello stupore stesso
        di sé-rottami inani   currunt

Papaveri, chi cerca che?   bah bah

Like the hornets they grow ever more enormous
                CRABRO CRABRO
and almost deformed by every destiny
and slimy viscera blasted upon the verdure:
away! away! it's time to strip away this spring
of puddles of blood from sniper fire
Run run
out of breath covering heads and arms and blind bodies
run run for the one who
runs and runs under the hornets and snipers
and died in horrid poppies

(1993–95)

Currunt

Poppies everywhere, today, obsessively oozed out,
sweatings of bloods of an
absolutely
strung out   exhausted   landscape,
spy sweat
of who knows what invasive illness
—mala mala bah bah tempora currunt   bah bah—
                or slumped epilepsy
Now not layers upon attuned layers
in fervid hiatuses or contacts or scores
but fibs of mental confusion
and no, no, never
interceptable by minds   currunt
Fields-ramshackle-furnaces
    of new-sprung tiger mosquitoes
      of Lyme-ticks
        of mother rapes
          of fatherlands pus-puzzles
under skies collapsed in the selfsame rape
        of inane self-wrecks   currunt

Poppies, who seeks what?   bah bah

Di che, papaveri, esantemi teoremi
      stridii?
            Ii Ii Ii?   bah bah

*

Nessun consuntivo   Papaveri,
mie anime già miriadi e in mille,
siti e situazioni sempre vigili,
o così finemente accorti nel più soave
           appena-esistere

(anni '91–93)

Colle, ala

I

C
Colline, ascendere, faglie—
      certa e dolce umbra mundi,
      ancora spiegata ala mundi
      pur se da avide
           alee
           truccata succhiata
Ascissa—
      già ben tracciata dal palpito
      dell'umbra mundi
      qui dove cielo fu. E anelò
      a non essere. E non ritornò.

★ ★ ★

P
Procedimento?   parto?
Ti proponi, rapina inesplicabile
in tenerezze, inospitate valenze
là-sotto, oltre la sonda—sorti
in ordinate ed ascisse:

What, poppies, poxes theorems
                    screechings?
                         Ii Ii Ii?   bah bah

                              ★

No stocktaking   Poppies,
my souls already myriad and innumerable,
sites and situations ever vigilant
or thus subtly cunning in the gentlest
                              edge-existence

                         ('91–93)

Hill, wing

       I

       H
Hills, ascending, faults—
            certain and gentle earth shadow,
            earth wing re-explained
            even if by avid
                    wings
                    bedecked suckled
Abscissa—
            already well charted from the throb
            of the earth shadow
            here where the sky was. And it encircled
            into non-being. And it won't come back.

                         ★ ★ ★

       S
Shall we continue?   Shall I leave?
You offer yourself, inexplicable theft
with tenderness, unwelcomed valencies
down-under, beyond the probe—fates
in ordinates and abscissae:

garante suadente e pur sempre
sostenutamente lontano
           (VERDE)?

                ★ ★ ★

Luce giusta d'autunno, ridonami
nelle tue diffrangenti prospettive
la mia giustizia che lenti cattive
confinarono al di là della porta

           II
Colle-ala che s'annuncia, che
si propaga e poi forse s'acqueta
           ma-non-mai
Stabilità e pure   indulgere
      a vertigine di echi
agli Arti nostri s'acclaude,
a Tenerezza
           del profondo
           del mai-stato abbandono
S'appone
           largheggiando di sé
           l'Allineato ||
           in più-che-futuro (tense)
E benigno di noi si scorda
a noi dato per accaderci—così—
           o-oink-in
           pronuncia trisecata
           pagina rattratta condomata
               microgrugniti forse?

                               (1988?)

                ★

E ti protendi come silenzio
ti protendi al silenzio,

suasive guarantor and forever
standoffishly distant
        (GREEN)?

★ ★ ★

Precise autumnal light, restore to me
in your diffracting vistas
my justice that rotten lenses
locked up beyond the door

    II

Hill-wing that heralds itself, that
propagates and then perhaps subsides
       but-no-never
Stability and pure   indulging
       whirling echoes
ending aslant our Arts,
Tenderness
       of the depths
       of the never-existed desertion
It adjoins
       lavishing itself
       the Aligned ||
       in more-than-future (tense)
And benign it forgets us
given to us to plunge down—thus—
       o-oink-ing
       trisected pronunciation
       skeletally shrunken page
          microgruntings perhaps?

              (1988?)

★

And you lean out like silence
you lean out into the silence,

generi, sei silenzio,
    SEI CASA
nell'idea stessa, nell'inane
    in-sé dell'idea,
    SEI CROLLO
    e libertà di sprofondati tetti
    e inviolato persistere a denti
    che in te s'intimizzarono
    SEI SCHERZO
e nel verde verdissimo
degli alti nocciòli crollanti pur essi,
se stessi aspergendo, da poggioli,
lieti spettri in trasbordo e in accurate
    accanite voglio di residenza
    e acclamazioni sottovoce   cedi
    SEI SPECOLA
traluci dall'alto una vendita al minuto
di sole e ombre   di punto
in nonpunto, fruscio, dissoluzione
    di meridiane stelle!
    di miriadi, a mazzi, di nocciole!
carole   già-nocciole,
    già-invasioni e abbondanze
e tutte, tutte a San Rocco
        benedizioni!

        (1988?)

—Casa campestre in rovina invasa da arbusti di nocciolo. Le nocciole
giungono a maturazione a San Rocco, in agosto.

Topinambùr

                                      mostruoso
Dato informe e mostruoso   dato informe e mostruoso

Topinambùr tuffi del giallo
atti festivi improvvisi del giallo
gialli brividi baci
        bacilli-braci

you generate, you are silence,
    YOU ARE HOUSE
in the same idea, in the inane
    in-itself of the idea,
    YOU ARE COLLAPSE
    and freedom of fallen roofs
    and inviolate persistence of teeth
    that in you summon themselves
    YOU ARE FOLLY
and in the greenest green
of the tall hazelnuts—they too collapsing
sprinkling themselves, from balconies,
merry specters in transit and in accurate
    assiduous desires of residence
    and acclamations sottovoce   you yield
    YOU ARE OBSERVATORY
you let shine through a retail sale
of sun and shade   in points
and nonpoints, rustling, dissolution
    of midday stars!
    of myriads, in bunches, of hazelnuts!
ring-dances   already-hazelnuts,
    already-invasions and abundances
and all, all at San Roco
        benedictions!

(1988?)

—A rural house, collapsing and invaded by hazelnut shrubs. At San
Rocco hazelnuts reach maturity in August.

Topinambùr

                            monstrous
Amorphous and monstrous fact   amorphous and monstrous fact

Topinambùr divings of yellow
unexpected festive acts of yellow
yellow shivers kisses
    bacilli-blisterings

Difficoltà anche con i nomi
più usuali di
persone, cose, carezze, inflorescenze
schermi

Fallimento di ogni
pointing
out,
at,
up

⋆

Topinambùr
   to to torotorotix
     augellini lilix
       lontani insettini di
       vespificato giallo
       Ur-giallo lilix

memorizzazioni fallite
che scendono a picco nel
nel mai-stato

⋆

Topinambùr abbandonati
qua e là, cari pargoli,
abbandonati in incontri
precari o in infinite assemblee
ma sempre un po' distratti dall'infinito

⋆

O filiazione
forse infida, dicono,
della luce più irta,
provocatori di paroline e bisbigli:
provocare ad appelli ed a fini
rimproveri eh eh
             fin dentro i giardini

⋆

Ma più chiamate a soste o
ad aggiri, a manciate di
dispersioni, ad immortali
(senza per niente essere trionfali)
             addii

Difficulty even with the commonest
names of
persons, things, caressings, inflorescences

screens
                                        Failure of every
          ★
                                        pointing

                                        out,

                                        at,

                                        up
Topinambùr
  to to torotorotix
    augellini lilix
      distant insects of
        waspified yellow
        Ur-yellow lilix   failed memorizations
                                  descending precipitously into the
                                  into the never-been

              ★

Abandoned topinambùr
here and there, dear children,
abandoned in fleeting
meetings or in infinite assemblies
but always a bit distracted by the infinite

              ★

O filiation
perhaps treacherous, they say,
of the fuzziest light,
provokers of sweet talk and whisperings:
provoking appeals and subtle
reproaches eh eh
                    inside the gardens

              ★

But more called to stoppings or
to skirtings, to handfuls of
dispersions, to immortal
(without ever being triumphal)
              farewells

★

O semine semplicissime
o complessive induzioni e scie
poi divergenti
di sottomusici elementi—
Affondi birbi birichini del
giallo di minimi
            temi tempi

★

Da entro i mille circoli
dei topinambùr assidui nunzi
di lunatici autunni
si sfilano le luci
        dai più nascosti vincoli

★

Digressivi discorsi
fratti divieti ad ogni
bella pretesa del giallo—
suggerimenti d'altri autunni
    vellichii d'autunni
        già persi, ritornanti in gialli sorsi

★

Freschissimi risvegli del verde-blu
dopo che le piogge novelle l'addormirono
e che ora si disdaglia e scompiglia
a un raggio, più che di sole, di topinambùr

★

Teneri plagi compiuti
dal verde e dall'azzurro dei prati
sui topinambùr qui sbandati
da chissà dove, chissà prima o mai più

                    (1993)

*

O simplest seeds
or comprehensive inductions and traces
then diverging
of submusical elements—
Lungings scoundrels imps of the
yellow of minimal
                themes times

*

From within the thousand rings
of the assiduous topinambùr messengers
of moody autumns
unravel the lights
        from the most hidden bonds

*

Digressive discourses
fractions forbiddances of every
fine pretense of yellow—
suggestions of other autumns
    tinglings of autumns
    already lost, returning in yellow sips

*

Freshest reawakenings of the green-blue
after the early rains put it to sleep
and that now arises and muddles
a ray, more than of the sun, of topinambùr

*

Tender plagiaries performed
by the green and by the blue of the meadows
upon the topinambùr here scattered
from who knows where, who knows if before or ever again

(1993)

Altri topinambùr

Entro i manipoli qua e là sparsi
dei topinambùr lungo gli argini
ogni lustro del giallo si fa intimo
all'autunnale catarsi

★

Ori di affabili corollari—
topinambùr se è il caso di nominare
una scintillazione che pare casalinga
ed invece è stellare

★

Tamburini topinambùr
euforia di mille
divergenti intuizioni—
gemellaggi infiniti

★

Azzurro arriso dagli incorreggibili
topinambùr mai stanchi di frinire
di titillare, di adire
ai paradisi più facilmente leggibili

★

Favoleggiare di esigue
anarchie, conversioni di lingue
mai udite del giallo
in gelb jaune amarillo

★

Con affettuoso gusto
i furbissimi topinambùr
si affollano al cancello
come a scuola, nel giorno giusto

★

Dove ritroverò le mie infelicità
numerose quanto incontrollabili?—

Other Topinambùr

The patches of topinambùr
scattered here and there along the edges
every glimmer of yellow brings home
the autumnal catharsis

*

Golds of genial corollas—
topinambùr, if it's the case to name
a gleaming that seems homely
and instead is stellar

*

Tambourines topinambùr
euphoria of a thousand
diverging intuitions—
infinite twinnings

*

Smiling blue of the incorrigible
topinambùr never tiring of chirring
of titillating, of accepting
the most easily read paradises

*

Storytelling of scanty
anarchies, conversions of never-heard
tongues of yellow
in gelb jaune amarillo

*

With affectionate taste
the wiliest topinambùr
crowd at the gate
as at school, on the right day

*

Where will I find my sorrows
as numerous as uncontrollable?—

Ma ora coi topinambùr torneranno
attutite dai tocchi di altre deità

Sedi e siti

Sedi del grigiore
sedi delle disfatte vitalbe—
ma non vi è lesinata un po' di luna

★ ★ ★

Volo   del grigiore
    glomi e glomi delle superflue
                superfluenti vitalbe
                tu del superfluo
                e accanito raccogliersi-in-luogo
                        e intensità di luogo, testimone

★ ★ ★

Si accelera e pur s'acqueta
il superfluo del grigiore-vitalbe
così connaturato
a questo—a quello—del
luogo: vizza via d'inflorescenze
o esclamazioni riarse,
il superfluo così connaturato
        all'ispessirsi
        in testimonianze già sparse

★ ★ ★

S'acqueta e acquisisce
strenuo
strenuo stento di prati oltre i prati
fino ai livelli di vitalbe specchiate laggiù

But now with the topinambùr they'll return
appeased by the touch of other deities

Settlements and sites

Settlements of grayness
settlements of tattered clematises—
but you are not skimped a bit of moon

★ ★ ★

Flight   of grayness
     glomera upon glomera of the superfluous
               superfluent clematises
               you of the superfluous
               and relentless gathering-in-place
                    and intensity of place, witness

★ ★ ★

The surplus of grayness-clematises
quickens and yet quietens
thus naturalized
to this—to that—of the
place: withered way of inflorescences
or parched exclamations,
the surplus thus naturalized
     in the thickening
     in the already sparse testimony

★ ★ ★

The strenuous
strenuous hardship of fields beyond meadows
quietens and acquires
as far as the levels of clematises reflected down below

s'assopisce nei limiti limbi il bell'esempio
Ecco aprirsi lo scempio umilissimo

★ ★ ★

Prati e colori
già trapassati
da queste parti, come
da strenua ed arsa farsa
di fantascienza bellamente
ricaduti
con gioierie di vitalbe
e incontenibili soprusi di
  guizzi e vertigini, pensieri vizzi
    ma pur sempre,
       anche nella morte, primaticci!

★ ★ ★

Paese di Balocchi, milioni
di aeri stemmi-diamanti-vitalbe
mai stanche di soffrire, stranirsi, di giocarsi
l'ultimo filo

★ ★ ★

Sede del grigiore—già luogo,
recinzione vaga del superfluo—
ma non ti è lesinato il lucignolo di un verso

Erbe e Manes, Inverni

    Pietà per finiti e infiniti,
    memorie
    forse distorcenti, distorte

the good example dozes off in the limbo-limits
 Here begins the humblest anguish

★ ★ ★

Meadows and colors
already perforated
in these parts, as
by a strenuous and parched farce
of science-fiction beautifully
 backfired
with raptures of clematises
and irrepressible impositions of
   flickerings and vertigos, withered thoughts
      yet always,
         also in death, early-blooming!

★ ★ ★

Country of Playthings, millions
of airy crests-diamonds-clematises
never tired of suffering, worrying, of playing
the last thread

★ ★ ★

Settlement of grayness—already place,
vague fencing in of the surplus—
but you are not skimped the wick of a verse.

Grasses and Manes, Winters

Pity for finites and infinites,
memories
perhaps twisting, twisted

ma che ovunque   ovunque
da voi stesse crescete
e dai vostri intrinseci oblii,
            erbe ed erbe, Manes, nostre sere . . .

Limature d'iridio, fratti quarzi
nel cupo che inverno insuffla,
            ripidi acumi
            fatti fatui   dal viola
            ma pur sempre arrivati a voi stessi
            ad erbe, erbe-Manes . . .

Frivoli Pargoli Manes
zirlìi forse geliferi
grillìi d'elfi-fili
in supplicità mite
            poa pratensis, poa silvestris—
rattratte motilità e
basse frequenze del verde: ecco
già vi si aduna spronando   spronando
sì che in lati obnubilati prati
            consolate   al viola
            consolazioni sottraete   al viola

O là, via per le strette e trash
            poa pratensis, Manes, poa silvestris,
            alla non più inconsutile   veste
            del mondo   al divelto
            provvedereste?   Ttsch, sst, zzt
            Salvereste?

. . . .

but everywhere everywhere
arisen independently
by your intrinsic oblivions,
        grasses amid grasses, Manes, our evenings . . .

Iridium filings, crushed quartz
in winter's infused darkness,
        precipitous acumens
        made fatuous   by violet
        and yet always carried to you
        to grasses, grasses-Manes . . .

Trifling Tiny Manes
whistlings perhaps chilly
chirpings of elf-threads
in mild supplication
        poa pratensis, poa silvestris—
shrunken motility and
low frequencies of the green: here
it already gathers spurring   spurring
even in vast befogged fields
        consoled   to violet
        consolations you dislodge   from violet

O there, away through the narrows and trash
        poa pratensis, Manes, poa silvestris,
        would you care for the no longer seamless
        garment
        of the world   would you nurture
        the uprooted?   Ttsch, sst, zzt
        Would you save them?

. . . .

da Sovrimpressioni

---

from Superimpressions
[2001]

Verso i palù

o Val Bone
minacciati di estinzione

I

"Sono luoghi freddi, vergini, che
allontanano
la mano dell'uomo"—dice un uomo
triste; eppure egli è assorti, assunto in essi.
Intrecci d'acque e desideri
d'arborescenze pure,
dòmino di misteri
cadenti consecutivamente in se stessi
attirati nel folto del finire
senza fine, senza fine avventure.

II

Scioglilingua per ogni
specie dei verdi, sogni
d'acque ben circuite e circuenti
con altezze d'inflorescenze
leggere fin quasi all'invisibile—
verdi intenti a conoscenze
impossibili, ventilate
dalle raggiere radianze dell'estate.

III

Specchi del Lete
qui riposanti in se stessi
tra mille fratelli e sorelle,
specchi del verde
ad accoglierli attenti
fino a disfarsi in scintille
a crescere in cerchi d'arborescenze
per tocchi
di venti,
di trepidi occhi.

—Pan,
dove sei?
—Sì.

Towards the Palù
or Val Bone
threatened with extinction

I

"They're cold, virginal places, that
keep away
the hand of man"—says a sad
man; or else he is lost, absorbed in them.
Intertwinings of water and desires
of pure arborescences,
domino of mysteries
fallen consecutively into themselves
drawn into the thick of the end
without end, adventure without end.

II

Tongue-twister for every
type of plant, dream
of waters well circulated and circulating
with heights of inflorescences
weightless almost to invisibility —
greens intent on impossible
understandings, fanned
by the radiant sunbursts of summer.

III

Mirrors of Lethe
here resting in themselves
amidst thousands of brothers and sisters,
mirrors of green
gathering them attentive
till they come apart in circles of arborescences
for the touching
of winds,
of anxious eyes.

—Pan,
where are you?
—Yes.

Fulgore e fumo, più che palustre
verde,
acqua nel verde persino frigida,
fa ch'io t'interroghi
ripetutamente, perché
nel tuo silenzio si aggira letizia.

"*Verso i Palù*" per altre vie

Nei più nascosti recinti dell'acqua il ramo
il vero ramo arriva protendendosi
sempre più verde del suo non-arrivare

★

Proteggi dall'astuzia soave dei tralci
dissuffla dall'ordine denso delle biade
                    delle loro verdissimi spade
in cui si taglia e s'intaglia l'estate

★

Voi molli onnipresenze
e folla di sorprese
fittissimamente conversate—
                    sempre crescenti intese

★

Mosaici di luci specchiate speculate
sottrazioni di luci tracimate
acque immillanti
per prati ed accerchiati incanti

★

Ardui cammini del verde
sul filo di infinite inesistenze—
un ultimo raggio li perseguita

Radiance and vapor, more than marshy
green,
water in the green, even frigid,
makes me question you
again and again, because
in your silence wanders delight.

"Towards the Palù" along other paths

In the most hidden enclosures of water the branch
the true branch arrives extending outward
always greener in its non-arrival

★

You protect from the gentle astuteness of shoots
you emanate from the dense order of the fodder
of their deep green blades
in which the summer cuts and carves

★

You, soft omnipresences
and crowd of surprises
thickly you converse—
always growing understandings

★

Mosaics of mirroring mirrored lights
subtraction of overflowing lights
glimmering waters
amidst meadows and encircled enchantments

★

Arduous walks in the green
on the thread of infinite inexistencies—
a last ray pursues them

da Ligonàs

II

No, tu non mi hai mai tradito, [~~paesaggio~~]
su te ho
riversato tutto ciò che tu
infinito assente, infinito accoglimento
non puoi avere: il nero del fato/nuvola
avversa o della colpa, del gorgo implosivo.
Tu che stemperi in quinte/silenzi indifferenti
e pur tanto attinenti, dirimenti
l'idea stessa di trauma—
tu restio all'ultima umana
cupidità di disgregazione e torsione
tu forse ormai scheletro con pochi brandelli
ma che un raggio di sole basta a far rinvenire,
continui a darmi famiglia
     con le tue famiglie di colori
     e d'ombre quete ma
     pur mosse-da-quiete,
     tu dài, distribuisci con dolcezza
     e con lene distrazione il bene
     dell'identità, dell' "io", che perenne-
     mente poi torna, tessendo
     infinite autoconciliazioni: da te, per te, in te.

     . . . .

Tu mal noto, sempre a te davanti come stralucido schermo,
o dietro sfogliato in milioni di fogli,
mai camminato
quanto pur si desidera, da ben prima del nascere:
     ma perché
     furiosa-dispotica-inane
     l'ombra del disamore
     della disidentificazione
     s'imporrebbe qui nei giri, strati e
     salti, nelle tue dolci tane?
Ma no. Con frementi tormente di petali di meli

from Ligonàs

II

Ligonàs

No, you have never betrayed me, [~~landscape~~]
upon you I have
poured back all that which you—
infinite absentee, infinite acceptee—
cannot have: the gloom of destiny/inimical
clouds or guilt, the implosive vortex.
You who dissolve the idea itself of trauma
into fifths/indifferent yet pertinent,
nullifying silences—
you resistant to the final act
of disintigrative and twisted human cupidity
you perhaps by now skeletal with few tatters
but you who need only a sunbeam to revive,
continue to give me family
    with your families of colors
    and silent shadows yet
    movements-from-silence,
    you give, distribute with gentleness
    and with mild distraction the decency
    of identity, of the "I", that perenni-
    ally returns, weaving
    infinite autoconciliations: by you, for you, in you.

   . . . .

Notorious you, always ahead like a superlucid screen,
or behind scattered in millions of leaves,
never sauntered
much as one wants, from well before birth:
    but why
    furious-despotic-inane
    would the shadow of estrangement
    of misidentification
    impose itself here amid your rounds, layers and
    leapings, within your mild dens?
But no. With quivering blizzards of blossoms of apple

e di ciliegi con rapide rapide nubi di petali e baci
tu mi hai ieri, ieri? accarezzato?
Gremite assenze, ombre grementi alle spalle
di quanto fu e sarà,
petali petali amatamente dissolti
nelle alte dilavate erbe—e laggiù tra i meli
stralunati presagi di sera . . .
In petali, piogge pure, lune sottili
dacci secondo i nostri meriti
pochi ma come immensi,
dà che solo in mitezza per te mi pensi
e in reciproco scambio di sonni amori e sensi
da questa gran casa LIGONÀS
dalle sue finestrelle-occhi all'orlo del nulla
io ti individui per sempre e in te mi assuma.

da *Sere del dì di festa*

1

(È un puro autosufficiente luogo letterario
è una purezza che non chiede avalli
è un avallo ad un'acme dello stesso richiedere
È dèi / in avvento / in fuga / in disguido /
                    in eterno ritorno al nido)

Tutti gli dèi del 31 gennaio
si sono qui in un attimo affollati
qui nelle estreme
luci, strascichi, forze del 31 gennaio—
gli dèi e ciò che è ostile agli dèi
Noi non-dèi c'intagliamo
a questi diktat leggi ed eserciti
          di beltà invincibilmente candide
          attonite a sé
          da se stesse distratte
          traenti doni di inenarrabilità nel narrare
          tutta la loro ridesta
          fragranza doglia e voglia di sera-festa

and cherry trees with swift swift clouds of petals and kisses
yesterday you, yesterday? caressed me?
Crowded absences, shadows crowding in at my shoulders
inasmuch as you were and will be,
petals petals lovingly dissolved
in the tall ashen grass—and down there amid the apple trees
gaping intimations of evening . . .
In petals give us, according to our merits,
pure rains, slender moons
few but how immense,
give so that only in mildness for you I conceive of myself
and in mutual exchange of drowsings lovings and sensings
from this great tavern LIGONÀS
from its window-eyes on the edge of the void
I forever recognize you and gather you into myself.

from *Evenings of the festival day*

1

(It's a pure and self-sufficient literary place
it's a purity that doesn't ask for guarantees
it's a guarantee at an acme of the same insistence
It's gods/in arrival/in escape/in a hitch/
                    in eternal return to the nest)

All of the gods of January 31st
are here in a moment crowded
here in the extreme
lights, draggings, forces of January 31st—
the gods and that which is hostile to the gods
We non-gods carve ourselves
with these diktats laws and hosts
            of beauties invincibly candid
            astonished at themselves
            by themselves distracted
            pulling gifts of inexpressibility in narrating
            all of their reawakened
            fragrance pain and will of evening-festival

A tutti gli dèi del 31 di questo 31:
alligna un gesto unanime
da essi inseparabile,
    scatti / scarti / fronti
    assestamenti in monti
    per un'eternità che si chiama
    a shock a sbalzi, peso nitido, brama
    lustro e violenza del 31 gennaio

Dall'apice del 31, di gennaio, festa-sera
  mi lascio vendere, macellare, distribuire
    mi lascio, glorioso, scaltro, rinascere
      mi lascio singolmente, ciecamente, altrimenti,
      deflettere, ripensare, ritrattare

TUTTO SI APRE A SBARAGLIO   di luci-lotte
  rupi di glacialità si varano da sé esaltate:
    ovunque, senza riparo, senza stasi-tregua
    dolcissima durissima voluttà epifanica
      emarginante—corri corri—o già essa è margine
      con noi   marginali non magnanimi distimici tipi,
      ma forse, un poco,
        soffiati in infilate nivali di fati

    2

31-1: sera che non è sera di nulla,
      non v'è nulla, nel suo tutto, che si chiami sera.

    Sera che scende da se stessa come
      purissima immemore autoctonia del gelo.

    Sera che è festa di tratti unicizzanti
      hàpax di unicità qui implicate
      per orrore errore splendore 31-1, e poi
      dannata euforia di guerriglie del gelo.

    Sera del dì di festa: e ogni vana, infine,
      voluttà in lei ristagna
      e poi rimbalza e scivola
      e ogni grido-bisbiglio precipita

To all the gods of the 31st of this 31st:
a unanimous gesture takes root
from them inseparable,
        lurchings / swervings / frontings
        subsidences in mountains
        for an eternity that calls itself
        in shocks in fits, clear weight, craving
        luster and violence of January 31st

From the apex of the 31st, of January, festival-evening
  I leave myself to sell, to butcher, to distribute
  I leave myself, glorious, cunning, to be born again
  I leave myself singularly, blindly, otherwise,
      to deflect, to rethink, to reprocess

EVERYTHING OPENS IN DEFEAT   of wrestling lights
  glaciated crags run aground by themselves exalted:
    everywhere, without shelter, without stasis-break
    gentlest hardest epiphanic rapture
      marginalizing—hustle and bustle—or it is already the margin
        with us   marginal not magnanimous dysthymic types,
        but maybe, a bit,
            blown through intertwined snowfields of fates

    2

1-31: evening that isn't evening at all,
        that isn't anything, in its everything, that calls itself evening.

    Evening that descends by itself like
        the purest oblivious autochthony of the frost.

    Evening that's a festival of singularizing tracts
        hapax of singularity here implicated
        by horror error splendor 1-31, and then
        condemned euphoria of the frost's guerilla-warfare.

    Evening of the festival day: and every vain, eventually,
        rapture stagnates in it
        and then rebounds and slides
        and every shout-whisper plunges down

in luce umana scavata dentro vetri
in cui Beltà chances frammenti già ipèrmetri
sotto ogni grado zero
sotto la cuspide 31-1
vibrano allùcinano.

Sera che non vuole, anche se onnipotente,
   che abbandonaaccantona futuro e passato
   e pur nega il presente   ma
   sera che non tradisce, sparge
   duri perdoni, durissime consolazioni,
   lacrime gloriosamente
             folli-fossili.

Sera, immensa ti fai di suoni nani
   di tossici juke-box
   che nessuno mai rinvenne, udì, sostenne;
31-1, domenica, sera del dì di festa
   passione ghiacciooscura
   nota e maisempre ignota,
   sera fuori figura   sutura.

da Adempte mihi
(da Tonin)

II

Sopra i colli di Este   (Da Marco)

Forse movendo in poco lembo di spazi
ad altre terre in
      questo soffocante dover essere,
      situarmi nel futuro non tuo
      sempre più al largo o all'addiaccio—
fratello, oggi col piede rivolto a più
soleggiati e scabri colli che i nostri
proni da sempre ai diluvi,
tra olivi con stupore, entrambi ombre, ci rinveniamo
      individuiamo altre, altre svolte,

in human light excavated inside glass
in which Beauty chances fragments already hypermetrical
below every zero degrees
below the cusp 1-31
vibrate dazzle.

Evening that doesn't want, even if omnipotent,
　　that abandonsforegoes future and past
　　and yet negates the present　　　but
　　evening that doesn't betray, scatter
　　harsh pardons, very harsh consolations,
　　tears gloriously
　　　　　　　　　　foolish-fossils.

Evening, immense you become with dwarf sounds
　　of toxic jukeboxes
　　that no one ever revived, heard, sustained;
1-31, Sunday, evening of the festival day
　　ice-darkened passion
　　known and neveralways unknown,
　　evening outside figure　　　　　suture.

　　　　　　　　　　　　　　da Adempte mihi
　　　　　　　　　　　　　　　(at Tonin)

　II

On the hills of Este　　　　　　　　　　　　　(At Marco's)

Perhaps moving in narrow margins of spaces
over other lands in
　　　　this suffocating needing to be,
　　　　to situate myself in a future not yours
　　　　ever more distant or out in the open—
brother, today with feet turned towards
hills sunnier and rougher than ours
forever prone to flooding,
amid olive trees in amazement, both shadows, we revive ourselves
　　　　we recognize other, other crossroads,

tra sulfurei, sepolti dèi
disseminati in frotte,
tra erose ma pur delicate
pervadenze e insinuazioni del verde,
tra seriche stasi e secche, tra sorreggenti veri?

Ed è tutto un confabulio-saltellio di
paesaggi nel modesto, non distimico, per un attimo,   aprile
dal nostro sogno ad occhi bene allenati sgranato—
Ed è tutto un brusire di incinerati fuochi / paesaggi
"A noi venite"   "non importa"
"non fa nulla"   di limite in tramite discorrenti—
ma di voi sepolte / insepolte
                              tracce o mappe di furie
è giusto questo rincorrersi nel futuro?

Il caro fratello ed io senza dire affermiamo, affermiamo
e acconsentiamo al fiorire febbrile dei dossi
pur se in lingue   tra loro orribilmente ignare
"Deh paesaggi"   "Non importa"   "Non fa nulla"
La stradina verso mai narrati olivi ci guida, no ci disperde
"Quali, quali"   "Sì venite"   "Non fa nulla"
            (ansimiamo a cancellare a riprendere cose a volo
            a mettere in serbo a disacconsentire a
            far incrociare come stecchini o ad immettere
            come in giri di vitree palline
                              i nostri cammini-destini)

                    1993–1995

da *A Faèn*

Luogo preso in parola, luogo ossitono,
Faèn come punto-abbondanza
        di rivalsa e raccolta di fieno, di interi
        monti e mondi risolti
        dissolti o affastellati in un

amid sulphurous, buried gods
scattered in swarms,
amid eroded yet delicate
permeations and insinuations of the green,
amid silken stases and shoals, amid sustaining truths?

And it's all a confabulatory leaping of
landscapes in humble, not dysthymic, for a moment,   April
of our dream to well trained eyes crumbled—
And it's all a buzzing of fires/landscapes reduced to ash
"Come to us"   "it doesn't matter"
"it's alright"   discontinuous from edge to path—
but for you who are buried/unburied
traces or charts of frenzies
is this chasing after one another fair?

My dear brother and I without speaking affirm, affirm
and consent to the feverish flowering of the summits
even if in tongues   mutually hideously incomprehensible
"Ah landscapes" "It doesn't matter" "It's alright"
The little road to never-narrated olive trees guides us, no it scatters us
"Which, which" "Yes, come" "It's alright"
(gasping to undo to take another shot at fleeting things
to put in reserve to take back our assent to
make intersect like little sticks or to allow
like the spinning of vitreous globules
our pathways-destinies)

1993–1995

From *At Faèn*

Place taken at its word, oxytone place,
Faèn as plentitude-point
of reward and hay harvest, of entire
mountains and worlds unraveled
and dissolved or jumbled in an

interminato pluviale di fieno,
ghiotta edibilità, latte futuro

Quei monti-mostri come l'Erbanera
nati e cresciuti nel proprio nome
    esteso come un'era
monti di fieni come immani risorse incontabili
    incontrollabili inarrivabili, perfino ingiuste
Esempio e pratica fino allo horror
di liberazioni, di abolizioni, di metamorfosi
mote-immote, sopraffazioni
    di obliterate-riscattate stagioni
Non esiste botanica, né bisogno di botanica
    è essa atona a questi fieni
    e a tutto il vegetabile ogni idea di botanica;
    essa allontana la vostra—per così dire—
    quidditas, giacimenti fienali
    essa vi sbanca sfrana in grate
                in grinfie in diverticoli

. . . .

Ah sotto l'ombra di
    cieli allergizzanti se stessi e tutte le cavità terrene—
        trappole per alti venti e nubi,
        rimarginarsi sempre all'erta, fieni di Faèn
        contro   falci e scarti, sassi, stecchi
        luoghi-omasi dell'insistere del costringere
        del sovrastare fino al compattarsi tra voce e mutezza
            rigurgurigitogito rumirumnazioni a gogò
                spasimi, singhiozzi in glosse, tosi, talvolta falò

. . . .

[. . .]

endless downpour of hay,
tempting edibility, future milk

Those monster-mountains such as Erbanera
their names kernals of birth and growth
   expansive as epochs
mountains of hay like immense uncountable uncontrollable
   unattainable even unjust resources
Example and practice up to the horror
   of liberations, abolitions, mobile-immobile
metamorphoses, browbeating
   of obliterated-liberated seasons
Neither botany exists, nor the need for botany
     every botanic idea is atonic to these hayfields
     and to all that which vegetates,
     estranging your—so to speak—
     quiddities, hayloft deposits
     bankrupting collapsing you in gratings
                 in clutches in asylums

. . . .

Ah in the shadow of
   allergizing skies themselves and all the terrestrial cavities—
     snares for high winds and clouds,
       healing always on the alert, hayfields of Faèn
       for   scythes and scraps, stones, sticks
       omasum-places of insisting of compelling
       of overshadowing till being compacted amidst voice and muteness
           regurgurgitagitation rumiruminations galore
               spasms, hiccups in glosses, coughings, sometimes a
               bonfire

. . . .

[. . .]

Riletture di topinambùr

Mille burle   e saggezze in cui
svanisce ogni furto o trucco
desofisticarsi di ogni giallo
di lunazioni, in altri bui

★

Spargete tutt'intorno
semi incerti a manciate,
fogliole o petali, cose vostre
trapassate   subito riacciuffate

★

I topinambùr feriti
da una vampata solare
per oscillazioni del ciclo di Bethe (?¿) (meglio forse del ciclo di Hauser)
hanno smarrito foltezza fortezza quiete

★

Quale mai senso ebbe il donativo
se nessuna eco l'accolse
e solo il dubbio dovunque s'appose?
Ma ora voi, sì, favi di luce soavi . . .

★

Esitare, abdicare di laringi, gole—
mancano all'appuntamento
oggi i topinambùr, pur se il loro concento
      rilancerà domani istorie e fole

★

O voi bene affidati,
solerti nel servirci di giallori rari
sul ciglio d'incerti affiati,
      di fallibili itinerari

★

Cieli di azzurro appena allattato
per topinambùr in drappello

Rereadings of Topinambùr

A thousand jests   and wisdoms in which
every theft or gimmick vanishes
desophistication of every lunation's
yellowing, in other shadows

*

You scatter all around
handfuls of uncertain seeds,
leaflets or petals, your possessions
slipped away   reseized at once

*

The topinambùr wounded
by a solar flurry
by oscillations of Bethe's cycle (?¿) (better perhaps than Hauser's cycle)
have lost thickness quiet strength

*

Whatever sense had the gift
if no echo received it
and only doubt everywhere emanated?
But now you, yes, honeycombs of gentle light . . .

*

Hesitating, abdicating of larynxes, throats—
the topinambùr today
missed their appointment, even if their harmony
        will tomorrow relaunch stories and fables

*

O you well entrusted,
diligent in proffering us rare shades of yellow
on the edge of uncertain amities,
        of fallible itineraries

*

Skies of azure just milked
for platoons of topinambùr

a sorvegliare dal cancello
se e come mi senta amato

*

Portate alla più aggrediente evidenza
il vostro sapere per caso-assonanza-baldanza
ciò che mai viene dato per scienza

*

Tribù di signorini
o eroi o dèi strette in bonsai
topinambùr, irreggibile
trapungere dell'autunno

*

Con voi partirò, topinambùr
per meditazioni invisibili, acri,
su autunnali tranelli o avalli
su adynatal su mai

(1994–96)

Fora par al Furlàn

e ora—forse—mai—
sei nel farsi e disfarsi
di prati pensieri spini arsi
d'azzurro, attimo ad attimo,
dai piani a montani primordi
Non c'è nulla che valga
ad esaurire questa inimmaginabile
vibratilità
né mano che entri decidendo
un senso ultimativo
— come a un fossile film—alla tua vita

o Benandante

watching from the gate for
if and how I feel loved

★

You expose to the bones
your knowing by chance-assonance-assurance
that which for science is never a given

★

Tribes of little lords
or heroes or gods clasped in bonsai
topinambùr, uncontrollable
prickling of autumn

★

With you I'll depart, topinambùr
for invisible, bitter meditations,
on autumnal snares or surities
            on adynatal on nevermore

(1994–96)

Traversing Friuli

and now—perhaps—never—
you're in the making and unmaking
of sun-baked meadows thoughts thorns
    of the azure, moment to moment,
        from the plains to primordial peaks
There's nothing that's worth
exhausting this unimaginable
            vibratility
no hand that arises giving
an ultimate meaning
— as if in a fossil film—to your life

o Benandante

Quasi a tentoni e semiorbi ma quasi
lieti incrociamo di già
gli argentini grovigli dei tuoi percorsi
verso altri raccolti
    altri   elementi

. . . .

(gennaio '92)

L'altra stagione

Dov'è sparita, o finalmente
essa è vera nel suo sparire, nel suo nuovo look,
nel suo essersi fatta esodo senza lacrime?
Ssst di echi di mille nulle cose
       guscio o coffin di inaudibili addii
       ma non è proprio così   il suo puro esser qui?

      In questi siti di noncuranza pallida
      in questo strappo già avvenuto
      in cui nessun futuro simula,
      in questa oh amabile oh cara esanimità
      non è forse la raggiunta acme / difformità?

. . . .

      Forse lungi brillarono mine di
      rifioriture choc, staffilate di refoli / virus
      e a terra imputridite lame o scorticate crepe
      contro ogni calendario si affastellarono
      o lasciarono fondere
      in spalmatili creme dai colori di Taide
      e in altri laidi colorini che
      in sé con sé s'incollano e satollano, ma

      Solo un
      vuoto vuoto vuoto

Almost scrabbling and semi-bereft but almost
elated we already traverse
the silvery snarls of your wanderings
towards other harvests
    other   elements

. . . .

(January '92)

The other season

Where did it vanish, or at long last
is it true in its vanishing, in its new look,
in its transformation into a tearless exodus?
Ssst of echoes of a thousand nullified things
        shell or coffin of inaudible goodbyes
        but isn't it just like this   its pure being here?

           In these sites of pallid nonchalance
           in this stripping away already transpired
           in which no future feigns,
           in this so lovely so dear lifelessness
           isn't there perhaps the achieved acme / dissimilarity?

. . . .

           Perhaps distant bombs exploded with
           shocking reflorescences, afflicted with gusts / viruses
           and on earth, putrid swamps or excoriated crevices
           snarled themselves against every calendar
           or split apart to melt
           in spreadable creams in the colors of Taide
           and other dingy colors
           clinging to and within themselves satiating
               themselves, but

           Will a mere
           void void void

d'occhio   ci saprà accogliere
nel suo posthiroshima remoto?

*Incerti frammenti, anni '90
(variante)*

Per altri venti, fuori rosa

"Sorvoleremo insieme il firmamento
dove le stelle brilleranno a cento" e poi
precipiteremo dagli alti strabiliamenti
in annuvolamenti sbilenchi
a trascinarci a sfilacciarci
in mille e mille dissipazioni?

O finiremo, consustanziale sangue,
disseccati in mappe
in indizi per i meteosat
                    persi sull'orlo di ignizioni?

O saremo, soltanto,
insieme a mugghiarci addosso
stipati nel manufatto mostro:
non-uomo non-natura, in fondo al fosso

                    Tohu e Bohu?

Dirti "natura"

Che grande fu
        poterti chiamare Natura—
            ultima, ultime letture
                in chiave di natura,
                    su ciò che fu detto natura
                        e di cui sparì il nome
                            natura che poté aver nome e nomi

of the eyes   suffice to welcome us
to its remote post-Hiroshima?

Uncertain fragments, 1990s
(variant)

Amid Other Winds, out of the Lineup

"Will we soar together over the firmament
where the stars shine in the hundreds" and then
plunge headlong from the lofty wonders
in cock-eyed darkenings
to drag ourselves unraveling
in thousands upon thousands of dissipations?

Or will we end up, coessential blood,
dissected in maps
in weather-satellite tracings
                          lost on the edge of ignition?

Or will we only,
enveloped by our howlings,
be stuffed into the manufactured monster:
not-man not-nature, in the bottom of the pit

                    Tohu and Bohu?

To call you "nature"

How grand it was
    to be able to call you Nature—
        final, last readings
            in the key of nature,
                on that which was called nature
                    whose name vanished
                        nature that could have names upon names

che fu folla di nomi in un sol nome
che non era nome

Al labbro vieni mia ultima, sfinita goccia di
possibilità di
dirti natura—
non hai promesso né ingannato, perché
mai fu natura—
mai fu—ma vieni
gocciola o lacrima scaturisci
dal labbro-natura
tu pura impura
pertinenza dis-pertinenza
di nomenclatura
ardente e vana
spenta e sacramentana
tu sbagliata lettura

ora travolta in visura di loschi affari
fatta da bulbi oculari
incendiati
dal re di denari

Visura

Il mondo è puro dispetto
è puro dispetto a se stesso
non è oggi né ieri né domani
è un "mai" stizzoso
stizzito stinto sterpo
che non riesce, ma forse
fuoresce a irretire
un suo intimo
de-definire,
sdefinirsi da sé
da me da ogni una
delle ubique oblique
ubiquità

that was myriad names within a single name
that was no name

To my lips comes the last, exhausted drop of
possibility of
calling you nature—
you neither promised nor deceived, because
you never were nature—
you never were—but emerge
as a tear or drop that seeps
from the nature-lip
pure impure you
relevance ir-relevance
of nomenclature
burning and vain
spent and sacrilized
you, mistaken reading

crushed now in the clutches of shady affairs
crafted by eyes
aglow
with the master of money

Inspection

The world is pure spite
pure spite at itself
it's not today nor yesterday nor tomorrow
but a peevish "never"
a vexed pallid twig
that though stunted perhaps
seeps out to ensnare
a secret
de-defining,
undefining of itself
of myself of each
of the ubiquitous oblique
ubiquities

Il mondo è l'altissimo o il bassissimo
che si fa scritta incisa su una stenta panchina
è il capoverso che spezza tutto l'esclamare ESCLAMARE
qui dentro qui fuori diffuso—
    il falso dire, udire, ardire
    trafigge e frigge in ire
    di arsi e tesi sconnesse
    tutte le sue vecchie scommesse

ma
forse
indizi-tizzi-fumi
di sue nuove convulsioni-stazioni
propone in uno scemo
memo
freddo e freddura che vedilà s'espande
e affiora e figlia
ancora in mille autismi, o se si vuole, trismi.

Kēpos

Qual è, dimmi, il tuo più riposto kēpos,
l'orto in cui divini
brillano in rari scintillii, rare ombricole
i tuoi *semplici*
che nessuno ha mai
immaginato abbastanza . . .
Non indagabili nella loro essenza
nella loro radente carezza-eleganza
nel loro alitare
    col Tutto tra dolci-brevi salvezze
    oscillare fino in fondo alle pozze più amare?
O era il tuo kēpos, Matrità remota

    . . . .

quella dispersa aiola di spine
implacabili bacche rosse
come fuoco che mai s'estingua

The world is the highest or the lowest
that becomes scribblings incisions on a rickety bench
it's the paragraph that splits everything exclaiming EXCLAIMING
here within scattered here without—
> to say, to hear, to dare falsehood
> it furiously pierces and sears
> all its old wagers
> with disjointed arses and theses

but
perhaps
traces-embers-smolderings
of its new convulsions-positions
suggest in a senseless
memo
frigid weather that beyond sight's margins expands
and emerges and continues to spawn
in thousands of autisms, or if you like, jaw-clenchings.

Kēpos

What is, tell me, your most secluded kēpos,
the garden in which
your divine healing herbs
gleam in slender glints, slender shadowy flickerings
herbs that no one ever
imagined enough . . .
Inscrutable in their essence
in their delicate-dear elegant caress
in their breathing
> with the All among gentle-ephemeral reprieves
> oscillating to the depths of the bitterest pools?
O was it your kēpos, distant Materniality

. . . .

that scattered flowerbed of implacable
thorns and berries
red as undying fire

nell'estremo del dire   del sentire
            sentinella ferita?
Giardini-diamanti
giardini-fonti
loci amoeni
        cui non riguardano i nostri veleni—
        loci a cui vanamente mi protendo
        ceu fumus in aëra anelando?

. . . .

Topinambùr e sole

Oggi il sole è bravo e giusto
è tornato un po' indietro
ed è là che guarda col gusto
di guardar da vicino,
senza farli appassire, i suoi figliolini
topinambùr—

ed essi davvero ne combinano, storie,
inventando tipi e raggiere di giallo e dovunque
mostrandosi con innocente sfacciata semplicità
che è dell'apparire e poi rapido sparire:
ma intanto oggi sono qua e sono là
sotto l'occhio benevolo di papà
e perfino oltre l'aia cent'anni fa
sulla concimaia   cinquant'anni fa
sbandierano carezze e cristalli gialli
                disponibili a sazietà
                fin nell'estrema delle valli   chissà.

—   "Su, venite anche con me
        all'osteria, a prendere un caffè."

348

at the extreme of saying   of hearing
         wounded sentry?
Diamond-gardens
fountain-gardens
loci amoeni
     untouched by our poisons—
     loci towards which gasping I vainly reach
     ceu fumus in aëra?

. . . .

Topinambùr and Sun

Today the sun is bold and befitting
arisen a little late
and watching with the zeal
of watching from up close,
without withering them, its little children
the topinambùr—

they truly stir up stories, inventing
shades and fannings of yellow everywhere
popping up with an impudent innocent
appearing-swiftly-disappearing simplicity:
but today they're here and there
under papa's benevolent eye
and even beyond the farmyard a hundred years ago
on the muckheap   fifty years ago
waving caresses and yellow crystals
        inclined to satiety
           as far as the farthest reaches of the valleys   who
            knows.

—   "Come on, come with me
       to the bar for a coffee."

New Poems

lievissime rotelle del 2000
come si pattina bene su di voi—
è vero che tutto è come prima
però che oliato scorrere
di giorni incastonati di rotelle
che sono freschi nel dare le più belle
invenzioni// 2-2-2000 che delizia
che letizia di vedere e non vedere,
di scender dentro mente e uscir di mente,
il significante ha guidato l'utente
l'ha pilotato in begli scioglilingua
sciogli niente.

Al "monte" Villa

Mai non vien meno mai quel
cupo importi sottraendo verde
per eccesso di verde, in ostinante gare
con altri rilievi
eterni raggelati foschi
    nella cupezza d'un agosto da buttare.
Riconosco i tuoi, che non son mai tradimenti,
ma carboni possenti di amore
di uno stridere che i silenzi intorba:
e vien sera da sera, come lumen de lumine,
vien cecità dalla tua fame-orba
di esistere, t'inghippi e plachi in soffocati
accenni   poi
alluvialmente aperti in grembi   lembi

Ma qui, sull'inferriata nera
dove si autogenera un'altra era,
dolcemente arriva un   soffio
di forti fiori che nome non vogliono—
               continuità
ancor più nere bilanciando, e insieme
sbilanciandole in folli "chissà."

well-nigh weightless wheels of 2000
how easily one glides over you—
it's true that everything's as it was
and yet what a greased pouring forth
of wheel-studded days
brisk in the generating of beautiful
inventions// 2-2-2000 what delight
what joy of seeing and not seeing,
of diving into the mind and leaving it behind,
the signifier has guided and piloted
the user in dazzling tongue-twisters
nothing-twisters.

At "mount" Villa

That dark enveloping of you never fades,
sucking green from superabundant green,
in stubborn contests
with other hills
eternal frozen murky
    in the gloom of a throw-away August.
I recognize your heights, that are never betrayals,
but powerful loving coals
of a rasping that muddies the silences:
and evening comes from evening, as light from lights,
blindness from your blind hunger
for existing, you deceive and appease yourself in stifled
inklings   then
alluvially open in laps   limbs

But here, on the black railing
where another era autogenerates,
a gust gently   blows in
of fragrant flowers that don't want a name—
                balancing
even blacker continuities, and together
unbalancing them in demented "maybes."

CASA pericolante

(Giù, lungo la stradella nella forra
con viva corrente)

CASA pericolante
cucita e ricucita con tiranti
onnidirezionali e con denti-zeppe
di ferrolegno, ma soprattutto
madre di una mutante finestra vuota,
ma affamata del nulla
e fatta di sostanza pura rivolta al fuori—
Ah casa, gentilissima e dura d'animo a un tempo
gelosa dei tuoi resti ampi d'intonaco
grondanti e gaudenti di scritte obsolete
(il primo Vasco Rossi) (erotici richiami con
nome e cognome e i più recenti col K dei ragazzini),
tu, tempi sovrapposti e collegati appunto
da quanto si possa immaginare di mezzi
intimi della razza degli stecchi forti come spiedi
e soprattutto da voluttà di abitar là,
di sentirsi, abitandovi, co-desideranti rammendi
connessi non v'è dubbio, all'eterno ||
    CASA, pericola in avanti
    o indietro o da tutti i lati e tetti e scoraggia
    chi pensa tu non possa ulteriormente pericolare
    inventa incroci calettature, incastronerie di
    materie che il tempo diversamente inebriò, disorientò,
    fece quasi svenire-svanire
    ubicò, traslocò in niente e in tutto
    rassodò fino a farli terribilmente gioire
    o soffrir lutto.

Ora, superba sei anche di LAPIDE, fissata nel punto
che non può non apparire il più giusto
e ti consacra come   CASA PERICOLANTE
agli occhi del passante
che ben ti conosce come tipo d'infinito
o non ti conosce, e certo chi non seppe com'eri

Unstable HOUSE

(Down along the little lane in the
stream-lined ravine)

unstable HOUSE
sewn and resewn with omnidirectional
tie-rods and ironwood
chock-teeth, but above all
mother of a mutant window, empty
but hungry for nothing
and made of pure substance facing outward–
Ah house, simultaneously kind- and hard-hearted
jealous of your own still-stuccoed remains
dripping and rakish with vestigial scribblings
(the first Vasco Rossi) (erotic beckonings with
names and surnames, the most recent with the K of young kids),
you, epochs overlain and coupled precisely
by what one's able to imagine of intimate
means such as sticks strong as skewers
and above all by the rapture of living there,
of feeling oneself, dwelling there, co-desiring mending
connected there's no doubt, to the eternal
      HOUSE, tottering forwards
      or backwards or to all sides and roofs discouraging
      those who think you can't totter any further
      who concoct crossings couplings junctions of
      materials that time differently disoriented, inebriated,
      almost made to faint-fade
      shifted, situated in nothing and everything
      stiffened until causing terrible exultation
      or sufferance in grief.

Now you even boast a SIGN, affixed to what
can't be but the most fitting spot,
that consecrates you as   UNSTABLE HOUSE
to the eyes of passersby who quickly recognize you
as an element of the infinite, or don't recognize you,
and those who surely don't know what you were like

come t'inventavi all'inizio del tuo pericolare
o, più avanti, quando eri abitata
dalla famiglia, per definizione, più disastrata
del paese: ma che avevano
una benedizione di latte tutti i mattini;
e da chi? dalla maestra Marini:
lei vi portava un bel vaso di latta colmo
del bianco, appetitoso perché forse unico, cibo.
Era anche chiacchierata
perché qualche volta andava a ballare
e fumava da un lungo bocchino
e non era granché sorridente: ora è dono
stupendo alla memoria, scomparsa la famiglia
sussidiata, scomparsi i tic beneficenti.

      Mah mah mah, come si pericola grandiosamente
      eppure umilissimamente
      con te, amata CASA, col tuo passato assente
      con tuo futuro invece
      garantito da tutti quegli zampini, rampini, spiedini.
      Ma anche dal buco della finestra che
      in qualche modo geometricamente impera—
            quale occhio mancato di benigna megera?

      In più, forte, come per fondare una città coi suoi comodi
      e superdotata, guarda mo', ecco ad ergersi
      a saggia distanza
      ampia cabina per uso corporale,
      altrettanto pericolante,
      e, pur ella, una sissignora vera
      con un enorme cappello-boschetto di vari piantami sul tetto
      quella sì, ben spudorata, a porta sempre spalancata
      quella sì riferimento a pace
      e benefizio, ed equilibrio perfetto:
      chiave, scheda magnetica,
      lucido, bozza, coppiglia, e quant'altro mai—
      garante operosa, nel suo pericolare
      per tutto il paese vocato a mangiare e ad espellere
      un fecondo di più: completando il tutto
      quale elegante sineddoche
      del meccano che mondo chiamiamo

how you devised yourself at the outset of your tottering
or, later on, when you were inhabited
by the clearly most wretched family
of the village, who yet had
a blessing of milk every morning;
and from whom? from schoolmistress Marini,
who brought a tin pitcher brimming
with the white, tasty because perhaps only, food.
She was gossiped about
because she sometimes went dancing
smoked from a long cigarette holder
and wasn't especially cheery: now a stupendous
boon to the memory, with the subsidized family
vanished, beneficent idiosyncrasies gone.
    Ah but how one totters majestically
    and yet humbly
    with you, beloved HOUSE, with your absent past
    with your future instead
    guaranteed by all those clasps, catches, skewers
    But also by the window-hole that
    geometrically rules in some way—
        as a benign shrew's missing eye?

    What's more: strong, as if to found a city with its comforts,
    and well equipped, look there, rising
    at a wise distance
    a commodious hut for bodily use,
    it tottery too,
    and yet a true ladylike latrine
    with an enormous sylvan bonnet of various shrubs atop its
        roof
    so shameless, with its door always flung open
    an allusion to peace
    and well-being, and perfect equilibrium:
    key, magnetic card,
    transparency, outline, linchpin, and all the rest—
    in its tottering an industrious guarantor
    of the entire town called to eat and expel
    an excess bounty: wrapping up everything
    what an elegant synecdoche
    for the plaything we call the world

Qual mai ALTAVISTA d'architetto
e mago di colori crudi e cotti
dei materiali, e della lor potenza
avrebbe meglio colto i segreti che dal fondo di ogni fondo
ispirando s'insinuando? Ma esistono mai simili
architetti a sposare
l'eterno stare (del presente mondo) col pericolare
che gli è necessario al tremito
del   —sine   fine—   vivacchiare?

YAHOO

What architectural, magical ALTAVISTA
of clear and cloudy colors
could have ever better cultivated the subterranean secrets
of the materials and their power
that inspire as they worm their way in? But is it possible
that architects of such ilk exist who wed
the eternal existing (of the present world) with the tottering
so much a part of the shuddering
of the   —sine   fine—   scraping along?

YAHOO

Selected Prose
_____

A Poetry Determined to Hope

Perhaps interest in poetry may take root in children through reading the illustrated verse of the *Corriere dei Piccoli;* perhaps the strange design of its "broken lines" may make an incomparable impression before one is fully conscious—before one is even vaguely self-aware. It is possible to find yourself at a young age—it happened to me and my peers—breathing in an atmosphere drugged more with poetry than any other daydream.

I developed as a writer, haphazardly and anxiously no doubt, during the years in which poetry—necessity and ever invincible joy—appeared as "ultimate" and "singular," the only shelter allowed humanity, supreme among its ambitions. The words of Sergio Solmi, who defined it as *novissima dea* (a reverberation of a passage by Ugo Foscolo reduced to its essential meaning), indicated the crafting of poetry as a maximal act, still "emergent" within the sinking of life and the acknowledged disintegration of values.

True decadentism, with its daring or humble or ironic *voluptates,* had already been for the most part surpassed; irrationalistic implications were substituted with existential ones; poetry no longer tended to direct its discourses "into the schism," into the realm of velleities of evasion and irresponsibility (those moving in this direction did so in a spirit quite unlike that of the daring writers of the early twentieth century), but rather "over the schism"—to become a living, accepted problematic. The poetic act was, nonetheless, extremely clear and rigorous even in its two divergent "modes." The response to this awareness, to this vitality, which only pretended to ignore history, was the concretizing of a style, the constant renewing of truth on the page, on the plane of art. Even in that climate of loss, poetry, with its call for a "higher" and "other" order, implicitly raised the problem of an organicity, of an integrality from which we felt far removed; it was the most resilient and mindful appeal to an eternal harmony of reality, even under the sort of anarchy and work "in the tower."

The historical events that followed that period could moreover be well explained as an acute manifestation of the general crisis that was a prelude to that poetry. That same postwar period, which left unresolved all the most pressing problems stirred up in the past, served as a test. The only fact, new to a point, was the need to wrestle against a chaos that by then had infiltrated the conditions of daily life, and the need for resistance at the biological level. The demand for any possible form of well-being became ever more pressing as the crisis grew more extreme. It was this situation that lent credence to certain strivings for renewal, which, even if truly "generous," were no less uncritical: legitimate, but based on inexact and partial diagnoses. Thus, only adhesion to comfortable mythologies made it possible to believe in a "restoration" in the making; the blind then pretended to save others, who were blind as well, but certainly less so than their aspiring saviors. And the new schemes in which this struggling was supposed to congeal led to a beating of our already-thin hides—a stripping away of yet more of the sense of what it was to be human. This brought about every possible form of confusion: from the resurrection of formulas already a thousand times forsworn to the application of old, fully entrenched literary conventions, to even the negation of that which characterized poetry itself. Particularly revealing was the accusation of narcissism and of indifference towards lyric poetry in general; so too was the bundling together of decadent smugness and the terrible battle of existentialism.

The accusation was then aimed at poetry of not knowing how to save humanity; doctrines of "health" were also concocted so as to unload on poetry the irresponsibility that instead tormented, most likely, the selfsame accusers. Because they hadn't grasped the actual extent of the crisis, they were all the more unable to understand either the humanity of the crisis or humanity in general; as a result, they could neither understand poetry: not a certain way of crafting poetry, but poetry *sic et simpliciter*. From this came either confessed annoyance at or hypocritical acceptance of the "broken lines" as well as treading into (but without overly believing) the "new." In reality, poetry has never been a savior in the form designated by the theorists of its myriad functions, even if in certain periods and in the work of certain poets it has more distinctly drawn nearer to history (or more accurately, to a more common and conventional idea of history). It was for itself, in any case, a source of well-being and has always been the most likely apparition of truth, of liberty, and thus of history: even poetry labeled as not politically *engagée* can boast to its high regard to have displeased both yesterday's despots as well as today's.

This does not mean that humanity cannot and must not move ahead so as to overcome the current and difficult impasse, using all its energies, including poetry understood only in its guise as a cultural and spiritual force among other forces. But what impedes the overcoming of the crisis is precisely believing, or faking believing, pretending to have already succeeded. And such is also the case with a more narrowly literary or poetic "progress": it is enough to pull out the reasoning reason together with the sentimental sentiment and juxtapose them, to put the lot through the preestablished cleft in the sky and then to dust off "idea harmony image—aura of abundant love," which merge "into one" as in the little verse by Niccolò Tommaseo—all this to bring into being the new man, with his not quite articulated "expression." On the other hand, to those who have more knowingly trodden these paths, the conventional nature of the results is clear; perhaps precisely due to this awareness they attain a paradoxical authenticity and, despite themselves, join the existential *côté* of culture and poetry. The preceding *ars* thus must continue to have meaning, to maintain its capacity for intimation, even in the mutating of spirits, expressions, and historic context; "post-hermeticism" for this reason dies so hard, while all that has remained from the great uproar of new approaches is a few themes without so much as the glimmer of a new language; these themes certainly matter, but, inadequate to found a new *ars,* tend to take refuge under the wings of "allegiant" poetry. This recognizes the inheritance of the problems and propositions of past poetry as its own; even if it doesn't resolve them, at least it doesn't elude them. It has the courage to confront face-to-face the true even if with infinite difficulty and with the danger of wandering through labyrinths; its "honor" is in this.

It seemed to me that one must aim for this, even if faced with a dearth of strength and reason; I was able to recognize myself in doing just this, in believing in a poetry determined to reconcile the irreconcilable, and which hoped (if the recollection is warranted)

as if not hoping, lived as if not living, moved in remaining im-
mobile, was faithful in not negating itself as conventional, offered
itself as a hypothesis of sheer grammatical occurrence yet without
conceding not being "word," revealed the eternity of today in its
admitting of fragile impermanence, and clung to the "beyond"
of a possible absoluteness even at the cost of seeming abstract.
The broken line and rhythm continued to overwhelm as a final
allusion to a transcendence or as an illusion: in any case they were
not, as for some, a scheme emptied of necessity and therefore
mute, incomprehensible, able only to reawaken a sort of obscure
remorse—and accepted for this.

In my case, from the first to most recent collections of my
verse, new experiences have taught me much, I believe, about
human reality, confirming what I had thought yet forcing me to
better understand the "pardonable" necessity of a certain type
of more effusive language, more open than past forms of poetic
expression, yet also provisional and awaiting other forms.

But if poetic expression has yet to reach fullness—and it will,
even if for the moment it is difficult to see how and when, because
of humanity's need to believe, or, at least, one knows that it is out-
rageous to speak of negation as if it were a revelation—this expres-
sion must always resurface at the vertex of reality, to be gathered,
developed, recovered: in the end, invented. To mention one who is
démodé, Hölderlin, the "was hier wir sind," will be made consum-
mate "dort"; what we are here will be made true only there, in
the broken lines, "mit Harmonien und ewigen Lohn un Frieden,"
with harmony, gain, and peace intermingling. And perhaps the
things of "here," before being said "in that way," existed neither
in the sky nor on earth nor in any place—they didn't count on
their existing. From the alpha poetry, if you will, of hermeticism,
to omega poetry, but always along the same line of development
and also of reversibility. Old and repeated things, which yet are still
fitting to repeat. Even to ourselves who, believing in it, though we
dare—cannot but do it—cannot but write poetry.

(1959)

Some Perspectives on Poetry Today

There are many perspectives from which one may attempt to recognize the currents and problems that characterize contemporary Italian poetry. Of particular interest today would likely be a linguistic classification (and someone is already at work at it), but there nonetheless remains much to say in respect to other areas of study, such as sociology (and ethnology), as well as psychology.

One notes, meanwhile, that in our country two components of civilization are in conflict: the "European" variety with others—so to speak—"Afro-Asiatic" in origin. This makes for a sort of privilege, as much due to the breadth of the field of experimentation and inquiry offered by a situation of this sort, as due to the possibility of transforming into a synthesis, a meditation what at the outset must be discordant. The difficult elaboration of new equilibriums meanwhile makes the panorama of our poetry (and literature in general) appear markedly more diversified than in other countries. Also, the elements that constitute it tend to converge and contaminate one another, or to be thrown into relief in unexpected forms in the attempt to make sense of one another—even if in appearance each appears to impose itself as if in total negation of the others.

In this way, a certain type of avant-garde research, doubtlessly in relation to an advanced neocapitalist society, to a consumer society, frequently reemerges here in Italy sunk in an ideological context close to Marxism, often in its most extremist forms. Opposing this is an old neo–realistic-populist wing of the literary ranks, evidently connected to a climate of depressed areas that reactivates itself in new forms, confronting the world of technology understood above all as a shaping force of human situations en masse. There persists, moreover, the defense of a certain idea of literature that, even if originating from a distant tradition (and so with archaic-aristocratic nuances paralleling social structures of other times), was able to internalize the literary tribulations of the late nineteenth century and the early twentieth, and to widen the broad area of risk that it had opened. The defense of this idea of literature ended up, in recent years, simply coinciding with the defense of a distinctive meaning of literature itself (and "espace littéraire" or "poétique") threatened by other proposals in which literature tends to be reduced to another function or to become muddled, as a barely definable element, with diverse forms of artistic expression. This last approach, which remains faithful without rejecting what is newly acquired, seeks to establish itself as a preliminary condition to any research, experiment, or adventure based on elements offered by a reality in ferment; it remains open in every direction and yet requires more rigorous scrutiny. Also detectable in this position is what has often been viewed as a negative aspect of our literature, namely, its capacity to absorb the riskiest forms of experimentalism, enriching itself as has happened many times in its history: evidently this is not a matter of defending the academy; on the contrary, this attitude is ultimately only related to a warning in favor of a vital continuity that impedes the formation of an "arcadia" of tradition as well as of innovation—which probably occurs more often than is usually willingly admitted.

Alongside this hint of reconnaissance carried out within facts of social nature, today it seems permissible to suggest another that further clarifies the picture using allusions drawn from psychology. In a time like ours, so burdened with divergent tensions, both positive and negative, every exploration must at the outset come to terms with the crisis that has beset an idea of humanity remaining relatively stable for millennia as a profound norm, for which we are still far from discovering a substitute. Science and technology have created a blockage, an engorgement of "revelations" (inventions and discoveries), which in large part justifies the use of the epithet "apocalyptic" to describe our times. The final unmasking, the demystifying-demythologizing, has particularly turned against that which—up till yesterday was understood as "macrohistory" (guided by transcendence or dialectics)—has transformed itself into "microhistory" thwarting itself with ahistoricity. The end of this history, of this idea of humanity and history, of this aeon, at the minimum could not but provoke the birth of an entire literary theme extremely differentiated and complex but also felt as a shock born of apocalyptic fears, while every possible integration (or in other words, every formation of new "security systems") appeared as difficult and distant the more it was responsible and conscious. In relation to these facts, to this rupture of norms, more than in the past (even in conditions of grave crisis), a psychological metaphor is becoming acceptable in the classifying of the various literary tendencies with a discourse that evidently is of concern not only to the national realm.

There are thus those who take for granted the existence, the persistence of a (collective or individual) "normality" that would appear to be founded on single "positive" ideologies accepted more or less consciously and dogmatically. This group loses more influence every day, even if many of their proposals are destined to remain above the horizon as necessary-temporary conventions—and perhaps to be picked up again in new contexts. This position is more commonly encountered in prose than in poetry.

There exists then a vast alignment with great variations—including many of the poets of the third and fourth generations here in Italy—which presents and interprets a largely "neurotic" psychology; the norm is thus challenged, run through with deep faults, but considered valid at least in its categorical nature if not fully accepted in its traditional forms. Here work is carried out that is almost always hard-earned, in which every *novum* is "sustained-assessed," or expelled in the name of a continuity that resists becoming conservation but instead seeks verification and supersedence along an arc of a certain idea of what is human, aware of having living roots in the past. It is a matter thus of a combined reception and destruction with a special sensitivity for the relationship between exterior stimulus and emotional past experiences, as well as between these experiences and the linguistic sign. In essence, the extent of this group corresponds to the analogous one ascertained above along another route.

You then have an entirely different sector, considered *novissimo* (as well as, or above all, in the apocalyptic sense of the term) that hasn't hesitated to recognize its stance as "schizomorphic" and that has established its role within the idea of the forceful predominance of a decisively pathological element over that considered "normal"; thus destructuration and rupture are institutionalized in a fusillade of proposals that burn themselves out one after the other—precisely out of the refusal of the selfsame image of the continuity-norm in favor of a punctiform time that "should" always be "the end of times." That which is eccentric-pathological here, by definition, would remain as such—even if while posturing as normality, in complying with it. But this type of complete disintegration can very rarely be guaranteed by the totality of an experience (as much at a sociological as a psychological level); it must thus clear the path to a mannerism of the negative, the more increasingly kaleidoscopic and rich with inflorescences the less rooted in past experiences. Poetry's latching onto the visual (or ex-visual, or tomorrow, invisible?) arts, with the loss of this or that distinctive trait, according to a feverish rhythm of thieving mad transformations and confusion, may effectively correspond with the last and lowest grades of schizophrenic dissolution. The degradation and asperity of the findings, however sustained by the defensive apparatus based on the terrorism of a pedantry inexhaustible in its *ergotare* and in its spinning of sophisms, characterize a large part of the "production for consumption" offered by this sector.

In short, there is no want of research departing from a ground-zero recognition and an aspiration to restore stable values, at least by way of an initial affirmation of biological presence; however, imperatively suggesting that "everything that presumes to be novel is done badly and in a rush" risks distorting the meaning and direction of the research.

Secondarily, it is important to recognize the necessary deepening of the awareness of the relationship between poet and reader that took place in Italy after the war—in terms of both motives and modalities. The concern for a suitable structuring of this relationship has often had a radical effect on the study of all forms of literature, first in a populist-Marxist climate, then in one of mass communication, when the cultural industry that developed aimed at conquering or establishing a market. An entire set of problems was born that is still widespread today. But an old postulate endures: those who write, who write poetry, are those inclined to speak and perhaps to hope to be able to listen as much as talk, even if this doesn't exclude the possibility of establishing a minimal relation with the edge, the void, and silence—which then dialectically transform the meaning of this monologizing aperture. In these individuals there is, however, a minimal form of violence and presumption that pushes them to formulate a game—but also because others help them to understand the true sense of that which they themselves are saying (see, for example, the work of Barthes in this regard). In reality there naturally exist infinite barriers interposed between possible interlocutors, barriers that must be destroyed and that are destroying themselves, even if in chaotic form. Here there exists an analogy with what occurs in authentic teaching experience, in that one becomes a "teacher" to a degree despite oneself and has a great desire to learn as much as teach: in any case there never exists for him the problem of dialogue with "a crowd" or "the masses": beyond this, he attempts to communicate with individual personalities even if closely interacting among them as a group. Responses to pedagogical invitation and thus to literary invitation will thus always be highly varied, even in a society in which all of the barriers between "authors" and readers have fallen and in which the institutions of school, publishing, and criticism have been perfectly synchronized in order to effect the development of a "total" culture—involving the relation of groups with groups or individuals with individuals with great dynamism and litheness. There will always be infinite ways of approaching the book—even that which wishes only to make a decorative object out of it.

As for massification and the market: these are phenomena present in every era ("dal dì che nozze tribunali ed are?"); they are closely associated with power and with the inborn violence found in every form of power: but for a true literary, a poetic act (as well as an analogous pedagogical one), the prospects are different. Acts of this sort tend always to situate themselves beyond the undifferentiated, precisely in order to reduce to zero the situation of "crowding" over which the measurements and theorems of statistics and the pressures of the market have sway—even if this "zero" will in fact never be reached. And certainly the present in this regard is different in many ways from the past: but not deep down, in its most primal elements.

There has always existed a love market alongside love; indeed, in the past the contract-market was more common, in this field, and in its more varied forms. Thus, alongside the sanctuary flowered the trafficking of icons, or even deities; there was always a Peter and a Simon Mago. In each of us there is always a bit of this and bit of that. The market is there ready to seduce and condition because it comes from that part of human nature that desires to be seduced and conditioned; but if one doesn't believe that humanity can overcome conditionings and self-conditionings (each person in some such if only minimal measure), all discourse must cease. The ruling classes in society—including the tendency to create dominant elements or classes—will always attempt to bring about massification. In the past, massification succeeded with a bewitching terribleness and a temporal duration certainly much greater than those designed today, despite the mass media's great efficiency. It is undeniable that a certain shoddy type of pseudoreligious "propaganda" (the term, from religious background, has ended up in taking on its current meaning) has succeeded in swaying spirits with another species of tenacity; its effects are much more negative than those caused by publicity for industrial or cultural products—if for no other reason than because this pseudoreligious propaganda is condemned to unceasingly conceive of ever-new idols.

One will counter that "statistically" massification exists and thus it must be reckoned with; its procedures and techniques should be studied. True: there's no reason to entirely disclaim the validity of such a study. But the books never balance out perfectly; someone escapes from massification, many escape; everyone escapes "for only an instant." Everyone experiences the old no, the initial refusal, knows the "point," and comes to find themselves once "at the point" at which escape-liberty is possible. And the literary establishment (like the pedagogical one, as well as others), with its favoring of the possibility of genuine "acts," tends to produce an ever-vaster number of single and singular entities, demassified and released, if not from the market, from the "spirit of the market."

As far, then, as our own Italian situation is concerned, the little market that exists for our poetry is still so restricted that almost all the buyers-sellers know one another. With poetry, excepting a few big names, one returns to the innocence of the primitives, to the giving and trading of books that always pass through the same cycle of hands. Perhaps things will change, but the obsession with the recipient, with the "to whom, to whom, to whom does one turn" (a theme much discussed in these years) should settle into a (modest) trust emerging from the source of the impulse to leave, and of the metaphorizing tension located at the base of every poetic discourse, which generates the pronoun *you* (with the first letter more or less capitalized) and thus *we, they,* etc., and creates a field where these are made possible. Perhaps this field merits the name "fedeltà d'amore"—a suspect expression, to be revived in terms as yet unthinkably divergent from those that it adopted, or attempted to adopt, in the past. Thus one can hypothesize that Tyrtaeuses move armies, or that Tassos cause the gondoliers to sing their verses, or that Yevtushenkos fill theaters most likely in a frame of *epoche:* all of this is just fine, and this initial encounter with the mass-magna useful: it nonetheless remains beyond the essence of the poetic invitation as such. This invitation tolerates armies and theaters, but only the ones that become something greater: gleaming "masses" of pluralities, of elements destined to become clear in all grammatical persons possible, and even in empty stains, places of the nonresponse, which is yet able to congeal in meaning. The hint reemerges of a poetry that is made neither by a lone person nor by everyone, nor for a lone person nor for everyone, and that crosses no place and that comes from no place, because the poetry itself is "the place," the condition, the beginning.

(1966)

Self-portrait

To speak of oneself entails without doubt some distortion; the image we have of ourselves surely corresponds very little, almost not at all, to the reality of what we are. In any case, when one attempts to speak of an itinerary claiming to have wandered along the borderlands of poetry, the possibility of distortion increases, one might say, infinitely. But in this respect I feel relatively free from blame in the sense that I have never "aspired" to anything having precise edges when considering poetry: but neither have I been able to keep from thinking into the beyond, even painfully, overshadowed by a sense of powerlessness. And yet I delight in remembering certain distant moments from my early childhood: I used to experience something infinitely sweet while listening to lullabies, nursery rhymes, and little poems (of the sort in the *Corriere dei Piccoli*), not in how they were sung, but in how they were pronounced or even simply read, in relation to a harmony directly connected to the interworkings of language, to its internal song. I have an extremely vivid and immediate memory of these distant experiences in which a vague, elusive "idea" or "presence of poetry" took shape for me. My paternal grandmother, to whom I owe special gratitude, stressed the fact that these sounds of the language were not song in the most common sense of the word but were in fact poetry. And my grandmother, endowed with that unique cultural mix of both popular and classic influences that often in the past was found in the so-called lower strata of society, used to recite verses by Torquato Tasso to me (a common tradition in the Veneto: reminiscent too are gondoliers singing Tasso and Ariosto). The harmony of this glorious Tuscan verse filtered through me like a dream, a veritable phonic drug, together with fragments of other languages, true xenoglossies, over the slightly "wild" continuum of our spoken dialect.

I remember also the profundity of certain states of mind so rich that still today when I think of them something tangible wells up—moments of fertile stupor while facing some element of nature, the landscape, the living, all that which surrounded me. At certain moments I sought out a feverish, overwhelming intoxication of existing in order to attempt to contemplate certain things, or rather, to participate in their secret lives. I felt that there emanated—from a leaf, a tree, a flower, a landscape, a human face, virtually anything at all, including later on, a book—a current of energy, a feeling of relatedness that I longed for; there was a sort of interchange between my interior being and the external world composed of "burning points," summits or sloughs, distinctive emanations in any case. From there came the more insistent apparitions that pushed me in the direction of poetry. And at this point I must reiterate that in my opinion poetry is, above all, an irrepressible desire to extol reality, to extol the world "in so much as it exists." Poetry is a type of celebration of life as such because it is life itself that speaks of itself (in some way) to an ear that listens (in some way); it speaks in its own way, perhaps mistakenly; and yet life and reality "grow" in their lauding, at the same time creating, almost as if expecting it. And yet through poetry there not only emerges praise (and this is a sentiment, and a concept, that we find in an entire poetic tradition); there looms a veritable "testing" of reality. In what sense? Reality also appears early on to children in the tragedy of its contradictions; it even allows glimpses of its final nullity; and yet it always possesses moments (that are in no way "rare" or "privileged," because they are able to surprise us at any time, even during the deepest, most stagnant depression) in which it reveals its absolute dignity, or better, its "worthiness" in existing, which has reasons solely within itself—all to be recognized, never all recognizable.

In a certain sense, poetry assays reality, connecting itself to the lauding of reality, which it does so powerfully as to become a test of endurance, a test of worth. Clearly all of this may seem related to forms of narcissism and autistic "consolation" in as much as those who assume such an attitude toward reality tend not to take account of the interiority and conditions of other people, of those around them. But if it is true that Narcissus is the first mode in which existence appears to itself, the tendency then is to surpass oneself in establishing something in a different vein. And there is "much" to be said of this primordial self-consolation: it is the state of being "much," of being abundant. The monologue in fact longs to open itself into a dialogue, precisely as an act of pure and simple lauding tends to transform into one of assaying which can and must be of use to someone, to everyone, to everything.

From this point of view, my childhood was rich even if not happy; on the crest of these emotions I also found myself prey to terribly depressing phenomena. But above all, I believe that what bore most heavily on my childhood and adolescence was the gradual seeping into me of an aberrant idea: that of the impossibility of fully joining the game of life because I would have been at once excluded. I suffered from various allergies, and at that time diagnoses could be rather confused and ambiguous. At times I believed that the asthma and hay fever that tormented me were phenomena that could worsen, in theory, with little notice. In daydreams I saw myself gripped by sinister illnesses and infirmities; I thought that I wouldn't live long "enough"—certainly not long enough to be able to express what I felt. I lived in a strange duplicity, in uncertainty, in emptiness. There grew in me a feeling of detachment from reality; I saw the world of history and its conflicts as if on a distant screen: he who imagines himself, and with some foundation, as a "temporary guest," inevitably comes to think of himself more a spectator than an actor. From the very beginning I was more often faced with surviving than living.

I started at an early age to "compose"—almost always poetry, less often prose. But it was only after the war that I was able to begin to think of an actual publication, because I hadn't been at all satisfied with what I had written and felt that I had overlooked the most and best despite coming close. In the end I don't believe that I was suckled by the Muses with particular blessing; rather it was I who long courted the sacred world of the Muses or even the most mundane world of those who are mistaken for Muses and in reality are only the husks of mirages—some already living in the past, others already dead even when they had been devised for the future. The world of poetry is one of mistakes, hallucinations, torpors, windings around nothing, in which one rarely stumbles upon the golden bough. My books were in any event born out of their nearly demanding, even threatening, necessity outside of every "program," even if my bent was to absorb and assimilate the themes as they slowly emerged over time. Or I myself recognized them in my own way, in remaining aloof, from a relatively unpredictable perspective. And I found every book readymade, like a series of layers of dust come to rest on something, or a *fallout* of minimal secrete explosions that as they accumulate acquire thickness. Over the course of four to five years each of my books was born in this way, all very different from each other, almost like the links in a chain, each clearly distinct yet placed according to those preceding it: even if in fact a revision, a new focalization of old themes, of the old me, constituted the activating nucleus of the emerging collection. Some critics have identified a violent separation between the first part of my work and the most recent part. And yet, even if it is true that disturbing traumas gave rise to this clear difference between my various books, including a shift in language, I think that they have continuity precisely because they are tightly connected by ordinary, everyday life. It is not that I write every day; on the contrary, I go for long periods without writing anything, in the dullest wretchedness. And yet I "ponder"; when verses, words—individually or in little clusters—begin to hatch and "grow fond of each other," I transcribe them, always by hand, using pens that give me the sensation of almost designing on paper, or even of perforating it, traversing it. I then accumulate this material in drawers, not even clearly knowing what it is. When there passes that period that roughly corresponds to a "grande mese" of life, I conduct a sort of examination, a reconnaissance of this material, and suddenly the outline of a book appears to me. Then the title emerges, which for me has great importance; the semantics of the title are telling and decisive. The title is born for me as the singling out of structure in the midst of a vast assemblage. In this way I came to see my various works, from *Behind the Landscape* to *Vocative, IX Eclogues, Beauty, Easters,* the trilogy, and *Filò,* which emerged according to their own internal dynamism, even if not entirely blurred to my conscious mind, and without doubt bound to unconscious elements of extreme arrogance, of terrible arrogance.

I admit that in this sense my life has not been easy and that my encounter with psychoanalysis—and above all, with crossroads, or rather cross-bearing, consisting of psychoanalysis and linguistics—

was motivated by more than a general interest in culture. Violent disturbances in my daily life instead have compelled me for many years to repeatedly seek a method of cure within psychoanalysis.

Today I feel as if I have said almost nothing of what I needed to say. This is an impression that has always been with me, even if the work I have done, accumulated over time, has given me the sense that I have satisfied a certain degree of my responsibility. *Quod potui feci; faciant meliora potentes,* I did what I could; those who can, must do better: it will be my joy to read the results—because I see no possible rivalry between those who write poetry, if they write "for" poetry. Every presence is a plant and a flower, a diamond, even a simple colored stone, or a simple lump of earth, which could not have failed to come, with "reason," into existence. Thus what I have written has accumulated beyond any personal sense of joy or satisfaction. It existed. This fact has given me a reverberatory form of consolation in the sense of having accomplished a minimum "duty"; but, I repeat, I have always had the sensation of circling around something without truly reaching it. Only rarely, in looking back over some of my writing, does it seem that I touched that gratitude, grace, gratuitousness that is poetry, which mobilizes around itself, or around its not-yet-having-arrived, pressing necessity.

In any case, even now after the dialectal experience of *Filò,* my most recent book inspired by amiable, fervid talks with Fellini, I've realized that in the darkness of the drawer there's already material for what will perhaps become a new book. Indeed, I can already glimpse it—I can see its rough shape. In the coming months I'll try to come nearer to this reality that is always burning—because to verify if it is or isn't a book is a countercheck, a yes, a no, that always pierces, a countercheck that is never certain, after all . . .

(1977)

from "Intervento": A Conversation with Middle School Students in Parma

The stylistic virtuosity of the poem "Diffractions, erythema" particularly struck me. How would you explain this virtuosity?

The poem you mention is relatively complicated and difficult but need not be incomprehensible. When we remember, or rather, struggle to remember things with exactness, memories stream through our minds in clouds, in layers; we ourselves are unable to control the flow of our memories, and it often happens that we are even dragged into the vortex of an unpleasant memory which we can in no way distance from our minds (and this is so-called obsession or obsessive memory). Memories emerge with their own strange law, and we can say that our brains often save us not because they cause us to remember but because they cause us to forget. It seems to me that it was Bergson who said that the brain is the organ not of memory but of oblivion, of forgetting. There is thus an equilibrium that must establish itself between memory and oblivion. When someone writes poetry, very often the person is swept along by a subterranean current of personal memories, which, however, when closely examined, are also the memories of others, of people who have around them a strange, collective memory. At times it is very difficult to distinguish a true memory from a fantasized one; it is something like a meandering passage of clouds that at one moment casts a shadow upon the earth and at another vanishes in the face of a blinding sun that illuminates things not willingly remembered.

In this little poem I imagined a sort of *gioco scenico* revolving around a game of cards. Picture walking by a tavern in which people are playing cards: from outside you can hear the sound of the cards being shuffled and slapped onto the table. The game is nothing but the arranging and disarranging inside our minds of memories, not only personal ones, but also collective ones. Imagine now a deteriorated film, full of jumps and interruptions; these represent the jerky progress of memory, with the rapid succession of periods that can be chronologically very scattered. Into this film I concentrate an extensive historic journey, which begins long ago when the woods (which are still existent, even if now heavily degraded) were full of wolves—so much so that hunters were paid to kill them. There were severe penalties for those who despoiled the woods, or rather, stole from them because they had absolutely no food to eat, or fuel with which to warm themselves. In these woods there flourished legends of strange wizards such as Barba Zhucòn, or Uncle Zhucòn, who makes an appearance in the poem. Events that I describe involving these figures occur in an indeterminate epoch of the far distant past. The poem then passes to other periods, to the sixteenth and seventeenth centuries, when in the woods there were beautiful abbeys, visited by scholars, but also used as havens for brigands because sacred places carried the right of asylum. It happened precisely in these woods during the seventeenth century that the abbot of the convent actually became a ringleader of bandits. The Venetian Republic imprisoned and wanted to try him, but the pope, calling upon the principle of juridical separation, which asserted that clergymen had the right to be judged only by other clergymen, contested the claims of the Royal Highness. Of this was born a dispute, the so-called Judicial Question, which came close to causing a war between the pope and Venice.

Even in more recent times the woods have been the stage for more or less legendary events involving impoverished persons living at the margins of society who were, unfortunately, led by their destitution to banditry. In one very strange episode an entire village had agreed to steal a chest full of money from a very greedy count; it was more or less a collective reappropriation of the money that had been taken away from the poor. Amidst these people, however, were actual criminals who took advantage of the help of the village to steal the chest, but who then escaped into the forest leaving everyone in the lurch. There they rendezvoused with a notorious, mysterious old woman who was a usurer who lent money to those wanting to organize criminal undertakings. At this point the famous phrase was pronounced, "We killed the hag." The fact is that the usurer demanded too big of a cut; consequently the thieves strangled her, tossed her body aside, then without a trace escaped with the money.

These events, which could figure as themes in guitar-accompanied folksongs, are abruptly interrupted by another, much more frightening sound—that of war.

In this poem I persisted in the difficult arranging of memories and the recovering of the past in all of its aspects; for this reason I made reference to the peculiar photographic vision of a wide-angle lens—a vision that is deformed precisely because it wants to comprehend everything. But what is impossible to capture and comprehend is the final act, absolute and unmitigated, of violence: war.

Let me pause a minute in order to explain the title, which may seem a bit unclear. One speaks of "diffraction" when a single ray of light is split into many directions and hinders sight, which attempts to focus on a single point in history in order to see clearly and neatly. Why "erythemas"? We are always within range of offending light. Erythemas (which are commonly defined as irritations of the skin, often caused by solar rays) can be understood as the terrible reactions we have when observing at close range events under the violent light of historical illumination, which very nearly causes the sensation of a burn, of an ulcer.

There is then the idea of history as something undulating and contradictory, even if it seems linear. In *The Woodland Book of Manners* there often appear lines from the *Bollettino della vittoria* (Victory bulletin) of November 4, 1918. The area where I live is the setting for these wartime occurrences, which people not only lived through but turned into a series of personal episodes that were then later often memorialized and transformed in legends. The most extraordinary events were commemorated with a great number of monuments, in whose unveilings we children were obliged to take part. We lived as if within a type of funerary saga; it was as if we, who had not lived through the war (having been born afterwards), had been compelled to relive it almost to the point of participating in it.

This is the climate in which the entire book is set; the past and the present are constantly relived in reference to this tragic experience. It is said that history is the teacher of life: in as much as this is true, history is an unheeded teacher because it teaches that violence, war, and blood have never led to any solution; and yet there are always those who believe that they can reform the world with weapons. It is also important to add that, in the same area, during the sixteenth century there flourished a great civil society, evidenced by the Venetian villas in which there lived important humanists and painters. Thus there is a contrast between the beauty of a far-gone past, however short-lived, and the terrible presence of the war, which has extended to current times through the consumerist-driven destruction of nature. It can be said that this too causes "erythemas," sores, burns.

This explanation may seem very long in comparison to the dimensions of the poem; in effect, poetic language has the essential characteristic of being condensed, one might even say "short-circuited," and violent. The violence of the language is necessary to restore the inherent sense of tragedy of the historical events with as much of the same intensity as possible as was experienced by those who lived through the war.

The desire to reproduce with words the intensity and complexity of past experiences is never completely realized: thus the frequent stoppages, blockages, and deviations in the discourse, which correspond in the text to the little sketched signs "No Entry," "Private Property," the image of barbed wire, etc.

How do the images work in the text?

Poetry has many more aspirations than the case may seem. Some poets say that poetry is like painting (Horace long ago said as much), while others (such as Verlaine) compare it to music, while still others have said that it must teach, provide moral guidance, and produce elevated thoughts. One might compare poetry to the *pantera profumata* that Dante mentions in the *De vulgari eloquentia* when asserting that perfect language leaves its scent everywhere but is never made visible in any place. Poetry has many aspects: voice and recitation are essential but also very important is visual appearance. Think, for example, of adorned initial letters, which have an illustrative value, or of the symbolically shaped verse of Alexandrine poetry, which was composed in the form of amphorae, goblets, and various ornaments.

We might ask if such textual appearance adds something to the reality of poetry: I wouldn't say that it adds all that much, and yet it is important to remember that this visual aspect exists and should be kept in consideration. In "Diffractions, Erythemas," the little images act as punctuation marks: just as question or exclamation marks indicate a change in the tone of voice, so too do the images of the cups, clubs, etc., indicate changes in the tonality of a discourse that desires to be musically rich. As such, this poem is set in the key of "clubs," "cups," or "money"—in a similar way that a musical composition is set in the "D minor," "C minor" or "G major." These are effects that have (or rather should have) a combined musical and visual impact. It is difficult to specify what exactly comprises the key of "clubs" or that of "cups," since their realization is left to the interpreter . . . Let me give an example: for one reader the tonality of "cups" might be based on the sound of people boozing it up, guzzling alcohol; the tonality of "money" might likewise be based on the "clinking" of coins (which, more-over, seems to resonate on a daily basis in the pages of newspapers, especially during periods of great economic crises when governments are unable to keep their promises). Another unusual form of punctuation that I use are ellipses, not, however, arrayed in straight lines, but in curving ones that return back on top of themselves, almost wandering over the page; these indicate a state of suspended thought: not a linear suspension, but one of a person who is "pondering," perhaps muttering or whistling to himself.

How does one become a poet?

This is a good question, particularly because poetry can prove rather tedious to the great majority of people. It is a fact that the readers of poetry are few; the little bit of poetry commonly encountered by most people is read at school. A popular novel might have a print run of 100,000 copies, while a book of poetry may have one of about 5,000 copies (if printed as a cheaper paper-back this figure might climb to between 10,000 and 15,000). The concentration, the accumulation of meanings in and the ambiguity of poetic language, evoke a sense of obscurity that estranges many readers. In addition, common prose (not that of greater value, which is difficult or impossible to distinguish from poetry) often depends on narrative formulas, on the taste for knowing "how the story is going to end." In poetry, on the other hand, nothing "is going to end" because everything begins again. Books of poetry are like serpents biting their tails: the beginning returns at the end;

the final verse is equal to the first, or is so similar that it gives the idea of something reentering itself, indicating in the process that the human presence is never exhaustive, that it is never capable of saying everything. Our discourse collapses in the face of the complexity of being; of surrounding reality there remains in us the desire to deepen our knowledge of things, to render on the page the snarl of reality just as it is, without sweetening it, without inserting additives to make it easier to digest. Unfortunately reality continually slips stones into our soup; thus poetic discourse cannot but be strewn with similar nasty surprises. On the other hand, it can also offer flashes of insight, sublime moments that are not found in prose discourse.

Prose discourse is something of a swift means of communication that travels about on roads, while poetic discourse often tends to climb into the stratosphere and swoop about in vertiginous nosedives. It has no rules; it is a bit like an amphibious mechanism, one of those strange machines in science fiction films: it dives into the water, then in exiting extracts wheels, then wings, and finally flies away. How in the world does a person ever aspire to use this sort of discourse? You might say that people come to write poetry thanks to a special disposition that greatly varies from person to person. If I try to recall the experiences that pushed me to write poetry, I need to go far back, to when I was in elementary school, or even earlier, when I used to read *Corriere dei Piccoli* with its stories in verse of Signor Bonaventura and his millions, who perhaps you too may know. I easily memorized these verses, which gave me a sense of euphoria—the joy of hearing words that had an internal music. Rhymes and lullabies fascinated me, which are profoundly connected to the roots of poetry. The same lullabies and children's songs disappear into the night of time and often correspond to spells, to magic rituals of prehistoric origin.

I also remember experiencing extraordinary emotions in front of a very beautiful landscape, a tree, a leaf, a person. When nature creates something that is harmonious or perfect, it diverts attention, a type of attention that we might call contemplative; simultaneously it often happens that we feel compelled to say, to write something in praise of the beautiful image we have seen. It isn't true that poetry is born out of sadness. It is commonly said that poets are persons filled with sadness who write in order to give expression to their grief. This fact is undeniable, but it is important to more fully examine it. Poets have a particular sensitivity for linguistic phenomena and are able to hear the peculiar melody of words; they are also very "sensitive" in general. Given that in life, unfortunately, periods of sadness and frustration are more common than those of exaltation, it is common for poets to write in order to repair the damage to their psyches caused by sadness, a process that, through the internal music of language, verges on a form of "auto-hypnosis." It happens that these verses, comparable to the incantations of the primitive world, serve to liberate from sadness not only the poet but eventually also others who read the poetry. One sees from this how important poetry can be, even if, in an immediate and direct sense, it doubtlessly "serves" no purpose.

When a person feels the need to withdraw into him- or herself, to meditate not only with the rational intellect but also with the heart in order to take stock, he or she will probably feel the desire to write poetry and will very easily come into contact with a number of poets. Although poets come to better understand one another, it is true, through the at times very elaborate and interesting writings of critics, before all else they must establish contact through a form of affinity. A poet may be a genius and not interest me, while on the other hand there are very mediocre poets who, for example, in books of little value, have written four or five verses that are, for me, unforgettable. It seems to me undeniable that everyone possesses the poetic instinct—as is seen in the numerous collections of poetry written by children. Why do children write poetry? Because they feel naturally stimulated by this language game that ferments within themselves, and because, reacting with a powerful emotional attraction to certain beautiful aspects of reality, they want to express their joy—just as we, when watching an entertaining spectacle, feel the need to "cry out" or clap our hands. These are some of the more general motives behind poetry, but everyone has their own personal story, especially in our times, which aren't easy. But when have the times ever been easy?

(1980)

Poetic and Bodily Perception

We cannot tell with certainty what a "text" might be, or if such a thing exists at all. Provided, however, that it does exist, there is no doubt that it is independent of whatever gave it birth in a process of genesis and hence separation. Even if one thinks of it as a scrap of debris or a relict, a secretion or excretion, a text takes off on its own—it flies off "on a tangent," as they used to say, and enters into an ill-defined orbit. A text is certainly also an "alien," similar to those in science fiction that come from "the beyond," capture a living creature, a living body-psyche of this earth, and pierce it with probes, thus mastering it and transforming it into one of its own. The captured being, however, in its own small way modifies the UFO (if that is what we want to call it) and there emerges a type of chimera or minotaur that is simultaneously here and not here.

We cannot thus in any way overlook the pretext, the extra-text and the like, if not some of the causes, which have made the existence of the text possible. The fact that a text is above all a linguistic vestige inevitably reconnects it to historic and biological time, and lowers it to an act of the "tongue," causing all of the more or less metaphysical baldachins and garrets that hold it up to fall to the dust (these must however be postulated, and remain continually there in a clutter, unless one concedes the presence of a text as a "fact in and of itself"). It is true that a text generally tends to appear firmly connected to the head, the tongue, the eyes, ears, and finally, to the celestiality of the cortex of the brain, after having vaporously filtered upward from the phylogenetically, as well as physiologically, lowest part of the brain.

It soon becomes clear, however, that a text is never "sufficiently born" to be able to detach itself from the body-psyche that made it possible and of which, perhaps, it is only a projection, rather than a true filiation. The body-psyche itself is an entity frighteningly written, inscribed, rewritten, sculpted, embossed, modeled, colored, and infiltrated by an infinite ensemble of elements within that limitless soup, that unmitigated plasma in which it is no more than a lump or ganglion. It is unclear then whether a text is a function of a feedback of reading to be directed much more toward the body-psyche in which, thanks to which, notwithstanding its objections, the text was formed. In turn the selfsame body-psyche counts for something only because it is a more transparent point, a warning light flashing red or an observation post overlooking the ecosystem of which the body-psyche is still a part and of which it "expresses" or "invents" at least some meaning, or indication of sense, which otherwise would remain latent: and in so doing, the body-psyche produces texts. At this point there reappears the idea of a text as necessary autobiography, to be read according to the two indicators of coming and going, and also with reference to the underlying assumptions that every biography tends to be pangraphy—even pushing or squeezing out the fact that the *grapheme* was already in the *pan-*. Body-psyche: but no body exists except as a finely structured psychic phenomenon (beware of disrupting the scheme of the body as the psyche or ego seizes it in the normal kinesthesia). Is that body real that is transcribed/described by the eye, or rather by the microscope, or even by the electronic microscope, and ever more downward? And the psyche, prickly little wretch, riddled all over with holes (as today it is so popularly described) and all tied in knots, and yet a-spatial and a-temporal, in its own way—does it not float upon that immense atomic-molecular vortex that is the body to which it pertains? Is it not born from the "reflexes" of each of the elementary particles that constitute that atomic-molecular castle in which it, false mistress, if it isn't careful, shipwrecks? Don't lean out over your own body: it may be more dizzying than leaning out over a *seven-hundred*-meter-high cliff. Watch out! Be careful! Or when it finally comes down to it, isn't the text, in the end, a most wretched and scrawny parapet that obstructs certain psyches from plunging down into the Lautréamontian abysses of "their" body, and through them into the abysses of the Immense All? Precisely because the text has been dead since the day of Plutarch (at least), does it not cease to be very dangerous, even under the guise of seduction, and not only of infernal agony?

Those who still "mythicize" makers of literature (and not instead crafters of jingles or the like) make the best readers, because they enter into communication with their saints by smooching up to relicts, perhaps to a scrap of greasy shirt, which for years suffered and rejoiced in close contact with the saint, to the point of understanding that the shirt or shred of it was in the end the actual place of sanctity. As perhaps, every minimum emaciated *quantum* of sadness or joy—that which is truth—can have "no place" if not within writing, destined in any event to become illegible, to be solemnly returned to the closed and definitive level of the detritus-enigma.

(1980)

Sundials

To delve into the problem of time—from the matrix of everyday life to the most intricate theories, such as those of modern physics—is to delve into what is perhaps the most complex problem of human nature over terrain that can never truly be subjected to external definitions. From the very beginnings of civilization humankind has felt the need to create a fabric of conventions within which time, interwoven into the matrix of everyday life, is rationalized, made "explicit," and eventually worked into a system of what we may call machines rich with utility.

If we consider the sundial, there is a certain amount of delight in seeing how it, one of the earliest "machines" designed to measure time, still today powerfully persists as an image or metaphor of a certain way of perceiving time. The sundials that are still now being made—despite the perfection of watches, or rather of ever newer and more sophisticated instruments destined to manipulate time in what appear to be the most unpredictable ways—carry richly vital, multifaceted layers of meaning. The sundial, born as an expression of the will to understand the flux of time (a concept here inseparable from the weather), has always been closely connected to the natural environment. It is a machine that may or may not work: it is even attractive when it doesn't work or when it suddenly starts working again at the most unexpected moments, thus reminding us that even the most perfect human machines are subject to breakdowns and shortcomings. The sundial, for example, contains within itself an acceptance of meteorological risks implying a noncoercive desire to remain in close contact with the flux of natural events. An observation by Goffredo Parise in his novel *Il padrone* (*The Boss*) comes to mind in this regard: within its process of "creating," nature makes space for errors and incredibly long losses of time, whereas technology tends to use every little scrap of time in its drive to maximize functionality to the highest possible extreme of efficiency.

Perhaps if tomorrow the world were to be rebuilt according to a highly technological plan, it would end up being covered in truly monstrous deformities as a result of obsessive technical perfectionism. When nature errs it may be that hidden within the mistake is a new prospect that we would have never otherwise discovered. In its erratic progress over very long stretches of time, nature is able to rebuild itself and move towards the unknown. Technology casts aside all that is considered "defective," even if it also learns much from mistakes; and yet, due to its hurried perfectionism divided into oftentimes disconnected sectors, technology at times gives way to death, as is evident in the effects of uncontrolled pollution and military rearmament.

And at the heart of the matter it is precisely what we are seeing today.

In considering sundials and their relationship with the (until now) uncontrollable weather, it is with delight that a personality comes to mind such as Colonel Bernacca, who interprets the eccentricities of the weather on television (which perhaps in short time will all become strict forecasts) and in sweetening them, helps us to digest them; in short, he gives "meteorology a human face." In the past the weather was always viewed as a phenomenon that escaped every possible control: Bernacca almost seems to take responsibility for weather that isn't as pleasant as we would like it to be, or that doesn't follow the course of our desires; he also seems to imply that "For now it's like this, but in the future . . . ." Meteorology with a human face, in short, is the desire to give an appealing and brightening image to what instead hides itself as a perpetual enigma not only within the unpredictability of meteorology but within all that which pertains to nature. The almost unreal sundial is a machine highly refined and yet at the same time primitive, at the mercy of the never completely calculable order of cosmic forces; it carries out an important part in reminding us of these forces while simultaneously often silently descrying the disturbing presence of them. Sundials are also simply beautiful to look at (evidenced by the new ones still being made today) scattered in remote gardens, or inscribed on roving stones, with their mysterious and ephemeral message issued directly from nature, which at any given moment may seem to point auspiciously towards an order kindred to humanity and cast forth messages that are no longer secret.

Upon sundials there are thus transcribed cosmic rhythms, something missing from watches.

Within the small space of a sundial, we can directly observe the all-encompassing phenomenon of the perpetual oscillation of the earth (which moves in accordance with many laws) and gather the transcribed immensity of the earth's actual movement and the apparent (as well as perhaps actual) movement of the sun. From sundials we may thus learn something of reality and may experience a clear and precise sensation of the minuteness and irrelevance of the earth, which is like a blade of grass lost within the universe yet run by laws that are miraculously stable, at least in terms of the span of human existence.

We participate then in the barely detectable oscillation of the enormous forces in which the cosmos rocks us: because if we carefully observe the transcription of seasonal terrestrial movement, as is apparent in the figuration of a sundial, we discover a likeness to the rhythmic movement of rocking arms, containing within them a maternal spirit, that of the *magna mater,* of nature in its totality.

In sundials we can also observe another very important phenomenon: on one part there are curves, quadrants, and markings that trace the eternal return of natural and ritual cycles, and on the other there is instead a line, an arrow, the gnomon that can speak either through its shadow or through a ray of sun that penetrates the small opening at the point at which it widens and ends. Sundials exemplify two ways in which humanity coexists with time: as a rhythm of eternal return in relation to terrestrial cycles and yet also as an arrow pointed ahead, an irreversibility linked to the never-ending flux, to the "hurling" through time, in relation to history and culture. Consider that to attain the slightest accord between the time of eternal return and the time of schedules, of moving ahead, or rather of rushing, escaping ahead, is perhaps the most important quandary that we find ourselves faced with having to resolve, particularly today.

Sayings and adages incised on sundials can also be extraordinarily suggestive; there is a collection, one might say, of many such wise expressions originating both from popular and more sophisticated layers of culture. Sundials indeed lend themselves to being experienced as cultural phenomena, as sources of instruction, aphorisms, and maxims, even heraldic inscriptions, but remain forever linked to a common wisdom that emerges from the experience of everyone.

Adages on sundials obviously tend to overlap with those concerning clocks, because clocks, especially those adorning bell towers, are often illustrated with various kindred proverbs. And yet only sundials truly possess the sense of the swift transience, the precariousness, that results from the fact they may suddenly stop working, while clocks are presumed to perpetually tick away.

There is a long tradition of related inscriptions stemming from ancient times, crossing the Middle Ages, and extending to our current era. In any case, the most dominant theme therein is the unstoppable flow of time. The arrow of the gnomon symbolizes the passage of "our" time as an irreversible phenomenon. Both in the mediations of ancient philosophers and in Christian thought there appear adages mainly moralizing in nature, justly aimed at more deeply understanding the act of looking at sundials or clocks. "Why do you ask what time it is? By the time you're told, it will have already fled," one maxim says, while another warns that "All strike, the last kills" (speaking of hours), and still another intones that "As soon as you glance at the time, the sundial, you will have already grown older." We find an abundant choice of meditative cues within these sayings; the most pressing injunction to be found within telling time reunites time with ethics: the hours constantly escape, and in so doing carry blame; in other words, whenever we look at the time there arises a feeling of negligence over all that which we have put off doing, all that we should have done but have not done.

There also exists an entire tradition of sayings more spiritual in nature, more elegant, and more connected to common, everyday life: one, for example, is to notice the time at the moment the polenta is poured out of the pot, ready not for what can properly be referred to as consumption but rather collective intake, as was often the case in old farming society.

In any case, the more or less ambiguous guidance of the sundial, despite centuries-old precision, gives to those who look upon it a sense of repose, subtly inspiring an unbinding attention that makes space for both digression and the fact that a little time is lost, first of all, in the deciphering itself of time, and then in the taste (that sundials arouse in us) for varying the "pace" of time—which can be either fast or slow, depending on our inner frames of mind. There exists, moreover, a psychological time, a way in which everyone lives according to a personal, interior sense of time: it is precisely in front of machines of this sort, bridges between the sky and human art, that this interior sense of time is awoken within everyone, made manifest in myriad reflections.

Clocks in this sense are much more limited. With their ticking, for example, clocks incessantly evoke a feeling of relentless, almost obsessive urgency, which is lacking in sundials. And in today's most recent indicators of time this ticking exists no more. New dimensions face us as we fall into a void, not knowing where it will carry us. In the past, both clocks and sundials offered us always in some fashion the possibility of seeing time within a certain unitary context. Clocks that were in use until recently, and in some cases are still used, have within their circular faces a line and a circle, elements that carry us forever closer to the profound reality of nature and humanity. In circular clocks, as in sundials, one can gather in a single glance the present, the past, and the future. Today instead, with clocks that electronically represent the precise "point" of time, a feeling for the past, and especially the future, is lost. With today's watches the fact that one cannot say "It's a quarter to nine," but instead "It's eight forty-five" creates an awkwardness in the way we sense time. We are left thus with an absolutely instantaneous and pointed time that sweeps from us a more "diffuse" time, haloed and harmonized in a circularity containing all three forms of time, present, past, and future. We are constantly thrown nearer the moment of supreme paradox, which incessantly nullifies itself, emerging as an obliteration in which the moment itself in appearing already self-destructs.

Long ago there existed an epoch in which time was not even recognized as such, because everything was immersed within it without means of measurement. This then passed to an epoch in which there emerged the necessity of measuring time so as to comfort humanity, to allow the setting of schedules, and to serve as a reminder of responsibilities on par with humanity's stature and potential. Today we are proceeding instead towards a mode of sensing time, and also of measuring it, which strays increasingly farther away from its two antecedents. Before us opens a void, an enigma contracted in occult throbbings, as far from eternally cyclical time as from rectilinear time. It is an "eternal point," a false eternity of the moment boiled down to pure form, breakable into ever smaller moments, into increasingly smaller fragments of time. In advanced technology there are processes that occur at the speed of thousandths of a second, of millionths of a second, of nanoseconds. This implosion of certain vortexes of time estranges us ever more from our everyday existence, from the possibility of fitting into the world harmoniously. Relentless technological development may perhaps someday bring about unforeseeable positive, certainly worthwhile, changes. But alongside today's triumphant, constant innovation and specialization, it is becoming increasingly necessary to refer back to our roots so as to gather a sense of the continuity of human experience, to win back a collective perspective in which everything has meaning: from sundials to clocks to electronic, or even atomic, measuring devices, to time perceived as our deepest dimension. Only in so doing will we be able to avoid the domination of a potential "technological alienation" generated by machines escaped from humanity itself.

It is important, moreover, to recognize the ever-present element of art in sundials and clocks, machines that invite artists to indulge their most creative whims, carrying us ever more and luckily within a parallel time, eternal yet historic: the time of art.

The time of art has nothing to do with time measured for industrial production or other such realistic, routine motives, and even less with time measured for the oftentimes frenetic velocity of cars. And yet the time of art is a time that contains all this and a little something more. To conceive of the sundial as a work of art is to find reconcilement with a sense of time destined to remain exquisitely human while making it possible to rediscover all the other forms of time in the flicker of fantasy that gives life to art, with and for humanity.

In the passing of recent years, the idea itself of "time," in its increasing sophistication, seems to have become ever more distanced from preceding conceptions. The saying "Time is money" has now become unusable as a paradox, metaphor, or witty remark. It has materialized "word for word" in the horrible convergence of the utterly abstract timetables of money, the ultimate symbol of metaphysical (infernal) finance; therein every millionth of a second, in time said to be "real" only out of convenience, mutates, ceaselessly racing across computer networks in a state of incessant overriding to serve speculations ever more rapid and destructive. Nothing could be farther from sundials than this most recent epiphany of time, freneticized and nearly bled dry of primitive origins in its fall into the void wherein time and money converge, reciprocally nullifying and depraving themselves along the fatal axis of confederated acceleration, greed, and fear.

Perhaps now from sundials seep tears of rain and gentle humidity, cloaked in shadows even when the sun vainly makes its mark. They remain, mute witnesses to when everything was innocent, in some way, and the time read upon them was dense, rich, perfumed with pure dewy air—when human time made space for gaps, pauses, pauses of delicate eternity.

(1984)

Between Minimal and Maximal Languages

In exploring dialectal texts one is prey to numerous and persistent hallucinations—with the fact remaining decisively important of whether one is or is not a dialect speaker. In the first case, one rediscovers the truly biologic taste of being in contact with, breathing in, and walking arm in arm with a dialect to the point of being aware of it not as a peculiar language somehow separated from other modes of speech but as a language that is "universal by default," by Edenic likeness, or even as a means so perfect that it disappears, that it leaves room only for being a means of communication, that it dissolves into communication itself, imperceptible amidst all of the movements, gestures, acts of physicality, of bodily presence, that are implicit within it, that accompany it, that complete it. But how many of those who write in dialect are true speakers and not simply knowledgeable users, who use it in their ordinary lives, literally day after day (with the transformations of spoken language that occur over months and years)? It is difficult to say, considering that situations are in any event differentiated by means of nuances or actual abysses. Perhaps the most authorized to write in dialect, if indeed the speaker has a particular responsibility-right, would have been Romano Pascutto, who recently passed away. In his village of San Stino di Livenza (near Venice), he was not only the excellent linguistic *auctor,* but even the mayor, and before that a constantly inspiring and leading force during the Resistance. But in fact there are a thousand paths that lead to the dialectal choice; this includes the well-justified right to write in dialect even when one does not use it on a daily basis.

Over the course of this century, the various dialects, increasingly less spoken, have been essentially transformed through the poetic experimentation and stylistic distinctiveness of numerous authors. And this according to paths, to existential and cultural experiences, that range from the sociopolitical debate over a sclerosis of "lingua alta" (as in the case of Noventa) to the choice to take refuge in pointedness, in hiding, in the jealously personal fact (as in Pierro).

Given the enormous number and variety of dialects, like a gleaming mosaic, still alive in Italy, the hallucinations that they produce, especially for speakers, at the moment of crossing over to other tesserae, are rich, creative, exciting, but capable of altering the judgment of the effective value of texts. When the tesserae are very close in color, one comes to feel that nearby dialects are variations of one's own dialect; it is thus common to be amazed while awaiting a familiar word to hear instead what turns out to be very different one—as often happens with the names of animals and plants. Where I live, for example, a mole is called a "solva," while only a few miles away the equivalent term, "musighèra," produces an effect of estrangement and surprise much beyond that of a literary text: all the more so in a text. As one slowly moves away from one's affiliated dialectal areas, the more impeded one feels; in evaluating as well as in understanding, one is subject to a game of attraction-repulsion, of connivance-vexation, because one feels directly involved in and yet in some way excluded from the profound anthropological and linguistic (rather than literary) truth diffused by the gravitation of familiarity present in the single idea that a dialect belongs to our national sphere.

When confronting a foreign language, which is studied as a "distant sphere," an entire series of alarms go off and precautionary maneuvers put into action to defend against an enigma; on the other hand, when confronting a dialect, which often is no less strange than an exotic language (even if meanings can more or less be guessed at), one remains dangling, half holding one's breath, simultaneously able and unable to deeply inhale the phonetic-semantic totality. Every syntactic turn, every idiomatic expression, every single word as inevitably "ours" together disappear or flit behind a mask (no matter how faint it may be at times) awaiting recognition. From this come idiosyncrasies or enthusiasms, circuit interruptions and sudden seductions (which dog criticism of dialectal texts, potentially knocking it off the track): in fact, thanks to the "jolt" of this situation, everyone finds themselves compelled to reread, to "rehear" (even with some sort of aftereffect) one's own dialects, the great phantasm of the national language, the mega-phantasm or myth or potential reality of the universal megalanguage, with all of the veritable traumas that it entails.

As far as I am concerned, a resolution that I *must* write in dialect gives me a sense of liberation and relief but also of impropriety. In the destructive reality of today, I see myself in dialect as participating in the ambiguous warmth of a tiny society of swarming little worms from whom a stone has been abruptly lifted that negated and yet also protected them. Naturally this does not come about when dealing with large urban dialects—true languages comparable to Italian, having extensive and complex literary traditions; and yet by now these are constantly being replaced by various forms of regional Italian. What is certain today is that most attention is given to dialects that have never, or almost never, existed in written form, to the most authentically (so to speak) indigenous spoken dialects of rural microcosms that reveal unexpected expressive riches, quickenings conserved intact beneath every form of corruption, buoyant and tenacious forces of resistance, even if in small areas. This includes the equations Guerra = Sant'Arcangelo di Romagna, Marin = Grado, Pola = Roncegno, Pascutto = San Stino di Livenza, Pierro = Tursi, to cite but a few of the most exemplary for their high literary value, and also for their quality of "idiomatic identification" so generous, loving, almost connivent in biologic form (or in metaphysical code of silence!) with the *numina loci*. This is the case even if there are doubtless no fewer authorial positions that return to forms of memory more generally regional, as Buttitta does for Sicilian and Loi for his Milanese—so astringently authentic, so "invented." It is important to recognize, in any case, that the spoken dialects of today—despite having fallen into an irreversible *deminutio* (primarily due to the break with the world of agriculture and handcrafts with its entire lexicon oriented to objects and acts today vanished)—are less worn out than it might seem at first glance. Today there are veritable words, drawn from foreign languages potentially panterrestrial in character, that are integrated into an internal rhythm of self-preservation, even enrichment. Consider words such as *inbulonà* or *parabris,* or expressions such as *son strach parchè ò vu massa stress* (which resonate here in my ears)—contaminations made possible especially in the northern dialects whose words frequently end in consonants. Certain innovations do not discordantly alter the phonological picture, so to speak, of these dialects, especially the more conservative rustic and marginal ones.

And what of the nature of a dialect, of dialects, especially the most bristly ones—of small villages, of minimal and isolated places—as regards "idioms" in the narrowest etymological sense of the word? Idiom means an exclusive fact, distinct to the highest degree, stripped down, across etymological diffractions of the word, a fundamental ambiguity: what is ἴδιον is incomparable, precious, irreplaceable "difference," but also devastating possibility of relapse into the "private," into the too closed, into "idiocy," at the edge. To know only dialect is a fact greatly and stupendously private but also stultified, deprived, and depriving. This is true all the more so for languages, that, when juxtaposed, render speakers and nonspeakers (reciprocally) mute and deaf. Barriers that in reality are extremely difficult to cross create murky mutenesses and reciprocal deafnesses. Beyond languages and dialects, there opens up an immense space of possible language known to everyone, happily catholic, gifted with "excessive" universality. A myth, a reality, that is abruptly satisfied by that natural-historical language that is today nominated as supreme, English, neo-English, vehicle of an enormous political, economic, scientific-technological, cultural, and even to a low degree mass-media power. But at the opposite extreme, the flicker of the thousands of persistent languages becomes even more feverish. Flickers, especially for dialects, "at the threshold." Destined, in any event, to bring into being the metaphor of the without-beginning and the without-end.

But what can a modest dialect amount to today (far distant even from the illustrious vernacular of the Veneto and its literary examples) above all for those who have always spoken it and feel it disappearing from their mouths, "from beneath" every intention? It is, in any case, the standard, tragically blurred for this time-life, in which all that is unstable, ephemeral, uncertain, presents itself. It is the story of a deafening and a silencing imposed from the outside in a way more insidious than a hex. Nor does this actually come about through the compensating force of a great language (great culture) that could have given the impression of being such (and in part was) an illustrious and monumental Italian, which imposed itself after the dialect, or rather, superimposed itself on it, leaving it practically unharmed, on the whole. Dialect, at any rate, for those who have found themselves speaking it alongside

Italian, in a kind of almost repressed diglossia, poses itself like a "first mystery," which evades every possible contemplation as well as every objectifying detachment. It is a situation that involves an exceptional number of Italians, even if in a diversity of forms that are difficult to compare and that statistics say vary from year to year. Today it is in a nebulous state, at a difficult-to-define intersection within families, small entourages, and small villages from the center to the periphery, between national language and the originating wellspring of dialect.

Semi-incompetent competency, performance that is almost not perceived as such, authentic means of contrast with respect to the luminous and hyperconscious phenomena that occur in "speaking a language," dialect appears as the metaphor—and it is, from a certain angle, the reality—of every excess, unimaginability, gushing superabundance or ambiguous stagnancy of the linguistic fact in its most profound nature. It remains laden with the vertigo of the past, of the megacenturies in which it extended, infiltrated, subdivided, recomposed itself, in which "the" language died and was reborn (song, rhythm, dancing muscles, dream, reason, functionality) within a very violent drift that causes us to tremble with unease because there we *touch,* with the tongue (physical organ and word system) our lack of knowledge from whence speech comes, and, in the moment in which it comes, rises like milk: in perfect opposition, here, to the other language, that "high one," valuable (at least apparently) as a distinct lexical and morphosyntactic totality, disposed to undergo use and maneuverings—while the lower current of the spoken dialect "makes do." It is the experimentation of an orality (zone of nourishment, "phase," etc.), an oracle, an oratory, minimal yet fortified with all the viscosity that permeates it, reconnecting it directly to all the environmental, biological, "cosmic" contexts, liberating *within* them the desire for expression and expression itself. Dialect is felt as coming from a place where no writing exists (the one that is only thousands of years old) nor "grammar": the location, therefore, of a *logos* that remains always *erchómenos,* which never freezes in a slice of event, which remains almost infantile even in its speaking, which is far from every throne. Poured back again into the earth, connected/disconnected in such "humility," this *logos* speaks through the thousand mouths of the "lowly" and, in any case, in the millions of "errors," of individual wanderings, highly mysterious rebels, in which the canons of yesterday and of today are consumed, and those of tomorrow are concealed: but only for being, in some way, made comic from the start.

Dialect announces itself as the vague location in which *langue* and *parole* tend to identify themselves, and every territoriality vanishes into those that are contiguous. And here would begin, particularly well articulated, a discussion of the neo-Latin situation, on the vortex from the bottom of which (with relative distortion in the perpetual orality) the arch-Latin language has been the object, arch-engraved on commemorative tables, the imperial and definitive language: but doubled in addition by one of its very fresh anti-institutional vernaculars. And we would need to mention the twists and turns, rebirths, metamorphoses, *splittings* (words of educated or popular origin) of every sort proper to the neo-Latin linguistic area and perhaps not discoverable in a form so garish and significant in another area. For this reason, for the "semi-diglossic person" who "sees double" and speaks on a double track of systems, very close in general, but wide apart in their destination, it must be frightening *to write* the dialect that guides the game although "feeling" relatively deficient with respect to the language and that permeates in its being ("wanting to be?") pulsation and somatic gurgling: of a continuum and of changeable pluriformities, similar to those of life, sunk in it and at the same time floating on its upper limits, towards symbol. In this context the enormous diversity of motivations of the individual dialect authors, mentioned above, proves even more moving.

Dialectality, nevertheless, for centuries had guaranteed a certain comfortable and implicit feeling of cohesion and duration, even though within narrow limits and according to the degrees of knowledge and lack of knowledge of the speakers. Currently, its nature, minute-fluid-interreticular and, above all, averse to the rigidity of the "national" reticules, its nature as an unconscious that, precisely, "explodes" slowly, reveals itself exactly in the moment when the source of orality itself is threatened, and every unconscious, every "maternality," risks being erased.

The avalanche of the media, with its barrage of stupefying luminescences, figures who oppress the word per se, and video clips, so to speak, that blend everything but make it tasteless, functions as a conscription that threatens even the pervasive Anglo-American influence, at the same moment in which it propounds it, launching—again—definitive deafnesses and mutenesses as from a universal discotheque. . .

On the other hand, the national language is in danger of becoming bloodless, amorphous, riddled with stereotypes and videobureaucratic waste just at the moment in which it is becoming popular, but late and when it already seems somewhat useless because it is spoken in an increasingly narrow area (with respect to the other major languages) and therefore "debased" in its turn to the level of a dialect but without having certain undefinable "faculties of adaptation" that dialect has. What a strange destiny Italian has: finally used by the masses after centuries of only written or elitist use, it is being pushed ever more to the margins of the international scene, a language reduced to miserable touristic bla-blas, or good for narrow layers of the culture for specialists in the arts or opera or for (most welcome) researchers of its roots. Therefore, the situation of the Italian speaker and writer is one of the most precarious, distressing, insane: genocide breathes around and inside it, even if still in a minor key. Moreover, the danger of a heavy cultural-linguistic homogenization concerns more or less all ethnic groups, putting to question the identity of languages and the peoples that in them recognize their most intimate truth. But perhaps electronics will be able to give us tomorrow a new, and for now improbable, miracle of Pentecost in which *logos* and pneuma will make use of *chips*.

To sacrifice oneself to a moment that is of rituality / conflict examining the dialect sites and writing-describing them with an inevitable effect of distortion and "indetermination" appears justified even if we don't know how productive. It remains linked, in any case, to an attitude that can only be outside of "this" time, precisely because it has ventured into a time of different directions and *durée;* and for this it has to do almost solely with poetry, rarely with prose (understood in their most obvious and necessary meanings). But for this reason the contact with dialects, killed but never dead, minimal but with linkages and echoes in the most incredible distances, is capable of framing, even if in encrypted terms, the most effulgent opening onto alterities, futures, active dissolvings. Dialect can have nothing to do with re-exhumations or embalmings "in reserve." It must be felt as a guide (beyond any hypothesis whatsoever concerning its destiny) to single out the signs of new realities that are pressing to emerge. One proceeds thus, from remote prehistory, perhaps prehuman (since which time without intermittence dialect has marked the advent of speech) to a future in which everything, radically called into question, is called to regenerate, beyond the terrible challenge emerging today, in the most magnificent, inconceivable forms.

(1987)

The Euganean Hills

There truly exist certain places, or rather, certain concretions
or archipelagos of places out of which—no matter how you
penetrate them and no matter how you think and rethink them
or gather them all together as in a model studied in perspective
from above—it is never possible to make a true "map" with fixed
itineraries. The desire that such places insinuate is one of almost
physically introjecting them, so intensely do they vibrate with
interwoven and concentrated vitalities. They exist in all the world
and in Italy are everywhere. That which pushes to identify them
is truly an exclusive love, "fatal" for the never-tiring violence with
which it rises from the bottom of the depths and pushes like
subterranean fire.

This is especially true, with brazen and bewitching evidence,
of the Euganean Hills (mountains). Even a simple promotional
brochure is more than sufficient to gain entrance to a flight of
visual surfaces, of matters of the earth and of human beings
who live there by choice or fate with their farmhouses, towns, or
castles, to give the sense of an "infinite" and an "eternal" belong-
ing. It is a reality that leads alluringly into a vortex of intrigues or
apparitions or confirmations: beginning with the near or enclosed
thermal "trickery" of healthful aquifers, lauded since ancient times
(Claudiano), and leaving Padua in the background.

To move around, to crawl over, to be in the Euganean Hills
and glide about in all the directions of the cosmos is to gather
the possibilities of the tortuosity of one or of ten paths upon ten
different horizons and to taste the healthy conviviality and calm-
ness of many olives and of many oils sufficient to forever feed
the interior lanterns and fluidity of fantasies. And at once we find
ourselves sweetly and bitterly entangled in successive paradises, in

accordance with the geologic body and with 30–35 million years, which hunch up their shoulders with boisterous herds of hill-mountains that end up weaving themselves into labyrinths.

At the extreme south of the range beckon the "radioactive" fragments of the sanctuary-scriptorium in Este, sacred to the ancient Venetian goddess Reitia, straightener of the world, weaver, and healer at the head of a pantheon almost entirely female. Reitia, who knows . . . a young girl of extreme unreality and elegance who emerges from a little woods, or a fruitful mother at work in a farmyard out of a play by Ruzante. All of it is in fragments and splinters, but also in well-turned vases, in pendants of unquiet passion, and in runes perhaps lunar. . .

Just beyond this, to the north there rise on the hills Baone and Calaone, home to the court of the Este marquises where in the thirteenth century the first and most important gathering of Provençal poets in Italy was kindled, including refugees from persecution in their homelands. The figures of Aimeric De Peguilhan, Lambertino Buvalelli, and the young Sordello, as detailed in the exciting studies of Gianfranco Folena, stand out amongst them in a dense interplay of relations between northern Italy and Provençe. Before her monastic retreat, the duchess Beatrice d'Este had been the noble "restaur" of the "Est" and had given much energy and joyous guidance to these writers.

The immense lyric patrimony from Provençe fittingly took root here after the Sicilian and Tuscan periods and found in Petrarch and in Arquà the climax of an entire tradition and an incredible beginning. With the gravitational force of a maximal star, Petrarch comes forth in the image of the autonomous poetic act and its necessary nourishing love-poison. Around him revolve events and crowds of admirers and illustrious imitators but also stodgy scholars.

Now in his "rosagiallo," the sarcophagus many times tampered with and restored, he camps out in the little square for tourists—but in the silent winter the space expands and expands again within the void. The sarcophagus is also perfumed with hoarfrost and nothing: it won't cease from being picked apart for this, just as the bronze head of the poet mounted above will never cease to be a target for flying stones. And is there still some remnant of the beehive that was found last century between the bare ribs of Petrarch during an inspection? Doesn't it bring to mind the bees of

Aristeo, symbol of the stubborn rebirth of poetry? And doesn't the unweighty, not-so-distant resting place of the poet inspire affection, before provoking reverence?

The secluded and rough aspect of the hills—which in certain areas are accessible only on foot along dirt paths where one can still encounter falcons—was certainly well suited to Petrarch and his long walks; here one can see the coalescing and spreading forth of the most varied intellectual and emotional experiences in the shelter of a "final limit." And if by now, almost by popular demand, the worst exploitation and eating away of the rocks has been to a degree halted, the rough scars nevertheless here and there all too often emerge: but perhaps these wounds might well workably fit within Petrarchian poetry. They bring to mind Dino Buzzati's *Miracoli di Val Morel* (Miracles of Val Morel), which speaks of the sudden volcanic resurgence that spewed forth rabid cats (973 to be exact) which were then destroyed thanks to Saint Rita in 1737; later on he predicts an eruption of panthers, this time instead caused by Rita in order to halt the destroyers of the hills. Here we may encounter great stories of local folklore, which are no less rich with truth and with fable than literary fantasies—and are more robust.

But in these more recent times another sort of destruction, amounting to a decapitation, begins to dog the mind. And the poets of these parts, some extremely talented such as Marco, are alarmed. Yes, because it seems that Laura herself, the lady of love of all Europe, is trembling and fading into myth. Just as well-read scholars have once again taken up the burden of disproving the existence of Laura, fortune has brought about the overlapping success of the song "Laura non c'è" (Laura's no more) at the Sanremo Music Festival. Nek is the name of the singer-songwriter who has come to underline this veritable *nex* (massacre) without even wanting it: meanwhile the teenagers of Italy hum along. For Padua, home to a widespread Petrarch craze—so deeply ingrained that the city's rugby team is named after the poet—it will be a hard blow. But wait: a few other philological authorities no less competent than the detractors will champion the fables, having no wish to deprive humanity, neither here nor in the entire world, of the "tangible presence" of Laura in history and the poetic Eucharist. The critical destiny of Petrarch, however, is as well off as ever—so much so that even Paul Celan, one of the greatest poets of our time, writing in German said that "Petrarch is once again in view." Coming from such an impervious and tormented vantage point, this is an assertion that calls for a reconsideration of the sense itself that poetry may have today.

Among the wide array of personages who have passed through this area in order to reinvigorate their various faiths, from Alfieri to Shelley to Byron, Ugo Foscolo holds an especially important place—he who madly dashed off towards the hills, jumping over hedges and ridges carrying a book of scattered rhymes, or who climbed up "to the sacred house of that sublime Italian." There, with the loved and rejected Teresa, Jacopo the suicidal protagonist of *Ortis* "prostrated himself"—in whom the author himself partially lurks. But the fact is that the dear hills, either reciprocating or enchanting, for Ugo were soothing to his erotic-political sadnesses—and who knows for how many others.

One gray spring day we were slowly wandering about by car amidst the press of the full, vaguely conical, roundish shapes of the hills, when at a bend in the road there appeared in the distance three geometrically perfect, outstretched, exquisitely pointed cones the color of lava ash that left us astonished. Possessed of their own nobility guaranteed by millions of years, carefree and yet somewhat devious children of the impossible—those cones appeared, they "were." "The Euganean Trimurti!" Simultaneously in Marco and me this dazzling, sharp wellspring of the divine spoke out, always present yet only in that moment manifest.

We remained long in contemplation (prayer, I would say) and then decided to return as soon as possible when we had more time. I hastily made a rough sketch that futilely pursued the precipitous and strict exactness, the subtle and mischievous haughtiness of those entities. We returned many times and never again encountered them. It seemed that . . . but no . . . they were partial resemblances, delusional scratchings. There was nothing to do but hope in another whim of the gods. In reality these are phenomena that continually take shape in any place, especially in the mountains: here hours, lights, seasons, and trifles incessantly come into conflict, making us starkly feel that nothing is stable, that everything changes even if it is motionless, because everything within itself is projected upon the unattainable essence of reality. And thus it comes to pass all the more so with the human spirit, even the most beloved human faces: everyone is the usual one / no one / one hundred thousand; everything was and will be landscapes diffracted and reassembled by wingbeats or gusts more or less caressing or malicious. And Yves Bonnefoy tells us that "places, like gods, are our dreams." Amidst the famous points on the hills that stand out, such as the garden, large villa, and labyrinth of Valsanzibio, the Castle of Cataio, or the Abbey of Praglia, are many nodes or quasi-Gordian knots created by the hilly shiftings, rough crags, or even by the various types of urban systems that emerge everywhere.

But—as if at the opposite pole of this space and time—it is worth lingering on the balcony in Teòlo, in anticipation of who knows what future of mechanisms ever more obsessive in the creation of exactitudes of pixels or apertures of omnidirectional compasses upon the infinite. At the regional center of experimental meteorological and hydrological study every atmospheric shift is recorded and forecast within the titillating gleamings and chromatics of computers. There the continuous writhing of the skies is interpreted, simultaneously collected throughout the entire region by hundreds of survey stations situated in the most varied points— stations whose sensitivity is every so often quashed by a plastic bag left by some farmer on the "eyes of the apparatus." Scientists at the center, each trained for specific tasks, prognosticate in millimetric units and with precision down to minutes and seconds, disaster or calm, here or there, so that if needed the best tactics of prevention can be organized in reasonable time. When exactly must the event at the Arena begin or be interrupted, or recommence without harm? Those in Teòlo can tell you.

Now it is night. The skillful young writer Giulio is enjoying the descent by bicycle from the hills towards Padua, whose sky is beginning to blaze with a pyrotechnic show. Perhaps he's returning from the popular Festival of the Jujubes in Arquà . . . Giulio is gliding downward content, bolstered by his hale phrase making, his good Italian—he could almost leap out into the void. "Listen"— perhaps everything might endure if faith in language endures?

(1997)

Between the Recent Past and the Distant Present

Dear Berardinelli,

Your letter is full of compelling observations and cues for reflection concerning familiar themes about which I have often thought and written.

But before diving into the heart of your ideas, I would like to call particular attention to the great change in human reality (so extensive as to entail, for example, the end of the agrarian world and the dialects connected to that world) that became apparent during the seventies. Before this there had been signs of disintegration noticeable only, however, when attempting to investigate the innermost connections between reality and language; this, however, came at the price of an instability that called back into doubt the same credibility of self-reference by means of language. This instability then led to an outlook particularly receptive to what managed to trickle out from diverse and disconnected forms of the present. And yet there always remained an unresolved uncertainty regarding the psychological unity and temporal permanence of the indispensable "I" that emerged at the center of discussion: an "I" in my case, devastated by periodic periods of depression.

Early on, in fact, I spoke of the place where I lived and the horizon of my everyday experience, sprinkled here and there with brief accounts subtly masked with hermetic-surrealist touches. In fact, among my writings there exists a brief foray into narrative prose, interwoven with my earliest poetry (*Sull'altopiano*, published by Neri Pozza). My poetry, in any case, has never lacked a certain narrativity. One can often find within it kernels or fragments of events, as well as figures and characters, spread over various spatial and temporal planes, that constitute a network of relatively abundant references, a more or less plausible map of the places where I have always lived.

I persisted for a time, overwhelmed and exhilarated, in my relationship with the environment; even if early on I came to recognize a threat looming over both locale and language, I must also make it clear that it was only with the passing of the seventies, and especially the late eighties, that this threat transformed into actual devastation—a devastation that is not solely the death of living beings. One knows this happens: one day something exists, and then the day after it disappears. I use the word devastation because there exists a metastasis-proliferation of distorted survivals, of synchronies and poisonous cacophonies, of reversals of sense even when symbols remain the same; it was also precisely at the end of the eighties that widespread corruption came to light. Previously, despite exposed or suspected grim episodes, there remained the long wake of postwar hope, fed by faith in economic development (generated, moreover, by the long and terrible travails of emigration, which I myself experienced for approximately two years, sustained by the goal of saving a bit of money in order return home for good): but it was precisely during the late seventies marred with terrorist acts and then in a flood in the eighties, that there emerged a loss of a sense of state, a cadaverization of our history, with all of the pertinent vital presence, more or less maggoty, concentrated in one or another part of the cadaver. Even language, in turn, was clearly shaken, devastated—and with it literature.

Poetry says all this, not being able to do any less, but it must say it from a type of "exile within reality": for Dante (*Par.* I) those associated with the laurel crown are either the King or the Poet. I am drawn to read this "or" not only as disjunctive but also exclusive, to read in it a contrast between a type of celestial city of poetry and a terrestrial one, that of the king. While there can never be harmony in the former, in the latter, the realm of poetry, it is possible. It should be. But the involvement, even when not overly apparent, with history, its conflicts, its follies, cannot but take place—all the more so because in continuous danger of becoming enslaved to the holders of true power. Poets are here "within" reality, but are also "exiled" from it as regards power, even when within power itself—in the event that they are claimed by an ethnic group or party. It is a matter, however, of a contrast that must have a liberating force: I have never agreed with Brecht when, in one of his poems, he laments that his are times in which one feels guilty even when speaking to a blossoming tree, because as long as there are tyrants, not even this should be done. This I cannot accept as true: no tyrant will ever be able gain power over those who, in some "distant" and "radical" way, truly believe in blossoming trees; in fact, tyrants cannot but sense a threat in the "lauding" of blossoming trees and the deep-set place of liberty from which this praise originates. And yet it is true that, in writing these words, I am conscious of the enormous complexity of reality, teeming with an incredible variety of historical situations. But the principle is valid. Because power, in nearing its own zero point, namely, tyranny, demands silence. The involvement of the Prince is decisively a silencing; (*Roma locuta, causa soluta*), he silences everything and thus resembles death—yet he also resembles life in that he is a continual source of death in order to survive as life. Even the worst beasts have made space for unexpected turns of reality. One cannot risk, however, falling into a relativism that would put in crisis every ethical principle that emerges from the *pòlemos* in Heraclitus and cruelly in the *Bhagavad Gita*. The evil that certainly exists, should, in any event, be observed from within an ethics that never completely succumbs to the idea of a nature "forever" malicious and that thus refuses to play the victim. Here we brush up against the Leopardian outlook, so "exalted," "exiled," and together so akin to the frightening *corpus vivens* of material reality, an outlook in continual self-contradiction.

When you, dear Berardinelli, ask if we should consider poetry as a message on the state of the world, perhaps something along these lines is in fact inevitable; it seems pertinent, however, to pose such a question with scathing irony and self-irony so as to avoid an emphasis more characteristic of speech-making politicians: for the poor intellectuals (?) or poets (?) there in any event remains the theme of bearing witness, and the sense that (if you'll permit me to quote myself), "So much, in these depths, / remains of the process of verbalization of the world."

There has always been a great deal of utopian tension in literature, important, if for nothing else, for comprehending a reality that is continually disappearing in its headlong escape into the future. Even when literary worlds arise that are all too revealingly "humanistic" or even "arcadian," in which values otherwise difficult to broach are made topical—even in these cases there is a "socio-anthropological necessity." Consider Heidegger's comparison of the concentration camps and mechanized, chemical-filled agriculture. Despite seeming an enormously cruel insult, his assessment contains some unavoidable truth: the distrust of technology, so giganticized in Heidegger, does not seem an exaggeration if one considers how fast technology is progressing, dragging us into the clutches of a treacherous scientific autonomy in directions that are impossible to foresee. If we do not want to fall into complete nihilism and accept a situation inspiring comments such as "Nothing can be done anymore" and "Everything's going to hell," we must in some way pursue stable forms of support and attempt to avert disaster, postulating a calculability of the scientific-technological mechanism.

Today, in the so-called Internet age, products abound that are frighteningly premature for a society that has not yet reached a potentially more collective and equitable form: but who can guarantee that panterrestrial communication will carry us in this direction? We know that great historic changes have occurred alongside outbreaks of violence, but the most disturbing form of violence that we currently must live with is not the threat of nuclear, biological, or chemical warfare but the ruination that looms over an unknown but immense number of places. We are compelled, in any case, to use obsolete criteria to judge slippery phenomena, not knowing what drives them or if they are controllable: from sudden, rapaciously bloody conflicts to AIDS and various new "sicknesses," it is in this climate that we have passed "from the killing fields to the killing of the fields." In fact, both predicaments have been thrust upon us simultaneously.

In speaking of places we also necessarily speak of times. The catastrophe of places (and precisely of the "dreams" that Yves Bonnefoy speaks of with magnificent "grace," to which you refer in your letter), is also the catastrophe of the fields—of memory—in which times are arranged according to an order: if we had remembered that scientific and technical progress was the product of humanistic civilization and was born from it as a rational development and ethical rigor, then all this utopian nucleus wouldn't have been lost from view—which is simply a request for orientation and in turn makes necessary the project (however makeshift and open to every form of criticism) for some "sense of reality."

The other writers of my generation who you mention, despite their diverse backgrounds and experiences, tend to converge upon just exactly this sort of line of demarcation.

If we consider, however, that science and technology in their most efficient forms have existed for little more than three or four centuries, it becomes clear that there is still a long way to go in order to reharmonize the dissonances brought about by this period—having caught sight of new world orders. For example, harmonizing historical time with biological time or, even better, geological time with cosmological time: only with great difficulty do we ascertain how human minds, especially those of the powerful, come to terms with our true condition. Indeed, if those in power were to think that they had control over a minor planet, a remote speck in a distant galaxy, and in the end possessed only that, their outlook would be more healthily depressed (as Hillman would say).

Our "alpha animals" instead are unrelentingly driven. If I think of that false god, the richest man in the world, I cannot but feel physical repugnance for him, his pennies, his schemes, his euphoric bespectacled gaze. The fact is that the progress that emerged with humanism, along with its advancement in knowledge, has given rise to problems of psychological readjustment, stripping us of false biblical and Ptolemaic time and thrusting us into an immense conception of time, consisting of millions upon millions of years. Perhaps only India, with its myriad epochs, can teach us something in this regard. In any event, it should be possible to compile a list of certain relatively inexpensive acts of courage. One small example of this would be to clearly state that we have already entered the new millennium—a fact implicitly admitted even by the church. But this entails confronting enormous economic interests, as well as mythologies and apocalyptism. It is far more common to turn a blind eye to the spreading of toxins that in turn propagate bizarre fantasies. Ours is a time of sects—religious, political, and otherwise—as well as analogous aggregations carrying labels advertising "alternative knowledge": we have arrived at the divine right of the masses in complete opposition to the liberating rationality of democracy. The most archaic and primordial instincts of the individual and of small groups have resulted in a form of absurd pretence. This "privilege" exists alongside the fundamentalism of the globalizers: two forms opposed to yet equivalent to terrorism. Here too in Italy the democracy of rights and needs has for the most part been disregarded; instead of leading to the abolishment of special rights and the control of consumerist lust, democracy has turned into a pretense of privileges for the masses and an unrelenting chain of consumption in which everyone wants their purchase to be exclusive or unique. Everyone is thus able to instantaneously transform themselves into geniuses capable of seducing and dominating, so much that every asinine television personality, whether in journalism or politics, is commonly deemed "charismatic"—given that all but the tiniest vestige has been lost of what can truly be called charisma.

Giacomo Novena comes to mind, whose poetry should be administered today as a compulsory vaccine; in one of his poems he revisits the famous maxim of Boileau: "Un sot trouve toujours un plus sot qui l'admire" (An idiot will always find a worse idiot to admire). Noventa corrects him thus: "Ah, Boileau!, la disgrazia xé massa / Più granda de quel che ti scrivi; / Un imbeçil trova un che lo amira / Anca in ùn de lù manco imbeçil" (Ah Boileau!, the offense is graver, much graver; / An idiot will find another to admire him / Even one less an idiot than him). These lines refer to the distant past. What would he say today? By now one feels the lingering sensation that in simply moving about, in simply presuming to be able to "indicate" something or bear witness to the existence of a stone, a plant, a cloud, a love (?), a *Witz*, it is difficult to express but fetid copies. In simply moving the air in speaking, taking part in (not merely beginning or even ending) any given discourse or action, one risks perceiving only a nauseating stench, ours and of others. Beyond all this there exists today not only a contrast between those who are and are not *imbeçil*, but, much worse, on a daily basis we bump up against every possible form of mental illness. This goes beyond the natural inclination towards madness in those in positions of power ("I signori tengono tutti un po' del matto"—Manzoni) to affect a great range of people in varying states of psychic disconnectedness, or zombiism, or borderlinism. To want everything and its exact opposite is the rule: for proof one need only look at the results of certain recent referendums.

The question is not only an Italian one; without doubt in the world there are far worse situations. And yet, some of our records and precedents are hard to overlook: the first country to have elected a prostitute (euphemized as a "porn star") as a deputy minister of parliament; the first country to have fostered a falling birth rate not as a legitimate need to slowly curb overpopulation, but to the masochistic point of not stopping at zero population growth and instead going in very short time to well below zero; the first country to chose dictatorship over democracy in the 1920s, abandoning a democratic tradition that was already reasonably solid (leaving out Russia, which having passed from a medieval tyranny to a dictatorship of "well-intentioned" origins, became increasingly grim and blind, nearly losing any possibility of continuance).

And then there is today's problem of the disappearing devotion, so to speak, to our national language, with its glorious cortège of dialects (which to many of the older generation offered the chance to be richly diglossic). Ours is a language threatened on all sides by an "anglosassone" ever more invasive and inept. The near future meanwhile promises increasingly more elderly people and fewer young ones, often stuffed and stupefied with all the "playthings" offered by our bulimic-anorexic society, by the capitalistic rotating and globalizing fundamentalism (mentioned above), maximally *schizo* because compelled to render the wealth of the few ever more turreted, pinnacled out of reach, and yet phantasmal—with the science and technology being developed for this small group's exclusive use. This it accomplishes together with sucking the blood out of the masses, while always leaving intact the worst residue of false faiths and the bloodlust of "ethnic cleansings."

Here too in this small corner of Italy, amidst the wasting away of the language and the dearth of a truly loving dedication of its speakers, dwells the Mammon-crazed proliferation of TV and media neologisms (in part benumbing, in part bureaucratic) of legal and administrative chimeras ever more complicated and nauseating. It is nearly impossible to read the text of a bureaucratic legal ordinance or regulation and keep from retching.

However, language will sustain life, either with or without us ("Contessa, che è mai la vita?" [Countess, whatever is life?] the troubadour Jaufré Rudel seems to say), preserving its inner drive, persistently and forever fashioning new formulas and sandcastles, despite the pull of entropy: new freedoms and interethnic understanding will perhaps come about despite enormous difficulties (Eibl-Eibesfeldt) on a biologic base for the moment still existent.

And yet the chance of this happening is greatly lessened given the human race's compulsion to frenetically, exponentially accelerate all movement to the point of nearly destroying the entire environment through incessantly increasing consumption: scholars of time and space, such as Paul Virilio, ever more concerned, are spreading the alarm.

Meanwhile here in Italy, amidst those who claim that our language is useless and that it would be better to go straight from dialect to English (who themselves ignore the former and can barely stutter a few words of the latter), there will triumph a new *grammelot* rich with sounds, including the most contorted borborygms, teeming with alternative-accompanying gestures. It is thus fitting that Dario Fo was awarded the Nobel Prize in literature, who long ago brought attention to the need to develop a mixed phonic and visual means of expression. And will Oliviero Toscani, with his photographs, films, and explosive visuality, not prophesy for everyone a future of only icons, brands, and "logos," an *embrasson-nous united colors,* in favor of the *impresa,* the *vendita,* the autopoiesis of *for sale* or *on sale?*

As far as poetry is concerned (so little spoken of here): in its meanderings more or less karstic, in its demented-infantile roots, in its eternal movement towards a future conceived as a *verbum* (including absorbing music and other arts), in its being a wound and (modest) unmarketable drug—to the side on the side—poetry will trudge ahead intoxicated with stubbornness and humility from its contact with the void. It will continue its endeavors misunderstood, understood, even at times turning creative in misunderstanding . . . Many conceive of poetry in this way, the old, the not quite so old, such as you, dear Berardinelli—even many of the young think in this way.

In regards to my "neurotic lyricism," as you say: I affirm that it comes in large part from the loss of the superior natural beauty so celebrated and enduring in the paintings of Titian, Giorgione, or Giovanni Bellini—and I might add—in the impassioned paintings of my father, who used to take me as a child to watch him paint en plein air; in these parts there isn't a church, however modest, that doesn't contain within itself some exceptional pictorial work that in its own way reverberates external harmonies. Every microcosm has its saint as well as its painter. I err. It had. The times are no more (without excessive nostalgia for the wretched day-to-day conditions of the inhabitants) when Hugo von Hoffmannsthal ecstatically described this area in his descent from the Alps towards Venice. Today there are poisonous factories, fetid industrial discharges, and horrible traffic jams on roads increasingly unfit for their loads and dangerous due to the unending of convoys of tractor-trailers and the crazed speeding of everyone. I, a puttering bicyclist, no longer feel safe anywhere. And yet there exist the marvelous colors of plants, weeds, if you will, but joyous, such as the yellow topinambur, which carelessly flout the careful order of gardens. They exist for those who search for them, scattered in clusters or throngs in remote places (but for how long will they last?) from which there still emanates a powerful eroticism that seems to waft up from the earth itself to become a form of feminine beauty expressive of the *terra,* sharp as a diamond point. Even if this sort of talk may seem obsolete or even offensive to a certain train of thought, I believe that it continues to have meaning.

And dark throbbings meanwhile arise from those places that retain the traces of past conflicts, such as the ossuaries commonly found here, some of which border on squalid discotheques—to say nothing of the major thoroughfares jammed late at night by the slaves of prostitution and their "beneficiaries" etc., etc. Places exist, consist, coexist; they call for new ways of thinking. And I repeat with Yves Bonnefoy, that places are our dream-nightmares and deity-landscapes, volcanic powers buried yet always lying in wait to send allusive tremors, from the Colli Euganei to the Lagune, to the Prealpi and the Dolomiti, in all of our beloved and accursed Italy, and all the beloved and accursed world. And the poets who will declare themselves, with a certain necessary sarcasm and tongue-in-cheek speech, perhaps will only say "Ich singe wie der Vogel singt / Ich singe wie der Vogel singt / in den Zweigen wognet." Noo! The legions of hunters are here—they too are ecological! Even little birds are a part of the ferocious food chain! Heavens, what good eaters!

Isn't it, in the end, that the writers of poetry also contribute to the massacre of the language, which, it seems clear, is destined to be continually wounded in order to truly exist?

Pardon me, dear Berardinelli, if I have obliged you to endure what amounts to a "parade" of well-known facts only in order to situate a few of the more relevant elements of our conversation.

(1999)

The Future and Languages

It has long been a favorite pastime of mine to thumb through grammar books and hunt out differences in declinations, conjunctions, syntactic forms, and orthographic antics. At heart, I have always been more of a "botanist" of grammars than a (mediocre at best) connoisseur of languages. Herein lies an obscure problem of mine, related in a certain way to my poetic expression. In haphazardly navigating these grammars, I often have the pleasure of stumbling across particular flowers, marvelous blossoms that can be compared to one another in all languages—blossoms that can also be dangerous. During our current period in history, with its many looming problems, the coexistence of languages will without doubt become more difficult than ever: simply consider English, which incessantly weaves its path everywhere, often escaping from the loom.

And yet another danger exists: America and no longer England is the matrix of this immense energy. There, among the ranks of the middle class, a passive indifference towards other languages is taking root—recalling a similarly infamous phenomenon of eighteenth-century Europe. Here I refer to the masses, because the upper echelons of society have always known how to get by. In the meantime, differences in pronunciation, orthography, and intonation are taking place within various social classes, ethnic groups, and geographic areas. A pressure is emerging in certain regions of Spain and Portugal, and in some areas of the United States, created by increasingly widespread forms of Spanish-English bilingualism. It is very dangerous, in any event, for a country to exclusively use a single language and not be familiar with any others: such a practice can create something of an implosive phenomenon, a tendency to constantly "reduce."

I recall an article by Anthony Burgess, filled with his character-
istic, brilliant paradoxes, in which he claimed that to learn English
one needed very little: to know how to whine using a few tricks
mixed with truncated vocal sounds spiced with various nuances.
Those who know how to use "on," "off," "out," etc. with the verb
"to get," have already learned half the language. These observa-
tions by waggish Burgess, despite their tomfoolery, have some very
serious truth to them.

Let us not forget that in ancient times things were very differ-
ent: for example, at the court of Augustus, both Greek and Latin
were spoken. Latin was the official language of the Roman Empire
because it was considered of high cultural prestige. Members of
the upper class, however, could not afford to ignore Greek. The
emperor Marcus Aurelius, wrote his extraordinary philosophi-
cal book in Greek—for himself, without intention for publica-
tion (though it expresses one of the highest moments of human
thought). It is very significant that the language of high culture
remained connected to the Greek matrix. The Romans actually
made a considerable contribution, but not at a level comparable
to the Greeks. But today, at the court of Washington, would a
language be commonly spoken simply for its cultural prestige?
(Keeping in mind, however, that Augustus was a conservative, even
linguistically speaking.)

I have spoken at length about this topic in order to stress how
important it is for leaders, in particular those of countries that have
international responsibilities, to be deeply involved in languages of
high cultural value that are different from their own. This would
obviously facilitate the reciprocal understanding of problems.
There have been numerous conflicts and diplomatic failures caused
by errors in the interpretation of messages and meetings (in 1919,
at the conference of Versailles, V. E. Orlando encountered serious
difficulties making decisions due in part to his poor knowledge of
French).

Today, moreover, the populations of ancient civilizations,
such as those of China and India, with their immense political and
cultural weight, are once again rising. This is contributing to the
present state of agitation in the world today, and consequently,
in linguistics. Difficult mediation is necessary to understand the
complex backgrounds of these powerful giants. And what can be
said of the Arab world, with its world ambitions and its problems

of bilingualism between modern Arabic and the different dialects used across vast areas?

For Italians, there is the urgent need to have good translations from English to Italian and vice versa. Without them we would be left without a voice and echo because our language is unfortunately becoming more and more marginalized. For example, the venerable magazine of physics, founded in Galileo's times, conserves only its title in Italian, *Il Nuovo Cimento* (the text is in English). By now it is a well-known, indisputable fact that when dealing with problems of general interest it is convenient to use a language understood far and wide.

There is also the question of "accessories," foreign words that are now part of our common language, which are often unnecessary and rather grotesque. And yet, in order to lessen the potential long-term damage to the identity of a language caused by this linguistic contamination, it is certainly not advisable to use legal impositions (such as France's Toubon law).

The methods of defense should be established according to each case and language on the basis of the historical contexts of the various affected countries (French supercentralism and Italian pulverization). In Italy's case, we must not forget that our national language developed alongside powerful dialectal structures (which are parallel languages) and Latin, an authoritative language used in the academic and scientific communities of Europe. A "flexible" defense, thus, is the only sustainable option in our case—keeping in mind that both Latin and the dialects continue to nourish our national language, which clearly can also be said of other languages. In these volatile and chaotic times, many oddities are taking place: at present, it is the television that lays down the rules, imposing linguistic models and expressions copied from "Americanoid" situations.

The Italian spoken today is often incorrect; when the pronunciation is not heavily marked by regional accents, it is affected by the Italian spoken by the cultural elite (actors, judges, etc.) of northern Italy. This causes a vacantly foolish admixture, reminiscent of sitcoms, which is the epitome of bad taste. One need only think of the first names, borrowed from English, that are given to children by "naive parents" influenced by soap operas such as *The Bold and the Beautiful*. It is one thing to use widely accepted foreign names as Sabrina, Samantha, or Deborah, but to impose

English versions of Italian names like Alex, Thomas, Christian, or even Anthony is another. When these names are accompanied by surnames from the Veneto, which often end in a consonant, and are then given an American accent, it seems as if the Morgan (rather than Morgàn) family has spread throughout the region—all thanks to the removal of an accent. As a final example, there is the well-known Benettón, first romanticized as Benettòn on national TV, then changed into the worldwide trademark, Bénetton.

This base habit of giving pointlessly foreign names is unmistakably common to other semantic areas as well. Comparable wonders can be often seen in the inscriptions of commercial signs whose use of foreign words is at times justified by the type of business, but not when it produces minotaurs (even if amusing) such as SNACK BAR AL CANTON and many other similar examples.

There are many practical reasons to have a global language, but we must not forget the danger it poses to ethnic and linguistic identities. Taking Italy's precarious situation as an example, we could hazard a guess that in two or three decades a new sort of linguistic proletariat will be created. In fact, those unable to speak at least some form of broken English will be excluded from all forms of power.

There will be many, who, despite having been introduced to English at an early age, will be unable to afford the expensive trips necessary for a full immersion. As a result, they will be discriminated against in the same way as those who, only two or three decades ago, knew only the dialect of their region and barely spoke Italian.

Then again, all these obstacles and terrors may be overcome, sooner than we think, by omnipresent technology and its mystical gadgets that instantly translate conversations. Research of this sort has been in the works for years, and sooner or later Sony, or some other company, will jauntily succeed; on the other hand, isn't the numen Internet, from which we can expect all manner of surprises, already working?

[n.d.]

January

Now brutalized by the industry of the snow—which, not having fallen here in my valley, nevertheless leaves a sensation of disquiet, as if the entire horizon of the mountains were worm-eaten, swarming with the crowds that in one way or another press close—January forever remains one of the most joyous and balanced months, leaving out its initial stretch overly congested with holidays. Exquisite tensions of lights and colors—the most unexpected hues of azure, violet, pink, and indigo—break apart and then gently fall to earth, dwelling with tranquility in every corner of the landscape: an order emanates from there within, continually recast in shapes forever strengthened with undercurrents of clarity, in reassuring forms of eternity. It is well known that winter is not the season of the death of things, of ruination; on the contrary, it is a powerful allusion to a time beyond time. It is in January that we are impelled to sense the circle that forever returns within itself, the year's cycle that breaks apart and slows to a standstill, making way for an overwhelming law of infinite stability joined, however, to an abyss, a splitting apart. Sublime explanations emerge speaking from a world beyond, certainly not against life, but seemingly "for" another form of life, in which the first, captured, is eternally preserved, gleaming with truth and lights "fixed" in a spell. This new life nonetheless remains ready to melt, when the moment comes, in the warmth and streaming sap of a process of regermination.

But it is especially from the whiteness, its slinking down just under the azure of the skies, from the enveloping whiteness of the mountains (a true synthesis of all colors), that January draws forth its manifold enchantments. Long ago it snowed more frequently, and January thickened everywhere: but in the valley and on the hills it lasted less than on the nearby mountains. Now there dominates in winter a disquieting aridity most extensive in January, a crystalline aridity: in the distance the prominent, downy outcroppings all quiver with glory and timid sparklings of glory. And yet everywhere there persists a luminous candor of another language, concentrated in all north-facing places, from hills to houses, low walls, gardens, and gentle slopes: miniature snow crystals and fringes of ice join layers of hoarfrost and rime survived for who knows how long. Thick, overbearing, spiny, and yet seductive, they gather in packs within every sinuous recess, amidst the dun of the ditches, the last dangling dry leaves, and the crying out, the indescribably pure and licit piercing of evergreen thickets laden with coralline berries encircling little fields hidden here and there within the hills' folds.

And it sometimes happens, after rare intense rainstorms, that the mountains, at a distance of two or three kilometers to the north, transform into a gigantic precipitous wall of whiteness with undertones of Himalayan mysteries; from it irradiates a phosphorescence that at twilight glows through windows into rooms and transfigures the people gathered round dinner tables into unrecognizable, nearly haloed entities. In those moments it is difficult to speak, so penetrating is the gleaming aura, and teeming with exceptional unrealities. As in the distant past, recalled now so clearly, conversations abate and movements thicken, seemingly part of a ritual in which the presence of January is celebrated, almost unconsciously. Meanwhile, everywhere outside in the vast world, violets, indigos, and shadowy grays in turn conquer one another and then are conquered by the electric lights kindling in the houses and streets. Everything then seems to break free from the spell's grip, and one feels the intimacy of kitchens enlivened with peaceful and modest dinners under the ordinary warmth of household lights. And such lights, especially if they are humbly yellowish, conjure up memories: of when stables welcomed the cheerful and pleasant communal warmth of the *filò*, the rustic vigils in which chatter and playacting, the comfort of simple drinks, and the reading of prayers prepared the ground for sweet, furtive encounters. This was life's pathway in January, but there are so many pathways, welling up like a gentle swarm of ice crystals.

Today, as if worming their way out from some sort of new, decidedly estranged or perversely soothing other-world, television screens tirelessly swirl their kaleidoscopes. And look, now it is time for the late-night "snow report," a most abstract and yet engrossing moment—despite initial appearances. A little tune that succeeds in winning over our attention accompanies a spectral, computer-generated landscape that slips without seeming into an irremediable nostalgia for a world in which there awake phony paradises with phony mountains and snow falling in rarefied simulations. There within, other Januaries, of divergent worlds, accompany the scrolling of place-names with individual readings of the snow's depth, poured into the most arcane of mirrors, "there in cyber-space." Nostalgias for futures overwhelm everyone, expectations of ever more inconceivable Januaries. And for an instant one forgets the vexing crush that presses in upon every nook of the mountains with its trail of filth.

[n.d.]

Rebirth of the Hills

Reverified today too the ineffable abundance, the perennial expand-
ing and shrinking of the hills, hills, hills, cilium, cilia, cilia, like
an inexhaustible crowd in mixed rescuing and abandoning, a gift
of presence variously distracted and returning back upon itself,
aimed towards the infinite. The rushing ahead of each single face
of amassed murky greens, of every serpentine meandering, green
upon green, was something more than simply born from nature
and reworked by man. From there was born something more than
human, madly abstract, but embodied from perception to percep-
tion. I rediscovered the sense too of great ideations, the vaster
valleys, the kindled wetlands—or the sense of a secret vortex in
the most clustered and precipitous thickets. I take note of every
place, every point within place: ephemeral and uncontrollable
perfections, but only because they are open, impatient for liberty,
for an extremely deep adhering to the terrible, flickering liberty of
chaos. And yet, nothing not homemade or not protecting, nothing
depersonalizing—rather, step by step, I set out upon perpetually
new paths of being, of seeing.

[n.d.]

June

June was always awaited with anxiety, almost with pain. Concern over the weather, its astounding intractability, reigned supreme. No advance of spring towards summer was secure enough to guarantee an end to sudden deluges, the "montanade" that lashed the countryside—at times accompanied by vicious and dazzling hailstorms, erratically aggressive and ferocious in their incredible, devastating, and scattered downpourings along the slopes and fields. And yet every rainfall came almost as if expected, as if hidden and then revealed by its particular duty or destiny, godsend or calamity. And in any case, in our parts June is the rainiest month.

But the enormous, vigorous growth of the earth, nearly breaking free from itself with every conceivable force, in summits and fecundities, emerged beneath our feet, drawing its thrust from the farthest abysses of the cosmos; it seemed as if the entire planet had fermented and swollen, anchoring itself to a sun ever more assuring and robust, doubtlessly demented with a precious arrogance. And yet, across the earth bursting with myriad plants, flowerings, and sunbeams, a veil of foggy-rainy-haze would at times rise up with an obstinate thickness that stuck in the lungs, filled with insistent obscurities unexpectedly creeping forth from every nook and cranny, challenging the irresistible upheaval of growth: and yet it was impossible to hate the damp velvet veil, that great abundance of water, because in reality it was an accessory and accomplice in the growth itself. Thus one felt torn between desires and nearly irreversible forms of death—but then the tide that rushed towards the solstice with its continually reborn mysteries and surgings grew overwhelming in its encircling. There was a dedication that we all felt within the great vegetal thickness and its nourishing pollinators, so conflicting, and together convergent in the stirring of their energy; they would leave a place intact yet in tatters, nearly bloody, an open sore. It was wonderful to wriggle through the meanderings of this oscillation between invasive honeyed sunlight and spiderwebs heavy with myriad diversiform droplets of water–often on horseback in the valleys riding low to the ground towards the nearby ridgelines and fields scattered in restless repose.

There were thousands of legends that emanated from the flowers, plants, and woods in their delicious, glistening, intersecting formulations. It was left to us to interpret and understand them, leaving out however—necessarily—their ultimate meaning. Of the many legends, the most everlastingly rich with stimulus, from episode to episode, was that of the poppies.

It would begin with the appearance of a single devious and tiny baby-gnome seeking to remain hidden or to be discovered only with effort or all of a sudden. They then began to appear here and there, audacious squads of the vanguard, nearly astonished to have dared so much. Then, over the course of days, storms, and the ripening of wheat into dripping gold, the poppies gathered into clusters or scattered about, leaving nothing untouched with their joyous yet ingenuous—and for this almost comic—scarlet conceit. From them arose a murmuring or dumbfounded abandonment, or insistent hinting at something, at a sense of wonderment that each poppy simultaneously saw in itself and shouted to the four winds. After the superabundance of the winds and rains had kicked up breezes through the encouraging soft azure, the poppies, scattered in the most unexpected places, quivered in unison, alluding to infinite mini-futures, both sweet and sour: they became mini-anemometers for the mystic gauging of joy, presences, absences, and loves, even if only in hints.

And meanwhile cathedrals, cupolas of cumuli or stratocumuli, drifted across the encircling horizon, slowly reddening as if in response to the inquiries of the poppies. But with the passing of the month, the shining yellow corn and wheat grew more assertive, taller, and thicker, while the poppies, beloved sprites, started to weaken, vanishing day by day as if swept away in clusters or scattered after a great battle; in the end there remained the straggling and dispirited rearguard to remind us of our shortcomings and losses, our weaknesses or small hidden hemorrhages, our longing for the will, increasingly pallid and enfeebled, to resist. And yet all this continued to give us endless joy, while other legends crowded the horizon, guarding and giving rise to silence. Was it then the glory of the solstice? It must have been, but it became something much more, because most of the sun's radiance was enfolded in freshly arisen hazy rains and atmospheric padding, while the entire landscape, fields and all, enjoyed to the very height of the sun a promiscuous convergence of heat and coolness, of dazzling sunbeams and dripping pools of water—in a variegated orgiastic promiscuity of opposites lost in their sufferings, of an inexpressibly extensive and nimble Eros.

The sun, great conqueror, was the center of everything, from the subterranean and terrestrial realms to the celestial heights; but the fact that the true map of its saunterings and clamberings remained so distant, so miraculously remote, better prepared the ritual reenactment, here celebrated every year, of Shakespeare's *A Midsummer Night's Dream.* The scenes were spun through with resounding intrigues, remembrances, and transformations of every sort, unloosed or reborn within a whim, powerfully redolent of a classicized foreignness, or even nonexistence; they felt like the flights of bees through slippery honey poked through with minimal entities. They lasted, untangling, for four days and nights, from the 21st to the 24th, ending on the evening of Saint John's Day. It was then, by unanimous traditional consensus, that every caress or gentle cuffing of the imagination transported us from hallucination to pearly hallucination, from the most stunning stunts of comic verse to everlasting poetry—which indeed triumphed in the end, with the highest ascension (altar) of the sun, able to generate in us a near-zenith of blazing, satiating nudity.

[*n.d.*]

Notes

Poetry

In the proceeding section, all notes are by Andrea Zanzotto, unless otherwise identified.

Da *Dietro il paesaggio* / From *Behind the landscape*

In various poems: Dolle, Lorna, and San Fedele are place-names, either true or fictitious.

Serica / Silky (pages 30–31)
The title "Silky" refers to the raising of silkworms, which was once widely practiced in Zanzotto's area of the Veneto—PATRICK BARRON.
LINE 3: "cadde la luna" ("the moon falls"): see Saffo's fragment 115, and Giacomo Leopardi's "La sera del dì di festa," line 3—PB.
For a possible influence on stanzas two and three, see Hölderlin's "Hälfte des Lebens"—PB.

Adunata / Gathering (pages 32–33)
Written in August–September, 1943, this poem refers to the retreat of soldiers, specifically to events surrounding Vittorio Veneto—PB.

L'Acqua di Dolle / The Water of Dolle (pages 34–37)
This poem, written in 1946, is set in the hamlet of Dolle (alias Rolle, located a few miles to the north of Pieve di Soligo); the river is the Lierza, a tributary of the Soligo—PB.

Là sul ponte / There on the Bridge (pages 38–41)
LINE 1: "San Fedele" is the name that Zanzotto gives to the pass of San Boldo (not far to the north of Pieve di Soligo)—PB.

Dietro il paesaggio / Behind the Landscape (pages 42–45)

LINE 21: "assistito da giorni tardi e scarsi," see Dante *Purgatorio* XX, 16—PB.

Nella valle / In the Valley (pages 44–47)

This poem describes Saint Silvester's Day (December 31) in 1945—PB.

Da *Elegia e altri versi* / From *Elegy and Other Poems*

Partenza per il Vaud / Departure for Vaud (pages 50–51)

"Vaud" was the Swiss canton (whose capital city is Losanna) to which
Zanzotto temporarily emigrated in 1946 following the end of the Second
World War—PB.

LINE 15: "the cold Montello," a wooded, hilly area approximately three
miles south of Pieve di Soligo; see also introductory note to *Galateo in
Bosco* (The Woodland book of manners) below—PB.

Ore calanti / Waning Hours (pages 50–55)

V

"Pedeguarda" is the name of a small hamlet to the northwest of Pieve di
Soligo, near Miane; for "Dolle" see note above under "The Water of
Dolle"—PB.

Da *Vocativo* / From *Vocative*

In various poems: Dolle and Lorna are place-names, either true or fictitious.

I paesaggi primi / The First Landscapes (pages 64–65)

"The First Landscapes" refer to those painted by Zanzotto's father in mu-
rals in their family home (some include images of the poet as a young
child)—PB.

Da un'altezza nuova / From a New Height (pages 64–69)

The setting of this poem is the hamlet of Nogarolo, nestled in the hills
above Lake Revine, about eight miles to the northeast of Pieve di
Soligo—PB.

Da *IX Ecloghe* / From *IX Eclogues*

Un libro di ecloghe / A Book of Eclogues (pages 84–85)

LINE 1: "Not of gods not of princes . . ." is an allusion to sixteenth-century forms of bucolic poetry dedicated to elevated themes and personages—PB.

LINE 11: The "butterflies" is a reference to Dante's angelica *farfalla* (angelic butterfly) (see *Purgatorio* X, 125; cf. also XII, 95)—PB.

LINE 15: Urania is the muse of astronomy—PB.

LINE 18: In his dream, Jacob's ladder joined heaven and earth (see Genesis 28:12)—PB.

Ecloga I / Eclogue I (pages 84–89)

LINE 21: "Oh kites" is a reference to Giovanni Pascoli's poem "L'Aquilone" (The kite)—PB.

LINE 32: "le mie labbra non freno" (I do not curb my lips) is from the Latin: "Ecce, labia mea non cohibui."

LINE 41: The Lazarus here is the one of the parable (Luke 16:19–31), not the one raised from the dead.

LINE 54: "cortese donna mia" (my gracious lady) is a standard rhetorical formula in chivalric poetry.

LINE 55: "sidera feriam vertice" is a paraphrase of Horace's first book of odes and means "I will touch the stars with my head and be exhalted"—PB.

Ecloga III / Eclogue III (pages 92–97)

LINE 3: "adyti," "adyta," slightly Italianized: the secret part of a temple from which the uninitiated are barred.

line 50: "hierophany," the moment in which the divinity shows itself—RUTH FELDMAN AND BRIAN SWANN.

Ecloga IV/ Eclogue IV (pages 98–101)

LINE 10: "pullus," here, "chicken embryo," "chick," but in the broader sense of the nascent form—RF AND BS.

LINE 13: "psychiod," with the value of the "embryonic psyche;" the psyche in formation—RF AND BS.

LINE 28: "Ah Sunday is always Sunday," like the quotation "I'd like to find new words" in the next stanza, is from a popular song—RF AND BS.

LINE 35: "cocci," the plural of the Latin "coccus," a spherical cell, as those of the genus micrococcus (streptococcus, staphylococcus, etc.). There is a play here on "coccus" and the Italian "cocco," egg (oval forms)—RF AND BS.

La quercia sradicata dal vento / The Oak Uprooted by the Wind (pages 102–105)

LINE 7: "Gordian snarl," as in the "Gordian knot" tied by King Gordius of Phrygia and cut by Alexander the Great after hearing an oracle promise that whoever could undo it would be the next ruler of Asia.

Notificazione di presenza sui colli Euganei / Notifying One's Presence in the Euganean Hills (pages 106–107)

For a possible influence, see Ugo Foscolo, *Ultime letter di Jacopo Ortis* (The Last Letters of Jacopo Ortis), letter 25. See also Zanzotto's essay "I Colli Euganei" ("The Euganean Hills")—PB.

Epilogo / Epilogue (pages 106–109)

LINE 2: "anancasm," the phenomenon by which a thought or gesture tends to repeat itself or be repeated obsessively—PB.

LINE 11: "omentum," membrane which enfolds and supports (literally, one of two pairs of peritoneal folds)—PB.

LINE 14: "O quale e quanto in quella viva stella," cf. "Il quale e il quanto della viva stella," *Paradiso* XXIII, 92.

LINE 19: "integrating" and "limit," in the mathematical sense.

LINE 24: The play in the last line of the poem on "mente," a common adverbial ending in Italian, or on its own, "mind," is lost in translation—PB.

Da *La Beltà* / From *Beauty*

La perfezione della neve / The Perfection of the Snow (pages 112–113)

LINE 4: "Assideramento" literally signifies frostbite, but here its meaning comes from a partly distorted etymology; "sideratus," the malign influence of a star or planet, is interpreted in a positive light; the Latin "sidera e coelos," "stars and skies."

LINE 23: "Lib. liberty," perhaps "libido" transforming into another word.

LINE 26: "Id-vid," apropos of life understood as "ideare-vedere" (ideating-seeing), with the common root cf. ἰδ(Γιδ); possible undercurrents of "Id" ("Es").

LINE 32: "Evoè" is a shout of Bacchic elation, ancient Greek in origin and particular to Dionysian rites—PB.

Sì, Ancora la neve / Yes, the Snow Again (pages 114–119)

LINE 8: "bambucci-ucci, odore di cristianucci," from an Italian fable—RF AND BS.

LINE 12: "we are a sign without interpretation," a variant of a phrase from Hölderlin's "Mnemosyne"—RF AND BS.

LINE 26: "evaso o morto / evaso o morta," the implications of Zanzotto's use of masculine and feminine cannot be conveyed in English—RF AND BS.

LINE 28: "glissate," used here in the sense of the musical glissando and also that of sliding or slipping away—RF AND BS.

LINE 35: "Cimbric gibberish" ("slambròt cimbrici"), the inhabitants of the Trent and Veneto regions refer thus to the dialects spoken by the very small groups erroneously thought to be of Cimbric origin and isolated in the lower Alpine areas. The Cimbri were a people encountered by the Romans in Styria c. 113 B.C. They were related to their allies, the Teutons, but it is not known whether they were Gauls or Germans by race.

LINE 44: "the big woods," perhaps the forest of Cansiglio, with a five-and-ten store in a small town at the forest's lower edge.

LINE 50: "umbra fuimus fumo e fumetto," a mixture of languages. The first two words are Latin for "we were shadow"; "fumo" and "fumetto" are Italian. There is a suggestion of the comic strip ("fumetto") balloon issuing like smoke ("fumo") from the mouth—RF AND BS.

LINE 52: "truffaldini," after the character Truffaldo in a comedy by Gozzi. The word is commonly used to denote a swindler—RF AND BS.

LINE 63: "and the snow rose," etc.: verses of an old popular song.

LINE 68: "clippety cloppety cl cl," recalls a line of Palazzeschi from his poem "La fontana malata"—RF AND BS.

LINE 76: "sciences, languages and prophecies," cf. I Cor. 13:8.

LINE 77: "cronaca bianca nera azzurra," a play on words. In Italy "cronaca bianca" is news of births, marriages, etc.; "cronaca nera" is crime reporting.

LINE 77: "Cronaca azzurra" does not exist—RF AND BS.

LINE 81: "water that swerves, etc.," from Zanzotto's poem "Al bivio" in *Dietro il paesaggio*.

Alla stagione / To the Season (pages 120–123)

TITLE: "season," "stagione" derives from the Latin "statio," meaning a stop, halt. Here it means the nonflow but, since a season passes, Zanzotto also intends the opposite—RF AND BS.

LINE 6: "stammering women," cf. *Purgatorio* XIX, 769. Dante's stammering woman symbolizes the sins of the flesh, purged in the three upper circles of Purgatory. See *Dante Alighieri The Divine Comedy: Purgatorio: 2, Commentary* by Charles S. Singleton (Princeton, 1973)—RF AND BS.

LINE 34: "mummi," Zanzotto has invented a masculine plural form of "mummia."

LINE 46: "infinite," Zanzotto is playing on both meanings of "infinitó," "infinite" and "infinitive"—RF AND BS.

LINE 59: "clio," Clio, the muse of history—RF AND BS.

LINE 59: "far su," Veneto dialect for "avvolgere."

LINE 60: "opus maxime oratorium," reference is to a Ciceronian definition of historiography.

Da *Possibili prefazi o riprese o conclusioni* / From *Possible Prefaces or Resumptions or Conclusions"* (pages 124–126)
LINE 11: "fifàus," shelter, in First World War military jargon.

Al mondo / To the World (pages 126–127)
LINE 2: The Latin "sistere" here means "to stand firmly on one's feet"—PB.
LINE 19: "chance," French term with no exact equivalent in Italian (or English); approximately it means "fortune," "luck," "odds," or "probability"—PB.
LINE 23: Baron Münchhausen escaped from the marsh by pulling himself up by his own hair—PB.

L'elegia in Petèl / The Elegy in Petèl (pages 128–133)
"Petél" is Veneto dialect for the caressing baby talk mothers and nurses address to small children, with which they try to approximate the children's own talk. It is the "Ammensprache," the language of wet nurses. Petèl is a prelanguage and at the same time suggests the end of language and of poetry. In this latter sense it is exemplified by two fragmentary passages from Hölderlin, already well on the way to total obscurity (from "Ihr sichergebauten Alpen," and from "Einst hab ich die Muse gefragt," translated as the last line of "The Elegy in Petèl": "Once I interrogated the Muse."). Petèl remains an undefined field of expression that could no longer exist; unprotected in the sense that it has no formal structure. It is as though it had no beginning and were reluctant to come to a formal poetic conclusion. In this middle ground, end and beginning encounter and circumscribe the flowering of little sketches referred to in the previous allusions to the marvelous atomization of Tallémant des Réaux's "historic" gossip and to the paradisiacal and comic-strip fantasy pornography of *L'Histoire d'O*.
LINE 23: "breakup," Zanzotto says "almost an explosion, a fragmentation as seen in a slow-motion film"—RF AND BS.
LINE 31: "The absence of the gods," from a celebrated passage of Hölderlin's, commented on extensively by Allemann and by Blanchot.
LINE 51: "the desire for fresh money," etc.: approximates an expression of the economist Di Fenizio.
LINE 57: "tutto fa brodo," literally, everything makes broth, an old maxim meaning roughly "anything goes." "Non è vero che tutto fa brodo" is a singing commercial meaning "it's not true that anything goes."
LINE 70: "Scardanelli," the pseudonym Hölderlin used to sign his mad poetry— RF AND BS.
LINE 71: *L'Histoire d'O* is by Pauline Réage—RF AND BS.

Da *Profezie o memorie o giornali murali* / From *Prophecies or Memories or Bulletin-Boards* (pages 132–137)

I

LINE 13: "munuscolo" ("small offering"), after Virgil.

III

The problems common to many mountain and hill areas in the process of being abandoned are seen here also from the point of view of the farmer Nino. He was the last survivor (or almost the last) in the Dolle area, with his enthusiasms and his taste for the great rites, among which are suppers, drinking bouts, etc. These symposia, often documented on film-strips, are always philosophical for him, a theorist in many sciences but especially in selenography, the science of the physical features of the moon, as well as an agricultural activist and prophet.

LINE 53: "clinami," in the Lucretian sense, of declivity, cleavage and climate ("declivio," "clivaggio" and "clima"). The Latin "clinatus" means "inclining," "leaning."

LINE 81: "summit," summit conference, used here obviously in the ironic sense.

LINE 82: "ombre," a Veneto word for glasses of wine, in quotation marks in the text to differentiate it from the Italian word meaning "shadows."

Da *Gli Squardi i fatti e senhal* / From *Glances, Facts and Senhals* (pages 140–147)

[The poem can be read as a] protocol relative to the first table of the Rorschach test, especially to the central detail, or as fifty-nine intervention-exchanges of as many characters (better than of one alone) in a colloquium of "contrasts" with another person who is stable, speaks within quotation marks, and is the same central detail. But the poem is also a panorama of a certain type of B-movie and more or less literary chatting of the day. And it is also fragments of an imprecise history of the human approach toward the moon goddess, up to the moment of contact. Etc.] [As here indicated, the poem in part deals with the U.S. lunar landing as a rending of the mythic fabric once surrounding the moon.—PB]

TITLE: "Senhal," public name that hides that which is true (for the finder), or simply "signal," or, if you like, "symbol of the symbol of the symbol" and so forth.

LINE 4: "the comics in ik," comics of the type "Diabolik," "Satanik," with relative annoying final hiccup.

LINE 6: "banal," also in the sense of "banal interpretation, (Ban)" in Rorschach.

LINE 15: "the geminated verb the quiescent," they exist (see Scerbo, *Grammatica della lingua ebraica* [Florence 1929], pp. 58–70).

LINE 31: "inerrancy," impossibility of being erroneous, specific to a dogmatic formula (in theology).

LINE 32: "usuals," here neutral plural.

LINE 44: "Flash," etc., Anglo-comicish voices; the "down" (used with "splash" to signify the moment of impact of a space capsule with the ocean surface) here it remains referred to in some way in all three voices.

LINE 47: "it is the first table . . . (center D)," the above-mentioned detail. It is often, but not necessarily, interpreted as a feminine figure. Here also little object, fetish, paleolithism, scale of superstition, and so on.

LINE 64: "phantasm," above all, in the psychoanalytic sense.

LINE 85: "oaks beeches firs . . . elders dill," cf. *Orlando Furioso* XXIII.

LINE 90: "desmìssiete" (wake up):, from "desmissiar" (dialect). This is the opposite of "missiar," to stir and therefore to make swirl in the negative sense (disturbance, illness, fainting). "Desmissiar" means then to make turn in the positive sense, to unscrew, to free from.

LINE 93: "bau-sette" (peek-a-boos), with the very young: one says "bau bau bau" (bow wow wow) keeping the face covered with a handkerchief or something similar, and then "sette" (seven): suddenly showing oneself with a laugh.

LINE 100: "six-here," etc., words of the game of morra.

LINE 109: *La beltà,* my book of verse.

Da *Pasque* / From *Easters*

Misteri della pedagogia / Mysteries of Pedagogy (pages 150–155)

LINE 1: "Reading Center," these centers are organized by the Ministry of Public Education as places for continuing education, open to all—those of school age and adults.

LINE 41: "Lume non è," etc.: cf. *Paradiso* XIX, 64–65.

LINE 70: "they go to the woods . . . they sleep like logs," these phrases refer to silkworms. Apple trees in flower and silkworms at work indicate two different seasons.

La Pace di Oliva / The Peace of Oliva (pages 154–155)

"The Peace of Oliva" Treaty was signed at Oliva (now a suburb of Gdansk) by Poland, Sweden, Brandenburg, and the Holy Roman Empire; Denmark was then forced to sign the Treaty of Copenhagen with Sweden, which ended the First Northern War (1655–1660).

LINE 7: "v v v," mathematical symbols referring to vector analysis—PB.

LINE 8: "Riss," etc., periods of glaciation during the Quaternary Era.

Per lumina, per limina / By Lights By Limits (pages 156–161)

The setting for this poem is a field of corn in the autumn illuminated at
night by the moon—PB.

Lanternina cieca / Small Dark Lantern (pages 160–163)

LINE 1: "mezz'oretta," from the Italian proverb, "da pasquetta una
mezz'oretta"—PB.

LINE 13: "acronìe," "atopìe," neologisms—RF AND BS.

LINE 16: "splitting/mirrors," to suggest an image repeated by a broken
mirror.

LINE 23: "Fordàn," fictitious name for a peasant family—RF AND BS.

LINE 23: "filò," a peasant evening in the cowsheds during the winter, but
also an interminable discourse that serves to pass the time (dialect). [See
also the essay "Gennaio" ("January"): "when stables welcomed the cheer-
ful and pleasant communal warmth of the *filò,* the rustic vigils in which
chatter and playacting, the comfort of simple drinks, and the reading of
prayers prepared the ground for sweet, furtive encounters"—PB.]

LINE 31: "s'immilla," used by Dante. See *Paradiso* XXVIII, 93—RF AND BS.

LINE 32–33: "Neta," "Toni" (called "Toni-oci" because of his eyes, "occhi"),
people dear to me and dead for many years.

LINE 34: "vi'tu," "varda," (dialect).

Codicillo / Codicil (pages 162–165)

LINE 3: ≅, symbol for approximate congruence.

LINE 18: "embricazione" (imbrication), an overlapping of edges like that of
tiles or shingles, the scales of buds or fish—RF AND BS.

LINE 24: "wholeness," in the mathematical sense—RF AND BS.

Da *Filò: Per il* Casanova *di Fellini* / From *Peasants Wake for
Fellini's* Casanova (pages 170–173)

"Filò": see note under "Small Dark-Lantern" (*Pasque* [Easters])—PB.

LINE 85: "posterno" ("postern"), the north-facing, shadowy part of build-
ings (or places).

For a complete translation of this book please see *Peasants Wake for Fellini's*
Casanova *and Other Poems,* translated and edited by John P. Welle and
Ruth Feldman (Urbana: University of Illinois Press, 1997)—PB.

Da *Il Galateo in Bosco* / From *The Woodland Book of Manners*

These poems were composed between 1975 and early 1978. The collection opens what could improperly be called a trilogy, in large part already written. Manners in the Woods (if in fact manners and woods exist), the collection of scant rules that maintain symbiosis and cohabitation, and the networks of the symbolic, from language to gestures and perhaps even perception: hovering like spiderwebs or buried, veiled like filigrees above / within that boiling of arrogance that is reality. The sonnets in particular refer to these improbable formulations of codes and subcodes of what is in no way codifiable.

The Woods are, to a certain degree—and by means of an inevitable series of crossings, passings, and hybridizations—also the Montello hill. There, as is well known, Giovanni Della Casa wrote his *Galateo;* a great many rhymes and verses in Italian and Latin were also written there, in both the Certosa and the abbey—the first of which has completely disappeared, while the other is now reduced to ruins. Despite being repeatedly exploited, the vast forest covering the Montello remained nearly intact for centuries—up until its destruction after national unification. The battles leading to the Italian victory over the Austro-Hungarian Empire in 1918 also took place there. What remains today of that singular place are strips of wilderness, weekend vacation homes, and farming developments. And yet something of the Great Forest is still left; something of its beauty and vigor settles like a regret, a memory, in some vague terrain. Everything is still possible on this hypersedimented terrain. The question is open, like those of all woods, both vegetal and human. So is the summons to see the squalid futility of all massacres, wars, and human sacrifices, and to suffer them to the fullest, to recomprehend them along with our own "so that others may be thwarted in the future"—so to speak (while every day the steady trickling of blood continues); a party of "continual vomiting" should be formed. Tens of thousands killed on and nearby the Montello alone: a tragedy that has remained ingrained in the earth and its people.

The topography indicated on the map is accurate, even if only a few markings and place-names are given, including the Line of the Ossuaries, which stretches to the east as far as the Adriatic Sea, and to the west through France as far as the English Channel: a line upon which Europe still stakes its life. And across the Montello the line indicates a terrestrial rift, overlaying the Periadriatic fault deep within the earth's crust . . .

Many titles, words, and short phrases appearing the poems are taken from the *Bollettino della Vittoria* (victory bulletin).

The verses that appear in electrotype facsimile are by the gentle poet and elegant writer of epigraphs Carlo Moretti of Montebelluno (1882–1960), taken from *Lauri e rose del Piave* (Pieve di Soligo, 1926).

The verses in Paduan dialect are by Nicolò Zotti (one of the Solleciti academicians, "Doctor and Lawyer" of the Communes of Montello on behalf of the Venetian Republic), who writes, following a well-established practice, under the pseudonym of the "peasant" Cecco Ceccogiato of Torreggia (Torreglia di Padova). The marvelously fresh composition "Rustic Ode" has the taste of the forest as it was in 1683 when the verses were written. Earlier noted by O. Battistella, they have been fished out of the Trevisio Municipal Library by Enzo Demattè and merit immediate republication.

LINE 1: Sweetness. Dearness. Little muffled slaps.

LINE 32: *Befehle* (orders, commands, injunctions) is a German word, but also a dialectal one (to the small extent it is by now used: befèl, plur. befèi = long, heated arguments and injunctions).

Gnessulógo / Noplace (pages 178–181)

The term "gnessulógo" (noplace) here reads as an adverb of place, derived from the phrase "in nessun luogo," but remains strangely free, as if an untranslatable negative complement to "ovunque" (everywhere).

LINE 5: "corries," round hollows in hillsides (possibly dolines)—PB.

Diffrazioni, eritemi / Diffractions, Erythemas (pages 180–187)

This is a modest homage to a certain "linea ludica" (ludic streak) quite popular in recent years. Treviso playing cards are a variant of the better-known Neapolitan ones. The sections in capital letters are taken in part from sayings or maxims found under the aces of spades, cups, coins, and clubs.

LINE 20: "I gravissimi Provveditori" (The very grave Providers), a reference to the *Oda Rusticale* (Rustic ode), strophe XXXI.

LINE 26: D^{ne}, "Domine" (Lord).

LINE 30: "sàntolo," godfather of baptism or confirmation (dialectal).

LINE 31: "Barba Zuchón," the protagonist of a fable told in many variants in Treviso folklore.

LINE 38: "Teodomiro," etc., found in the trademark of the cards, on the ace of coins.

LINE 39: "the rich old woman," confused references to a real story from the nineteenth century. The count is robbed of a chest full of money by a group of thieves ("francs" here are equivalent to "lire" [money] as is generally so in most of the northern dialects). Overlapping with this, inside the confusion of memories, is the mysterious "mutuante Cian" (money-lending Cian) (what loan? what relations did she have with the band?).

LINE 50: The phrase "Gavemo sbalà la vecia" (We killed the hag) was still in use in my childhood, repeated as a grim fable to send chills down the spines of children and also adults during vigils.

LINE 51: "vecchia di spade," knave of spades, in other words death or negation, as in the game of the same name.

LINE 63: "the Abbey," l'abbazia benedettina di Sant'Eustacchio (the Benedictine Abbey of Saint Eustachius), located near the town of Nervesa and the largest ossuary on the Montello. It dates to the second half of the eleventh century when it was founded by Benedictine monks from Cassino. It was first destroyed in 1229 during a war between Guelfs and Ghibellines, again in 1358 during a war between the city of Treviso and Hungarian invaders, and finally during the First World War—PB.

LINE 65: "The Archprior," in reality the abbot-bishop Marcantonio, central character of the celebrated case that gave rise to the dispute between Paul V and the Venetian Republic (see Paolo Sarpi, the Interdict, etc.) at the beginning of the seventeenth century.

LINE 70: "zhisanpe" (slatterns), disreputable or foolish women (dialect).

LINE 103: "deep hammering," in the gloomy, enchanting stories of my mother and relatives, who had stayed in the zone occupied by the Austrio-Hungarians, very close to the front.

LINE 105: "from the Stelvio to the Sea," see wartime bulletins.

NOTE: For a detailed discussion of this poem, see "'Intervento': A Conversation with Middle School Students in Parma"—PB.

(Certe forre circolari . . .) / (Certain circular chasms . . .) (pages 186–191)

TITLE: "circular chasms," dolines, or funnel-shaped subsidences that often terminate in deep, karstic caverns that have escaped cultivation and are still, in many cases, wooded.

LINE 37: "Don Abbondios," plural, generalized, of "Don Abbondio," a character from Alessandro Manzoni's novel *I promessi sposi*—PB.

LINE 54: "Vecchia di Spade," see note above under "Diffractions, Erythemas."

LINE 65: "morsura," as in etching [the reproducing of images or words by engraving a metal or stone surface with acids or corrosives].

"Rivolgersi agli ossari" / "Apply to the ossuaries. No ticket is needed" (pages 190–195)

LINE 29: "pazzi-di-guerra" (war-crazed-veterans), there were many, however little discussed (even if the expression was often used as an insult). There are still some alive today in mental hospitals from that distant time. Living ossuaries.

LINE 35: "Father and mother," cf. "Sul Piave" ("On the Piave") in *IX Eclogues*. [In this poem Zanzotto confronts the ossuaries in the Montello Wood both as disturbing, sacred resting places, and as tourist attractions—

which supply jobs to the local population, from the maintenance of the
charnel houses to the cataloguing of bones—PB.]

LINE 32: The Piave is a river that runs just to the northeast of the Montello,
close to the ossuaries—PB.

Stati maggiori contrapposti, loro piani / Conflicting Dominant States, Their Designs (pages 194–199)

LINE 4: "tesseract," a regular convex polychoron formed of eight cubical
cells—PB.

LINE 15: "lluvias, chuvas," both mean rain (Spanish and Portuguese, but
with a dialectal sound).

LINE 17: "HCl," exaggerated reference to commonplace hydrochloric acid,
here reconnected to the theme of the stomach, of digestion? (It is also
convergent with the theme of vitriol.)

LINE 51: "$\varepsilon <> \lambda$," pseudo-mathematical symbols, not to be taken seriously.

"Tentando e poi tagliuzzando a fette" / "Touching and then chopping into slices" (pages 198–199)

LINE 14: "the Solutrean" "the Magdalenian," periods of prehistory, cited ran-
domly [the former began approximately in 19,000 B.C..; the latter ended
in 13,000 B.C.—PB]. Neolithic artifacts [dating from approximately 7000
B.C. to 3000 B.C.—PB] have been found throughout the forest.

LINE 22: "mordaccia" (muzzle/bit), for those tortured or burned at the
stake. It was primarily used to immobilize the tongue—calling to mind
Giordano Bruno. [Bruno was burned at the stake by the Catholic Church
in 1600 for his beliefs; a wooden bit was put in his mouth to keep him
from speaking—PB.]

LINE 16: "karstic intentions" (or para-karstic): characteristic of the Montel-
lo's geologic configuration.

(Sono gli stessi) / (They're the same) (pages 200–203)

LINE 11: "bear bile" is supercharged with digestive juices!

LINE 12: "shuttle-like viruses," modifiers of RNA, carriers of genetic frag-
ments from species to species, rich with capricious, unpredictable "inven-
tions" that stitch together various aspects of the most distant species.

LINE 17: "available here," on the Montello there are still active military
bases—not only those of the past.

LINE 25: "transferase," an enzyme.

Da Ipersonetto / From Hypersonnet (pages 204–207)

"Hypersonnet" is formed of fourteen sonnets, each of which stands for one
line in an overall sonnet, plus a "Premessa" (preface) and a "Postilla"
(postil). It was written in homage to poets such as Gaspara and Della
Casa who wrote sonnets while living in the Montello Woods.

I

LINE 2: "hyphae," the threadlike filaments forming the mycelium of a fungus—PB.

LINE 5: "scientific lens," microscope—PB.

IV

LINE 6: "and yes" "and yes," cf. *Gerusalemme Liberata* XIII, strophe 10: "che sì? che sì." But also autumnal sneezes. The theme of allergic sneezing also appears in "Come Ultime Cene" (Like Last Suppers) in *Fosfeni* (Phosphenes), and at the end of "Tu sai che" (You Know That) in *Meteo;* see also the beginning of Zanzotto's essay "Autoritratto" (Self-portrait)—PB.

LINE 14: "pia lex: per te peribo," Latin for "pia legge: a causa tua morirò" (sacred law: because of you I will die)—PB.

LINES 6–11: The theme of the woods as a source of food appears in Della Casa's original *Galateo* (LXI)—PB.

(Che sotto l'alta guida) / *(That under the noble* guidance (pages 206–209)

The episode mentioned did not happen exactly in this way, but the gist of it is here. Cossimo provides an account of it in *Giorni di Guerra* (Days of War) in the section "La battaglia del Montello" (The battle of the Montello) near the end.

( )   ) ((pages 208–209)

LINE 1: *"Varo"* ("bowlegged"), bending inward.

LINE 1: *"valgo"* ("knock-kneed"), with deformed legs bending towards the outside.

(Milky) (pages 210–213)

LINE 24: "squish," the sound of rapid and animalesque defecation.

Da *Fosfeni* / From *Phospenes*

These poems took shape in large part alongside *Il Galateo in Bosco* (The Woodland book of manners), between 1975 and 1978; others were added during the preceding years, until 1981. The present collection thus more or less represents the second part of a rather improbable trilogy (which was earlier alluded to in *Il Galateo in Bosco*). It emerges here as a type of contrast, or residuum, a north that through other types of hilly shiftings fades into the space and geometries of the Dolomites, towards snow and abstractions, across fogs, frosts, gels, and scarce or nonexistent history.
Under the name of logos goes every insistent or benign power of memory, communication, and interconnection that crosses realities, fantasies,

and words, tending to "confer" these, to place them into relation with a foundation (?). And who knows what else goes under this name. The inscriptions in Greek—or pseudo-Greek—near or at the end of many poems, carry a value of "overturned," mirrored, or reflected titles.

TITLE: "Phosphenes," swirlings of signs and luminous points seen by keeping the eyes closed (and rubbing them) or also in pathological situations.

Come Ultime Cene / Like Last Suppers (pages 216–219)

LINE 7: "gel," as the rest of the book, this term means "frigid gelatin."
LINE 33: "miniorgasm in ahchoo," reference to the comparability between the sneeze and the erotic orgasm claimed by certain psychoanalysts.
LINE 72: "ΘΕΩΙΑ ΚΡΥΟΣ," theory, and also procession, of frost-crystal-gel.

(Da Ghène) / (At Ghène's) (pages 224–227)

Ghène, the tavern-keeper's nickname, in distant times.

"Ben disposti silenzi" / "Well-disposed silences" (pages 226–227)

LINE 17: μηδέν, etc., this means nothing more than a scribble, in error, even if it recalls the theme of giving without expecting anything in return.

Periscopi / Periscopes (pages 228–229)

LINE 10: "liquid crystals," with reference to their properties (today they are used in many common objects). [Liquid crystals are a phase of matter whose order is intermediate between that of a liquid and that of a crystal; they can be understood to be crystals which have lost some or all of their positional order, while maintaining full orientational order—PB.]

Vocabilità, fotoni / Vocabulary, Photons (pages 238–241)

LINE 2: "Eurosia" (or Orosia), saint venerated as a protectress of the town of Jaca in the Pyrenees, with popular followers in southern France and northern Italy; she is also popularly believed to protect against hailstorms—PB.
LINE 3: "Barbara," saint venerated as a protectress of miners, builders, firefighters, and shipbuilders and associated with protection against lightning (as well as building failure and bombs)—PB.
LINE 5: "Lùcia," Santa Lùcia (St. Lucy), on whose day (December 13th), according to an old dictum, the cold begins.
LINE 7: "niña," Spanish for "child" (fem.)—PB.

Tavoli, giornali, alba pratalia / Tables, Newspapers, Snow-Covered Fields (pages 242–245)

"Alba Pratalia" are the "snow-covered fields" of the *Indovinello Veronese* (Veronese Riddle), symbolic of a blank page. The Veronese Riddle, dating to the early ninth century, is considered to be the oldest literary text written in Italian *volgare:* "Se pareba boues / alba pratalia araba / & albo uersorio teneba / & negro semen seminaba" (he led cows in front of him / plowed white fields / held a white plow / and sowed black seed). The riddle can be approximately solved as follows: the cows symbolize the farmer's (monk's or poet's) fingers, which draw a plow (feather pen) across the white fields (blank paper), scattering black seed (ink)—PB.

Futuri semplici—o anteriori? / Futures—Simple or Anterior? (pages 244–247)

LINE 3: "Witz," German for "joke" (also a Freudian term used in dream analysis)—PB.

Da *Idioma* / From *Idiom*

This collection forms part of the group of books that includes *Il Galateo in bosco* (The Woodland book of manners) and *Fosfeni* (Phosphenes). It was written in part at the same time as these two previous volumes (1975–1982), and in part later on (1983–1984). Together they form a pseudo-trilogy: nonlinear moments of the same work that make constant reference to one another, even if with a certain discontinuity, including a certain reciprocal recantation.

TITLE: "Idioma" ("Idiom"), to be understood according to every etymological diffraction and beyond, from the fullness of nascent, irrepressible speech as a singular blossoming, to the opposite pole of closure in the peculiarity by which one arrives at the heading "idiocy." Language, private language, private and depriving fact; an excess of privacy and therefore of closure-privation-deprivation. An emphasis on peculiarity: but also, on the contrary, a linguistic means understood entirely as an upwelling from that peculiarity.

Genti / Peoples (pages 250–251)

Unfortunately this poem refers to situations by now unstable.

Sfere / Spheres (pages 252–253)

TITLE: "Sphere" ("Spheres"), soccer balls (in the jargon of the sport); the occasion for the poem was the live television broadcast of the 1982 World Cup in Spain, which Italy won—PB.

LINE 20: "Acufeni" ("Acouphenes"), whistling noises in the ears. [See also "Adorazioni, richieste, acufeni" in *La Beltà* (Beauty), and the introductory note to *Fosfeni* (Phosphenes).—PB]

Orizzoni / Horizons (pages 252–255)

LINE 6: "oh parents," and parents of parents ad infinitum.

LINE 10: "special effects," in a cinematic sense.

Nino negli anni ottanta / Nino in the Eighties (pages 254–257)

This poem refers to (and in fact updates) an earlier poem, "The Prophecies of Nino," from *La Beltà*. At that time (in the 1960s) Nino pedaled "between seventy and eighty, almost volage." [See also note under "Prophecies or Memories or Bulletin-Boards: III" (*La Beltà* [Beauty])—PB.]

Andar a cucire / Going Out to Sew (pages 256–261)

LINE 11: "Zauberkraft," "magical force," from Hegel.

LINE 25: "a broad, U-shaped valley," a technical geological expression. The U-shaped profile is typical of valleys of glacial origin (those of fluvial origin, on the other hand, are characterized by a profile in a V).

LINE 36: "Graphemes," a linguistic term. In homology with "phonemes," considered indivisible units of the sound chain, graphemes are the smallest units of writing that cannot be divided. In a wider sense, the word stands for the written trace of speech.

Onde éli / Where Are They? (pages 260–263)

TITLE: the dialect translation of the famous topos and theme "ubi sunt."

Par I otanta ani de Montale / For Eugenio Montale on His Eightieth Birthday (pages 262–265)

Eugenio Montale (1896–1981) is one of the masters of modern poetry and the greatest Italian poet since Leopardi. His three major collections of verse—*Ossi di seppia* (Cuttlefish Bones, 1939), *Le occasioni* (The Occasions, 1939), and *La bufera e altro* (The Storm and Other Things, 1956)—have been widely translated into English, most recently by William Arrowsmith, Dana Gioia, and Jonathan Galassi. Winner of the Nobel Prize for Literature in 1975, Montale was known as "Eusebius" to his friends—JOHN WELLE AND RUTH FELDMAN.

In ricordo de Pasolini / In Memory of Pasolini (pages 266–269)

Pier Paolo Pasolini (1922–1975), poet, novelist, filmmaker, and political gadfly, perhaps the most important cultural figure in postwar Italy, was murdered in obscure circumstances near Rome in November 1975. Known in the English-speaking world primarily for such films as *The Gospel according to Saint Matthew, The Decameron,* and *Salò, or the One Hundred and Twenty Days of Sodom,* Pasolini was instrumental in the contemporary rediscovery of the Italian dialects as vehicles for poetic expression. In addition to his poetic masterpiece in Italian, *Le ceneri di Gramsci*

(The Ashes of Gramsci, 1957), his books containing his Friulian dialect
poetry, *La meglio gioventù* (The Best Youth, 1954) and *La nuova gioventù*
(The New Youth, 1974), have been largely responsible for leading the
contemporary revival of writing poetry in the dialects, a phenomenon
known as "la poesia neodialettale" (new dialect poetry). Before moving
in 1950 to Rome, where he gradually gained fame as a poet, novelist, and
filmmaker, Pasolini spent a number of years from the middle to the late
1940s teaching Latin and Italian in rural schools in Friuli, his mother's
native region. Zanzotto, himself an active educator throughout his adult
life, first became aware of Pasolini through his renown as a teacher.
Although Zanzotto taught in a neighboring district of the Veneto, the
region bordering Friuli on the west, both young men had the same ad-
ministrator, who often sang the praises of Pasolini's ingenious teaching
methods—JW AND RF.

LINE 32: The phrase "alba pratalia" (literally, "white meadows," translated
here as "white expanses of snow") stems from one of the oldest extant
examples of written Italian in its evolution from Vulgar Latin: the
"Veronese riddle" (see note above under "Tables, Newspapers, Snow-
Covered Fields" in *Fosfeni*). The phrase, which also symbolizes the white-
ness of a blank sheet of paper, takes on added significance in Zanzotto's
poem because Pasolini, who had a deep love for Romance philology and
edited two important anthologies of Italian dialect poetry, himself uses
"alba pratalia" in one of his poems—JW AND RF.

Da *Mistieròi* / From *Small and Humble Occupations* (pages 268–273)

Dedicated to the dear and venerated memory of Angela Bertazzon and
Marina Bon. Many times published in plaquettes, this composition
was actually conceived as an integral part of the volume *Idioma*. It
is also a tribute to the series of woodcuts, *Le arti the vanno per via,* by
G. Zompini, with a verse commentary by Questini, published in Venice,
1785.

LINE 45: Mentioned in the poem "Herdsmen," Arcadia derives its name
from the bleak, mountainous region in the Peloponnesus. Celebrated
by Virgil in his *Eclogues,* it became the traditional, idealized world of the
pastoral, a literary genre that has lasted two thousand years, centered
around a fictionalized imitation of rural life usually set in a golden age.
Jacopo Sannazaro published a series of eclogues with the title *Arcadia*
circa 1504, which treats the laments, loves, and other activities of various
shepherds and shepherdesses in Arcadia. An immensely popular work,
Sannazaro's *Arcadia* was a link between the pastorals of Theocritus, Vir-
gil, and those of Sidney, Spenser, and later writers. Zanzotto himself has
written a book, *IX Ecloghe* (IX Eclogues, 1962), in tribute to what he calls
"the great shadow of Virgil"—JW AND RF.

LINES 42–51: When Zanzotto's dialect poem "Pastor" (Herdsmen) was read over the radio in his locality, the station received numerous enthusiastic calls from shepherds who heard the poem as they tended their flocks. "Variante 1984" *is* Zanzotto's response to their warm response: a gesture typical of the Arcadian tradition, which features numerous "responsive verses" or "singing matches." "Variante 1984" Anca adès no i val manco / e cola radiolina al fianco / sore 'l sol o le stele / i scolta le canzhon pi bele" (Today they're still highly prized / with their radios at their sides / under the sun or under the stars / they follow the hit songs on the charts)—JW AND RF.

Alto, altro linguaggio, fuori idioma / High, Other Language, beyond Idiom? (pages 272–275)

TITLE: Within the chain connected to the term "idiom."

LINE 37: "the piece of paper," see Dante *Paradiso* XXIII, 64–66; see also Zanzotto's poem "Genti" (Peoples)—PB.

Da *Meteo* / From *Meteo*

This book is intended as but a sample of work in progress. Here collected for the most part are "uncertain fragments," stemming from and in part contemporaneous with *Idiom* (Idiom, 1986). They are, in any event, provisionally organized according to themes that blend one into the other—not according to a precise temporal sequence, but perhaps a "meteorological" one.

Morèr Sachèr (pages 282–285)

TITLE: "Morèr," mulberries; "Sachèr," caprine willows. Here the terms are always used in the plural (invariable). [Parts from both trees were once widely used in the raising of silkworms; see also "Serica" ("Silky") in *Dietro il Paesaggio* (Behind the Landscape)—PB.]

Lanugini / Lanugos (pages 284–287)

TITLE: "Lanugos," dense cottony or downy growth, especially the fine, soft hair that covers the fetuses of some mammals—PB.

LINE 1: "pappi" (pl. of pappus), tufts of bristles that crown the ovaries or fruits in various seed plants, such as dandelions and thistles, and function as sails or parachutes in their dispersal—PB.

"Non si sa quanto verde" / "There's no telling how much green" (pages 288–291)

LINE 41: cf. "Da un'altezza nuova" ("From a New Height") in *Vocativo* (Vocative).

Leggende / *Legends* (pages 290–293)

In this poem local proverbs concerning the seasons and weather, in the face of recent, extreme environmental and climatic changes, lose their relevance. See also Zanzotto's essay "Meridiane" ("Sundials")—PB.

LINE 3: "the pallid little girl," the moon—PB.

LINES 27–38: "the darkest / May of the century," May, 1985—PB.

Stagione delle piogge / *Season of the Rains* (pages 292–295)

LINE 19: cf. Dante *Inferno, 34.*

Tu sai che / *You Know That* (pages 294–297)

TITLE: from a distant Sanremo music festival ("Tu sai che i papaveri . . .").

LINE 26: "immilare" has various meanings (most of which are lost in translation): to extemporize or improvise; to intuit; to multiply; and to distill drop by drop. See also Zanzotto's essay "Giugno" ("June") dedicated in part to the theme of poppies—PB.

LINE 27: "persiflage," light or frivolous banter, light raillery—PB.

Altri papaveri / *Other Poppies* (pages 296–299)

LINE 16: "crabro" is Latin for hornet.

Currunt / *Currunt* (pages 298–301)

LINE 15: "zanzare-tigri" (tiger mosquitoes), that breed in water collected in old abandonded car tires.

LINE 7: "mala tempora current," Latin for "these are ill-omened times"—PB.

Topinambùr (pages 304–309)

TITLE: "Topinambùr," a herbaceous, perennial plant whose tubers, having a taste similar to that of an artichoke, are used to feed both humans and animals; it is also called *tartufo di canna* (cane truffle). It has ovate leaves and yellow flowers and lingulas. From the French *topinambour,* after the name of a Native American tribe (from dictionaries). [Because of its resemblance to a small wild sunflower, the plant was given the name "girasol" in Spain (which was then misinterpreted by the English, who, confounding girasol with Jerusalem, named the plant "Jerusalem artichoke"); its Latin name is *Helianthus tuberosus*—PB.]

LINE 4: "bacilli-blisterings," hidden within the landscape are sicknesses and burns.

LINE 6: "torotorotix," allusion to Greek literature, as well as to the work of Giovanni Pascoli: as in the voice of a bird. [See also "Possibili prefazi o riprese o conclusioni," VI ("Possible Prefaces or Resumptions or Conclusions," VI) in *La Beltà* (Beauty)—PB.].

LINE 7: "augellini," little birds—PB.

LINE 8: "lilix," onomatopoeic sound of the flight of birds (and perhaps insects).

Sedi e siti / Settlements and Sites (pages 312–315)

LINE 5: "glomera" (pl. of glomus), the bulbous clusters of the invasive, intertwined clematises—PB.

Erbe e manes, inverni Grasses and Manes, Winters (pages 314–317)

LINE 18: "poa pratensis, poa silvestris," common species of grass.

LINE 7: "Manes," (from mānus, "good") a name given by the Romans to the spirits of the dead, which were believed to be immortal; they dwelt underground and only emerged during certain times of the year. On the Mons Palatinus at Rome, there was, as in other Italian towns, a deep pit with the shape of an inverted sky, known as a mundus, the lowest part of which was consecrated to the infernal gods and also to the Manes; it was closed with a stone (the lapis manalis) which was thought to be the gate of the nether world. This stone was raised three times a year (August 24, October 5, November 8): the Manes were then believed to ascend to the upper world—PB.

Da *Sovrimpressioni* / From *Superimpressions*

This collection continues the direction begun in *Meteo.* More than works in progress, herein are "works adrift" that tend here and there to cluster in relatively uniform groups—which at once shake off, and yet are also implicated in the current atmosphere, whipped up with frenzy and all manner of excess that cause everything to bend towards an omnivorous and annihilating plethora.

The title *Sovrimpressioni* (Superimpressions) should be read in relation to the return of memories and scriptural traces, together with a sense of suffocation, of menace, and perhaps of an imprinting invasiveness.

There exist numerous other nuclei contemporaneous to these, in part already developed.

Verso i Palù / Towards the Palù (pages 320–323)

TITLE: "The Palù," also called Val Bone, are marshy areas that since medieval times have been shaped into many forms, including earthen cisterns, and transformed into vast pool-shaped meadows encircled by flowing waters and planted with trees of many types, conserved with care for centuries. The current expansion of industrial and residential development, and the necessity of enlarging the road network (already clogged, especially in the Veneto), along with a blind and invasive agriculture, today threaten to erase these true masterworks of "land art"—which were once of economic value: from grain-growing fields to fish-rich waters.

LINE 19: "Lethe," the river of oblivion.

LINE 28: "Pan," Pan has long been considered dead (cf. Plutarch). But . . .

Da *Ligonàs* / From *Ligonàs* (pages 324–327)

TITLE: "Ligonàs," A large inn and tavern in the open countryside. Its name, of uncertain origin, was once displayed on its façade. In time it disappeared, but has now been restored.

Da *Sere del dì di festa* / From *Evenings of the festival day* (pages 326–331)

LINE 6: January 31 is the last of the "days of the female blackbird" and the peak of winter.

LINE 12: "diktat," an authoritative or dogmatic statement or decree—PB.

LINE 37: "Dysthymia," which literally means "depression of the spirit," is a chronic depression of mood. Sufferers usually have periods of days or weeks when they describe themselves as well, but most of the time (often for months at a time) they feel tired and depressed; everything is an effort and nothing is enjoyed—PB.

LINE 43: "Autochthony," the state of being indigenous or of an organism "having sprung from the ground it inhabits"—PB.

LINE 45: "Hapax" (legomena), words or forms evidenced by a single use by an author or occurrence in a text—PB.

LINE 53: The French term "chance" in the text has no exact equivalent in either Italian or English; it approximately means luck, fortune, or probability—PB.

LINE 53: To be "hypermetrical" is to be beyond measure or meter—PB.

GENERAL NOTE: See also Giacomo Leopardi's poem "La sera del dì di festa"—PB.

Da *Adempte Mihi* / From *Adempte Mihi* (pages 330–333)

In memory of my dear younger brother Ettore, who passed away in 1990.

TITLE: "*da Tonin*," name, now forgotten, of a locality in the hills to the north.

SUBTITLE: My friend Marco M. has since moved.

Da *A Faèn* / From *At Faen* (pages 332–335)

TITLE: "*Faèn*," "*Erbanera*," place-names, either true or fictitious.

LINE 1: "oxytone," word with a stress or an acute accent on the last syllable—PB.

LINE 29: "omasum," the third stomach of a ruminant animal located between the reticulum and the abomasum; also called "manyplies" and "psalterium"—PB.

Riletture di Topinambùr / Rereadings of Topinambùr (pages 336–339)

LINE 39: "adynaton" ("adynatal," pl.), a declaration of impossibility [usually in terms of an exaggerated comparison; sometimes, the expression of the impossibility of expression—PB.]

LINE 11: "Bethe's cycle," in reference to Hans Albrecht Bethe's carbon cycle (related to his study of the sun's energy production)—PB.

NOTE: See also Zanzotto's poem "Topinambùr" in *Meteo*—PB.

Fora par al Furlàn: "Traversing Fruili" (Veneto dialect) (pages 338–341)

Written in memory of Pier Paolo Pasolini, as a distant corrective allusion to his theory in which death intervenes to give an ultimate and definitive sense to life. Pasolini, here identified with a Benandente, escapes from this fate, in so much as it is true.

LINE 12: "Benandante," The Benandanti are restless but benign creatures in ancient Friulan folklore, of remote origins (cf. Carlo Ginsburg's studies on the subject).

L'altra stagione / The other season (pages 340–341)

LINE 17: "Taide," Finnish for art—PB.

Per altri venti, fuori rosa / Amid Other Winds, Out of the Lineup (pages 342–343)

LINES 1–2: the old song, "Vento, vento, portami via con te" (Wind, wind, carry me away with you).

LINE 13: "manufactured monster," in reference to the bull crafted by Perillo, commissioned by Falaride. [In the sixth century B.C. near the site of present day Agrigento, Sicily. The bull, hollow and made of bronze, was used as a torture chamber: the tyrant Falaride had his enemies put inside and a fire lit underneath; their muffled screams resembled the bellowing of cattle—PB.]

LINE 15: "Tohu e Bohu," one of the approximate transcriptions of the expression that in *Genesis* signifies the state of primordial chaos before the creation. In French, it has become a commonly used expression, meaning, among other things, commotion or turmoil. ["Tohu" can be roughly translated as "unformed," and "Bohu" as "unfilled."—PB]

Dirti "natura" / To Call You 'Nature' (pages 342–345)

LINE 25: "visura," bureaucratic inspection.

LINE 28: "king of coins," a playing card; see also "Diffractions, Erythemas" in *Il Galateo in bosco* (The Woodland book of manners)—PB.

Kēpos / Kēpos (pages 346–349)

TITLE: "Kēpos," Greek for garden—PB.

LINE 20: "loci amoeni," delightful or pleasant places—PB.

LINE 23: "ceu fumus in aëra," like smoke in the air (of Virgilian origin).

New Poems

Al "monte" Villa / At "mount" Villa (pages 352–353)

TITLE: "mount" Villa: A hill slightly higher than those surrounding it.

Casa Pericolante / Unstable House (pages 354–359)

This house is located along the Soligo river in the small village of Solighetto, just upstream of Pieve di Soligo—PB.

LINE 10: "Vasco Rossi," popular Italian rock musician, whose name is written on a battered wooden shutter of the house: "VASCO 6 UN MITO" ("Vasco, you're the best")—PB.

LINE 11: "the K of young kids," the use of the letter *k* as a substitute for *c* or *ch* in graffiti (on a nearby bench), such as in "kiamami" instead of "chiamami" (call me)—PB.

LINE 74: "ALTA VISTA," the name of an Internet search engine (Altavista), roughly meaning "lofty" or "sublime vision"—PB.

LINE 82: "sine fine," Latin for "without end"—PB.

LINE 83: "YAHOO": the name of an Internet search engine, also read here as a whoop of delight—PB.

Prose

All notes in this section are by PB.

A Poetry Determined to Hope (pages 363–366)

P. 363: "*Corriere dei Piccoli*," a popular children's magazine with many features, including the comic strip "Signor Bonaventura" noted for its captions written in rhymed verse.

P. 363: "Sergio Solmi," poet and literary critic (1899–1982).

P. 365: "Niccolò Tommaseo," poet and lexicographer (1802–1874).

P. 366: "Hölderlin," Johann Christian Friedrich Hölderlin, German poet, novelist, and dramatist (1770–1843).

Some Perspectives on Poetry Today (pages 367–373)

P. 371: "dal dì che nozze tribunali ed are?" roughly, since the day that weddings courts and altars?, line 91 from Ugo Foscolo's poem "Dei Sepulcri."

P. 373: "Tyrtaeus," Greek elegiac poet active in the middle of the seventh century B.C.

P. 373: "Tasso," Torquato Tasso, Italian poet, best known for *La Gerusalemme liberata* (Jerusalem Delivered; 1544–1595).

P. 373: "Yevtushenko," Yevgeny Yevtushenko, Soviet poet (1933–).

Self-portrait (pages 374–378)

P. 377: "'grande mese' of life," an important stage of life.

From "Intervento: A Conversation with Middle School Students in Parma" (pages 379–385)

P. 379: *"gioco scenico,"* theatrical stage set or scene.

Poetic and Bodily Perception (pages 386–388)

This is only an approximate translation of original title of this essay, "Vissuto poetico e corpo"; in Italian, "vissuto" means "lived" or "actual experience" which I have extended here, based on Zanzotto's use of the term, to also mean "perception." See also American poet Charles Olson's essay "Proprioception," for the intriguing parallels it contains to Zanzotto's essay.

Sundials (pages 389–395)

P. 389: In Italian the term "tempo" may mean both "weather" and "time," a double meaning played with in the original that is lost in translation.

P. 389: Goffredo Parise, Italian novelist (1929–1986).

P. 390: Colonnello Edmondo Bernacca: popular weatherman active in Italy from the late 1930s to the early 1980s.

Between Minimal and Maximal Languages (pages 396–403)

P. 397: *"lingua alta,"* high speech.

P. 398: *"inbulonà,"* from the Italian "imbullonare," or in English, "to bolt."

P. 398: *"parabris,"* parabrezza, or windshield.

P. 398: *"son strach parchè ò vu massa stress,"* "sono stanco perché ho accumulato stress," or "I'm tired because I've been stressed-out for days."

The Euganean Hills (pages 404–408)

The Euganean Hills: a clustered range of nearly one hundred round, green hills of volcanic origin that emerge from the encircling, flat expanse of the Venetian plain in northern Italy. Situated near Padua, they cover an area of roughly twenty thousand square hectares. In 1989 they were partially protected when the area became a regional park. Mixed oak and chestnut forests are widespread in the area, and alternate with fields and terraced slopes cultivated with a variety of plants, including olive trees and grapevines. The hills have been inhabited by humans for over 80,000 years and contain scattered ancient villages, isolated monasteries, the odd castle, and Renaissance-era villas.

P. 404: The Euganean hot springs, used since ancient times, are located close to Padua at the base of the hills and cover an area of about 36 square kilometers. The area hosts numerous hotels and health facilities and is renowned as an important mud therapy center.

P. 405: "Reitia," the Paleovenetian goddess, often represented next to animals and an egg with a key in her hand, and a nature deity linked to human and agricultural fertility; a sanctuary to her was built in what is now the town of Este at the southern edge of the hills. Reference is often made to her in *Filò* (*Peasants Wake*).

P. 405: "Ruzante," the pen-name of Paduan playwright Angelo Beolco (c. 1502–1542).

P. 405: Aimeric De Peguilhan, popular troubadour (c. 1170–1230).

P. 405: Lambertino Buvalelli, poet from Bologna (d. 1221).

P. 405: Sordello da Goita, poet known in part for his lament on the death of Ser Blacatz; P. XX: Gianfranco Folena: contemporary literary critic and historian (d. 1260).

P. 405: Beatrice d'Este, the first Beatrice of the Este family to be sainted (d. 1226). The former convent in the Euganean Hills where she lived for the last six years of her life was converted into a villa in the seventeenth century and is now a museum of local natural history, located atop Monte Gemola.

P. 405: Arquà (Petrarca): the site of Petrarch's final resting place, located at the end of a small, green valley in the southeast corner of the hills, a few miles from Montselice. His former house there has been turned into a museum and contains many manuscripts, documents, and artwork relating to the poet's life.

P. 406: Dino Buzzati, an influential writer from the Veneto and author of *Il deserto dei Tartari* (*The Tartar Steppe;* 1906–72).

P. 406: Petrarch first saw Laura in the spring of 1327 in the Church of Saint Clare in Avignon and immediately fell deeply in love with her. Although she was betrothed to, and eventually married, another man, Petrarch dedicated much of his artistic output to her, including the vast majority of his well-known *Canzoniere*.

P. 407: Ugo Foscolo (1778–1827) first became known for his book *Ultime lettere di Jacopo Ortis* (The last letters of Jacopo Ortis), which describes the young lovers Jacopo and Teresa's futile attempts to marry—due to the fact that after Napoleon's cession of Venice to Austria, Jacopo must seek foreign asylum. Teresa's father, already under state scrutiny, would be further compromised and potentially ruined by the match. Desperately unhappy, Jacopo eventually commits suicide.

P. 407: *Uno, nessuno, e centomila* (*One, No one and a Hundred Thousand*), completed by Luigi Pirandello in 1926, is a novel that challenges the idea of static identity; in it, the main protagonist, named Vitangelo Moscarda, becomes painfully aware of the thousands of faulty physical and mental identities, or masks, that he constantly creates in order to exist.

P. 408: Teòlo is a small town located along the northern edge of the Euganean Hills and is home to an important regional weather station.

"Between the Recent Past and Distant Present" (pages 409–417)

This essay first appeared in *Nel caldo cuore del mondo* (Florence: Liberal libri, 1999) with the title "Dai campi di sterminio allo stermino dei campi" (From the killing fields to the killing of the fields); it was written in response to a letter from the book's editor, Alfonso Berardinelli, entitled "La poesia come messaggio sullo stato del mondo" (Poetry as a message on the state of the world) in which Bernardinelli writes, "I think, dear Zanzotto, that yours is the last generation to have grown up in an Italy that was still premodern: the last generation, as it matured, to have lived through the trauma of a familiar and loved world transforming to the point of disappearing" (76–77). He adds later that "the best modern poetry . . . seems to me that which conserves within itself traces of a certain place, the linguistic colors and flavors of a microcosm: a city, a region, some particular stretch of coast, or a valley crossed by a river," and then defines Zanzotto's poetry as "completely cosmopolitan and yet no less provincial: abstract and astral, but also locally and geographically determined" (82). [This note is adapted from *Le poesie e prose scelte* (Milan: Mondadori, 1999), 1739.]

P. 411: *"Roma locuta, causa soluta,"* a phrase from *The Prince* meaning a controversy has been resolved through the intervention of the pope.

P. 411: "So much, in these depths, / remains of the process of verbalization of the world," from Zanzotto's poem "Profezie o Memorie o Giorniali Murali," XVI.

P. 414: *"Witz,"* see note under "Futures—Simple or Anterior?" in *Fosfeni* (Phosphenes).

P. 414: "I signori tengono tutti un po' del matto" (roughly, the seigneurs are all a bit mad), from Alessandro Manzoni's novel *I promessi sposi*.

P. 415: Jaufré Rudel, prince de Blaye, French poet and troubadour (1135–1210).

P. 415: Irenäus Eibl-Eibesfeldt: biologist, ethologist, and the author of *Ethology: The Biology of Behavior*, *The Biology of Peace and War*, and *Human Ethology*.

P. 416: Paul Virilio: French urbanist and philosopher, born in Paris in 1932.

P. 417: "topinambùr," see note under "Topinambùr" in *Meteo*.

Primary Works of Poetry and Prose by Andrea Zanzotto

A che valse? (Versi 1938–1942). Milan: Scheiwiller, 1970.

La Beltà. Milan: Mondadori, 1968.

Colloqui con Nino. Pievo di Soligo: Edizioni Bernardi, 2005.

Dietro il paesaggio. Milan: Mondadori, 1951.

IX Ecloghe. Milan: Mondadori, 1962.

Elegia e altri versi. Milan: Gramigna, 1954.

Filò. Per il Casanova *di Fellini*. Milan: Mondadori, 1976.

Fosfeni. Milan: Mondadori, 1983.

Idioma. Milan: Mondadori, 1986.

Il Galateo in Bosco. Milan: Mondadori, 1978.

Le poesie e prose scelte. Ed. Stefano Dal Bianco and Gian Mario Villata. Milan: Mondadori, 1999.

Ligonàs. Florence: Premio di Poesia Pandolfo, 1998.

Meteo. Rome: Donzelli, 1996.

Pasque. Milan: Mondadori, 1973.

Poesie (1938–1986). Ed. Stefano Agosti. Milan: Mondadori, 1993.

Racconti e prose. Milan: Mondadori, 1990.

Scritti sulla letteratura: Aure e disincanti nel Novecento letterario. 1994. Ed. Gian Mario Villata. Milan: Mondadori, 2001.

Scritti sulla letteratura: Fantasie di avvicinamento. 1991. Ed. Gian Mario Villata. Milan: Mondadori, 2001.

Sovrimpressioni. Milan: Mondadori, 2001.

Gli Sguardi i Fatti e Senhal. Bernardi, 1969.

Sull'Altopiano e prose varie. 1964. Vicenza: Neri Pozza, 1995.

Vocativo. Milan: Mondadori, 1957.

Contributors

PATRICK BARRON, an assistant professor of English at the University of Massachusetts, Boston, is the coeditor and cotranslator of *Italian Environmental Literature: An Anthology* (2003). He has won the Rome Prize in Modern Italian Studies, a Fulbright grant, and an award from the National Endowment for the Arts for his translations of Andrea Zanzotto's poetry.

RUTH FELDMAN was a poet and award-winning translator of Italian poetry whose honors included the John Florio Prize and the Calvino Prize. In 1999 she and John P. Welle received the Raiziss / de Palchi Prize for their translation of Andrea Zanzotto's work *Peasant's Wake for Fellini's* Casanova *and Other Poems*.

THOMAS J. HARRISON is a professor of Italian at the University of California, Los Angeles. He is the author of a multidisciplinary study of European expressionism, *1910: The Emancipation of Dissonance* (1996) and of *Essayism: Conrad, Musil and Pirandello* (1992).

BRIAN SWANN is a professor at the Cooper Union. His books include *The Middle of the Journey* (1982), *On the Translation of Native American Literatures* (1992), and *Coming to Light: Contemporary Translations of the Native Literatures of North America* (1996). He is also the coeditor and cotranslator of *The Collected Poems of Primo Levi* (1992).

JOHN P. WELLE, an associate professor of Italian at the University of Notre Dame, has received grants and fellowships from the Fulbright Commission and the National Endowment for the Humanities. He is the author of *The Poetry of Andrea Zanzotto* (1987) and the editor of *Italian Film and Literature: Annali d'Italianistica* (1988).

ELIZABETH A. WILKINS is a translator and writer. Her full-length translation of Zanzotto's *Gli Sguardi i Fatti e Senhal* appeared in *Forum Italicum*.

Index of Titles and First Lines